Problem-Solving Therapy

Arthur M. Nezu, PhD, ABPP, is distinguished university professor of psychology, professor of medicine, and professor of public health at Drexel University as well as honorary professor of community health sciences, the University of Nottingham in the United Kingdom. Dr. Nezu is currently editor of the *Journal of Consulting and Clinical Psychology*, associate editor of the *Archives of Scientific Psychology*, and consulting editor for numerous additional scientific and professional journals in psychology and behavioral medicine. He is also past president of the Association for Advancement of Behavior Therapy (now known as the Association of Behavioral and Cognitive Therapies) and the American Board of Cognitive and Behavioral Psychology. He is board certified by the American Board of Professional Psychology in three specialties (cognitive and behavioral psychology, clinical psychology, and clinical health psychology) and is a fellow of the American Psychological Association, the Association for Psychological Science, the Society of Behavioral Medicine, the Academy of Cognitive Therapy, the American Academy of Cognitive and Behavioral Psychology, and the American Academy of Clinical Psychology. Dr. Nezu has also been designated as a distinguished scholar/practitioner of psychology by the National Academies of Practice, is author or coauthor of over 200 scientific and professional publications, serves as a consultant to the Office of Mental Health Services of the Department of Veterans Affairs (DVA), is a member of the Special Medical Advisory Group, which advises the secretary and under secretary for health of the DVA, and is a member of the American Psychological Association's Treatment Guideline Development Panel for Depressive Disorders.

Christine Maguth Nezu, PhD, ABPP, is professor of psychology and professor of medicine at Drexel University and honorary professor of community health sciences, the University of Nottingham in the United Kingdom. She is past president of the American Board of Professional Psychology and designated as a distinguished scholar/practitioner of psychology by the National Academies of Practice. Dr. Maguth Nezu has contributed to scores of scientific publications, has presented extensively at professional conferences around the world, and is a member of multiple editorial boards of leading psychology journals in the United States and abroad. She is board certified in clinical psychology and cognitive and behavioral psychology by the American Board of Professional Psychology and the clinical director of Nezu Psychological Associates. She serves as a consultant and health sciences specialist to the Department of Veterans Affairs. Dr. Maguth Nezu has received awards for her contributions to the specialty of cognitive and behavioral psychology sponsored jointly by the American Board of Cognitive and Behavioral Psychology and the American Academy of Cognitive and Behavioral Psychology and is a fellow of the American Psychological Association.

Thomas J. D'Zurilla, PhD, is professor emeritus in the Department of Psychology at Stony Brook University. He has also been a practicing clinical psychologist, specializing in cognitive behavioral therapy, for more than 40 years. Dr. D'Zurilla was one of the pioneers in the cognitive-behavioral movement that developed within clinical psychology in the late 1960s and early 1970s. He participated in the development of the first behaviorally oriented clinical psychology training program. Collaborating with Marvin R. Goldfried, Dr. D'Zurilla developed the original model of problem-solving therapy, which was aimed at facilitating broader and more durable behavioral changes with cognitive and behavioral therapies. Their 1971 article titled "Problem Solving and Behavior Modification," published in the *Journal of Abnormal Psychology*, was recognized as a Citation Classic in Current Contents in 1984. Dr. D'Zurilla is an author on nearly 100 theoretical and research publications, most of them in the areas of social problem solving and problem-solving therapy. Together with Arthur M. Nezu and Albert Maydeu-Olivares, Dr. D'Zurilla developed the Social Problem-Solving Inventory-Revised (SPSI-R), which has become the most popular and useful measure in scientific studies on social problem solving and problem-solving therapy. Dr. D'Zurilla's work in these areas has been translated into several foreign languages, including Spanish, German, Japanese, Chinese, and French.

Problem-Solving Therapy

A Treatment Manual

Arthur M. Nezu, PhD, ABPP

Christine Maguth Nezu, PhD, ABPP

Thomas J. D'Zurilla, PhD

SPRINGER PUBLISHING COMPANY

NEW YORK

Springer Publishing Company, LLC
11 West 42nd Street
New York, NY 10036
www.springerpub.com

Acquisitions Editor: Sheri W. Sussman
Composition: Absolute Service, Inc.

ISBN: 978-0-8261-0940-8
e-book ISBN: 978-0-8261-0941-5
Online ancillary ISBN: 978-0-8261-9919-5

Appendices are available from www.springerpub.com/nezu

14 15/5 4 3 2

The author and the publisher of this Work have made every effort to use sources believed to be reliable to provide information that is accurate and compatible with the standards generally accepted at the time of publication. The author and publisher shall not be liable for any special, consequential, or exemplary damages resulting, in whole or in part, from the readers' use of, or reliance on, the information contained in this book. The publisher has no responsibility for the persistence or accuracy of URLs for external or third-party Internet websites referred to in this publication and does not guarantee that any content on such websites is, or will remain, accurate or appropriate.

Library of Congress Cataloging-in-Publication Data

Nezu, Arthur M.
  Problem-solving therapy : a treatment manual / Arthur M. Nezu, PhD, ABPP, Christine Maguth Nezu, PhD, ABPP, Thomas J. D'Zurilla, PhD.
    pages cm
    ISBN 978-0-8261-0940-8—ISBN 978-0-8261-0941-5 (e-book)—ISBN 978-0-8261-9919-5 (Patient handouts)
  1. Problem-solving therapy. I. Nezu, Christine M. II. D'Zurilla, Thomas J. III. Title.
  RC489.P68N49 2013
  616.89'14—dc23
                        2012043303

Printed in the United States of America by Gasch Printing.

This book is dedicated to U.S. veterans and service members

Contents

Preface

Problem-solving therapy (PST) is a psychosocial intervention, generally considered to be under a cognitive-behavioral umbrella, that is geared to enhance one's ability to cope effectively with both minor (e.g., chronic daily problems) and major (e.g., traumatic events) stressors in order to attenuate extant mental health and physical health problems.

Rather than representing an updated volume of the theoretical and empirical literature on PST or social problem solving, the purpose of this book is to serve as a detailed treatment manual and to delineate general intervention strategies of contemporary PST that are required to effectively conduct this intervention approach. This current version (why we refer to it as "contemporary PST") represents significant conceptual and clinical revisions of previous versions of this approach based in part on the authors' clinical and research experience, the extant treatment-outcome literature, and advances in related areas of research in psychology (e.g., decision theory, psychopathology) and neuroscience (e.g., neurobiology, stress, and emotions).

Because this volume is basically a treatment manual, in addition to describing the clinical guidelines, we provide multiple case examples and illustrations as well as worksheets, patient forms, and various handouts that serve as instructional aids.

This book is intended for a wide variety of professionals (e.g., psychologists, psychiatrists, social workers, primary care physicians, counselors, nurses, and teachers) who are interested in directive approaches to psychotherapy and skills training. Because PST has been adapted for a wide variety of populations and clinical problems, professionals should find this manual to be applicable for a multitude of their clients across multiple settings, including outpatient, inpatient, and primary care venues. We believe that clinical researchers interested in abnormal behavior, psychopathology, positive psychology, stress and coping, prevention, personal adjustment, creativity, decision making, and social problem solving will also find this book helpful. Last, this treatment manual, although very clinically oriented, can also serve as a text for a variety of upper-level undergraduate classes as well as applied graduate courses.

Note that the appendices, including the Patient Handouts contained in Appendices II and III, are also available for download on the publisher's website in order to provide them to clients as instructional and informational aids. To download, go to www.springerpub.com/nezu.

We wish to thank our research and clinical colleagues who have knowingly and unknowingly enhanced our thinking over the years, our graduate student assistants who helped immensely with multiple research projects related to this book, and the multitude of patients and clients with whom we have had the honor to work using this approach. We also wish to thank Sheri W. Sussman at Springer Publishing Company, without whom this book would never have been realized.

SECTION I

Conceptual and Empirical Considerations

ONE

Introduction, Brief History, and Social Problem-Solving Constructs

Problem-solving therapy (PST) is a psychosocial intervention, generally considered to be under a cognitive-behavioral umbrella, that is geared to enhance one's ability to cope effectively with both minor (e.g., chronic daily problems) and major (e.g., traumatic events) stressors in order to attenuate extant mental health and physical health problems.

The major treatment goals of PST include:

1. The adoption of an adaptive worldview or orientation toward problems in living (e.g., optimism, positive self-efficacy, acceptance that problems are common occurrences in life)
2. The effective implementation of specific problem-solving behaviors (e.g., emotional regulation and management, planful problem solving)

Overall, PST has been effective in helping individuals suffering from a variety of health and mental health problems, including depression, anxiety, emotional distress, suicidal ideation, cancer, heart disease, diabetes, stroke, traumatic brain injury, back pain, hypertension, and posttraumatic stress disorder (see D'Zurilla & Nezu, 2007, for a detailed overview of the extant outcome literature). It has also been effectively used to treat individuals with schizophrenia and mental retardation as well as implemented as a means of preventing emotional difficulties from initially occurring or becoming worse in certain vulnerable populations, such as veterans returning from combat war zones. PST has further been evaluated empirically as an adjunctive strategy in order to enhance one's adherence to other forms of medical or psychological treatments, as a means of improving the lives of caregivers as well as enhancing their ability to care for a loved one, and as a major treatment component of marital and couples therapy.

The purpose of this book is to serve as a basic treatment manual and to delineate general intervention strategies of contemporary PST that are required to effectively conduct this intervention approach. This current version (why we refer to it as contemporary PST) represents significant conceptual and clinical revisions of previous versions of this approach (e.g., D'Zurilla & Nezu, 2007; Nezu, Nezu, Friedman, Faddis, & Houts, 1998) based in part on the authors' clinical experience, the extant treatment-outcome literature, and advances in related areas of research in psychology (e.g., decision theory, psychopathology) and neuroscience (e.g., stress and emotions).

Whereas many fundamental aspects of contemporary PST remain the same as previous versions (e.g., the use of specific rational problem-solving steps to resolve or cope with stressful problems), this current manual especially emphasizes treatment strategies geared to help individuals better manage emotional dysregulation, a major barrier to effective problem solving. For example, rather than simply caution people to "STOP and THINK" when attempting to cope with a stressful problem as suggested in previous manuals, we have come to better understand the significant difficulties that individuals can have when attempting to do so if such problems are particularly stressful and associated with intense emotional arousal, including anger, depression, and anxiety. As such, we now advocate teaching people to use the "SSTA" method of coping with stress, where S = STOP; S = SLOW DOWN; T = THINK; and A = ACT (see Chapter 8 for a detailed explanation of this model).

PST has been conceptualized and implemented as both a system of psychotherapy (Nezu & Nezu, 2009) as well as a brief, skills-oriented training program (e.g., problem-solving skills training). This latter approach has tended to de-emphasize those PST treatment components geared to foster a positive problem orientation and enhance emotional regulation skills. Whereas programs representing this skills-only approach have been found to be effective, PST protocols encompassing the larger model (as advocated by Nezu, 2004) have fared significantly better regarding outcome (see Chapter 3; Malouff, Thorsteinsson, & Schutte, 2007; Nezu & Perri, 1989). However, given that both approaches have been effective, we present a case formulation approach of PST treatment in Chapter 4 that offers guidelines for PST treatment planning across various populations and circumstances.

STRUCTURE OF MANUAL

Whereas the major purpose of this volume is to provide specific treatment guidelines for effectively conducting PST, we believe it is important to initially provide both the conceptual and empirical underpinnings of this approach for two reasons. First, such information can help the clinician to better understand the fundamental principles inherent in PST and thus be able to apply it more effectively with a variety of individuals and situations. We suggest that the research literature regarding PST, similar to *all* other psychotherapy approaches, has not been able to address *every* individual patient demographic and characteristic (and combination of these characteristics), such as age, ethnicity, sexual orientation, socioeconomic status, comorbidity, and so forth. As such, no manual can offer specific guidelines for every individual or contingency. This notion underscores our basic commitment that it is adherence to understanding and addressing these principles and treatment goals that are important to the success of PST, rather than the specific activities, exercises, scripts, or homework assignments that even we, ourselves, describe and offer in this manual.

Second, we firmly believe that the greater the degree to which our patients and therapy clients understand our approach, the more likely it is that treatment will be effective. In other words, in most cases, if clients understand (and hopefully share) our therapeutic worldview (e.g., why PST is important, how problem solving relates to distress, whether it has been previously documented to be effective for problems similar to those experienced by that client), it is more likely that they will "be on the same page," making treatment activities and objectives more understandable and transparent. As such, we provide the background material in hopes that the clinician has such information in his or her "back pocket" when providing the purposes of PST, the rationale for why it may be important to engage with a particular patient (i.e., why it is relevant to the person or persons requesting treatment), and the evidence showing that PST has been found to be effective in order to instill confidence both in this approach and in the therapist providing PST.

Given the above, we briefly present in this first section of the manual an overview of the theory underlying PST (Chapter 2) as well as the supportive research that documents its efficacy across various populations and clinical problems (Chapter 3). The next section offers an overview of problem-solving assessment and treatment planning (Chapter 4) as well as general clinical considerations (Chapter 5), whereas the third major section provides for detailed clinical guidelines for conducting PST (Chapters 6 through 11). Where appropriate, we also provide examples of the various forms and worksheets that we have developed that can be helpful when conducting PST as well as sample scripts, clinical dialogues, and case examples to illustrate certain points and demonstrate how to conduct various strategies. Note that the Appendices, including the Patient Handouts contained in Appendices II and III, are also available for download on the publisher's website in order to provide them to clients as instructional and informational aids. For information, go to www.springerpub.com/nezu

A BRIEF HISTORY OF PROBLEM-SOLVING THERAPY

In 1971, Thomas D'Zurilla and Marvin Goldfried published a comprehensive review of the relevant theory and research related to real-life problem solving (later termed *social problem solving* (SPS); D'Zurilla & Nezu, 1982; Nezu & D'Zurilla, 1989) that cut across a wide range of related academic and professional fields, including creativity, abnormal behavior, experimental psychology, education, and industry. Based on this review, these behaviorally oriented psychologists developed a prescriptive model of problem solving that consisted of two different, albeit related, components: (a) general orientation (later relabeled *problem orientation*) and (b) problem-solving skills. *General orientation* was defined as a metacognitive process that primarily served a motivational function (i.e., the more positive one's general orientation, the more likely he or she would attempt to solve or handle a difficult problem in living). This process was described as involving a set of relatively stable cognitive-emotional schemas that reflect a person's general awareness and appraisals of problems in living as well as his or her own problem-solving ability (e.g., challenge appraisals, self-efficacy beliefs, or positive outcome expectancies).

Problem-solving skills referred to the set of cognitive-behavioral activities by which a person attempts to discover or develop effective solutions or ways of coping with real-life problems. According to this early model, four problem-solving skills were identified: (a) problem definition and formulation, (b) generation of alternatives, (c) decision making, and (d) solution implementation and verification. In addition to describing the components of this model, D'Zurilla and Goldfried (1971) further presented preliminary guidelines and procedures for training individuals in these skills in order to help overcome deficits in their ability to cope effectively with stressful problems.

Subsequently, by virtue of being a graduate student in clinical psychology under the mentorship of D'Zurilla, Art Nezu became especially interested in the clinical applications of this approach. His initial efforts involved confirming several of the theoretical tenets of the PST model, including the positive benefits of training individuals to better define social problems (Nezu & D'Zurilla, 1981a, 1981b), generate alternatives (D'Zurilla & Nezu, 1980), and make effective decisions regarding such problems (Nezu & D'Zurilla, 1979). Based on research regarding the stress-buffering properties of effective problem-solving coping (e.g., Nezu & Ronan, 1985, 1988), D'Zurilla and Nezu later developed the relational/problem-solving model of stress referred to in Chapter 2 (Nezu & D'Zurilla, 1989), which provided for a conceptual framework supporting the broad-based applicability of PST across a wide range of problems and populations.

In the 1980s, Nezu and colleagues focused their research activities on the relationship between problem solving and clinical depression, an effort resulting in the development of both a conceptual model of depression (Nezu, 1987) and an adapted version of PST for depression (Nezu, Nezu, & Perri, 1989). Since Nezu's earlier outcome studies evaluating the efficacy of PST for major depressive disorder (e.g., Nezu, 1986a, Nezu & Perri, 1989), PST has come to be viewed as an efficacious, evidence-based psychosocial treatment alternative for depression, as supported, for example, by recent meta-analyses of this literature (e.g., Bell & D'Zurilla, 2009b; Cuijpers, van Straten, & Warmerdam, 2007).

Since that time, we, as well as many other researchers and clinicians, have adapted this earlier model to treat a wide range of psychological problems and patient populations. Significant examples include geriatric depression (e.g., Areán et al., 1993; Areán et al., 2010); primary care patients (e.g., Barrett et al., 2001; Mynors-Wallis, Gath, Day, & Baker, 2000); caregivers of adults with various medical illnesses (e.g., Rivera, Elliott, Berry, & Grant, 2008; Wade et al., 2011 [traumatic brain injury]; Bucher et al., 2001 [cancer]); adults suffering from a variety of chronic diseases, including cancer (e.g., Allen et al., 2002; Nezu, Nezu, Felgoise, McClure, & Houts, 2003) and diabetes (e.g., Hill-Briggs & Gemmell, 2007; Toobert, Strycker, Glasgow, Barrera, & Bagdade, 2002); depressed, low-income minority adults (e.g., Ell et al., 2010; Ell et al., 2008); persons with mental retardation (e.g., Nezu, Nezu, & Areán, 1991); adults with personality disorders (e.g., Huband, McMurran, Evans, & Duggan, 2007; McMurran, Nezu, & Nezu, 2008); generalized anxiety disorder (e.g., Dugas et al., 2003; Provencher, Dugas, & Ladouceur, 2004); and sexual offenders (e.g., Nezu, D'Zurilla, & Nezu, 2005; Wakeling, 2007). The primary basis for such adaptations involved the hypothesis that the targeted problem is significantly related to ineffective real-life problem solving (Nezu & Nezu, 2010a; Nezu, Wilkins, & Nezu, 2004). In other words, ineffective SPS can serve as a vulnerability and/or maintaining factor regarding a wide range of psychological disorders and problems. This diathesis-stress model is explained in detail in Chapter 2.

DEFINITIONS OF CONSTRUCTS

The following are definitions of three major concepts integral to PST: problem solving, problem, and solution.

Problem Solving

We define *real-life problem solving* (frequently referred to in the literature as social problem solving in order to differentiate it from the type of problem solving typically not occurring within an interpersonal or social context) as the self-directed process by which individuals attempt to identify, discover, and/or develop adaptive coping solutions for problems, both acute and chronic, that they encounter in everyday living. More specifically, it reflects the process whereby people direct their coping efforts at altering

a. The nature of the situation such that it no longer represents a problem (referred to as problem-focused goals; for example, overcome a barrier to their goals, reduce the conflict between two sets of goals)
b. Their maladaptive reactions to such problems (referred to as emotion-focused goals; e.g., reduce negative emotional reactions, enhance ability to accept that problems are a normal part of life)
c. Both the situation itself and their maladaptive emotional responses to the problem

Rather than representing a singular type of coping behavior or activity, SPS is conceived of in our model as the multidimensional meta-process of ideographically identifying and selecting a set of coping responses to carry out in order to effectively address the particular (and potentially unique) features of a given stressful situation. Note that PST is geared to enhance the efficacy of the process of one's problem-solving activities in order to increase the likelihood that such efforts are ultimately successful. As such, it is important to remember that an effective solution for one individual may not be an effective solution for another person experiencing the same or similar problem. Further, a solution that previously worked for a given person at one point in time may not necessarily work again in a similar situation for the same person at a later date, as that person and/or circumstances may have changed. Therefore, one important feature of effective problem solving is the ability to match adaptive responses with the demands of a given problem while taking into account a variety of external and internal factors present at a given time.

Note that we particularly distinguish between the concepts of problem solving and solution implementation. These two processes are conceptually different and tend to require different sets of skills. Problem solving refers to the process of finding or developing solutions to specific problems, whereas solution implementation refers to the process of carrying out those solutions in the actual situation. Problem-solving skills are conceptualized as being general, whereas solution-implementation skills are expected to be specific to a given situation depending on the type of problem and type of solution. The range of possible solution-implementation skills includes all the cognitive and behavioral performance skills that might be required for effective functioning given a particular person's environment. Because they are different, problem-solving skills and solution-implementation skills are not always correlated. Hence, some individuals might possess poor problem-solving skills but good solution-implementation skills, or vice versa. Because both sets of skills are required for effective functioning, it may be necessary at times to combine PST with training in other social or behavioral skills (e.g., assertiveness skills, communication skills) in order to maximize positive outcomes.

Problem

We define a problem as a life situation, present or anticipated, that

a. Requires an adaptive response in order to prevent immediate or long-term negative consequences (e.g., difficulty regaining practical and/or emotional homeostasis)
b. Wherein an effective response is *not* immediately apparent or available to the person experiencing the situation due to the existence of various obstacles or barriers

Note that the demands engendered by the problem can originate in a person's own social or physical environment (e.g., breakup of a relationship; natural disaster) as well as internally or intrapersonally (e.g., desire to make more money, confusion about life goals, sadness due to a lack of social support).

The barriers that make the situation a problem for a given individual or set of individuals can involve a variety of factors. These can include:

a. Novelty (e.g., moving to a new environment)
b. Ambiguity (e.g., confusion about how a relationship is progressing)
c. Unpredictability (e.g., lack of control over one's career path)
d. Conflicting goals (e.g., differences of opinions about which house to buy)
e. Performance skills deficits (e.g., difficulties in communicating with one's coworkers)
f. Lack of resources (e.g., limited finances to pay a mortgage)

A person might be able to recognize that a problem exists immediately or only after repeated attempts to respond effectively have failed. A problem can be a single time-limited event (e.g., missing a train to work, dropping one's car keys down an elevator shaft); a series of similar or related events (e.g., repeated unreasonable demands from one's boss, repeated violations of a curfew by one's teenage daughter); or a chronic, ongoing situation (e.g., continuous pain, strong ongoing feelings of loneliness, or a significant medical illness).

As we define it, a problem is not a characteristic of either the environment or the person alone. Rather, it is best characterized as a person-environment relationship represented by a real or perceived imbalance or discrepancy between the demands of the situation and one's coping ability and reactions. Therefore, a problem can be expected to change in difficulty or significance over time, depending on changes in the environment, the person, or both. This relational view of a problem has major implications for problem-solving assessment, as it suggests that problems are very ideographic; in other words, what is a problem for one person may not be a problem for another person. Moreover, what a problem is for a given person at one point in time may not be a problem for this same person at a subsequent time.

Solution

A solution is a situation-specific coping response or response pattern that is the product or outcome of the problem-solving process when it is applied to a specific problem situation. An effective solution is one that achieves the problem-solving goal or set of goals (i.e., changes the situation for the better and/or reduces the distress that it produces), while at the same time maximizing other positive consequences and minimizing negative consequences. Important outcomes include the effects on others as well as oneself, long-term effects, and short-term consequences. Within this context, it should be noted that the quality or effectiveness of any particular solution can vary for different individuals or different environments, depending on the norms, values, and goals of the problem solver or significant others who are responsible for evaluating the individual's solutions or coping responses.

REVISED MODEL OF SOCIAL PROBLEM SOLVING

Based on decades of continuous research and program development, we have significantly revised the original D'Zurilla and Goldfried (1971) model of problem solving over the years. According to contemporary social problem-solving theory, attempts at coping with stressful problems are largely determined by two general but partially independent dimensions: (a) problem orientation and (b) problem-solving style (D'Zurilla, Nezu, & Maydeu-Olivares, 2004). Note that this basic model has been repeatedly validated across numerous populations, cultures, and age groups (D'Zurilla & Nezu, 2007).

Problem Orientation

Problem orientation is the set of relatively stable cognitive-affective schemas that represent a person's generalized beliefs, attitudes, and emotional reactions about problems in living and one's ability to successfully cope with such problems. Rather than being two ends of the same continuum, as the original D'Zurilla and Goldfried (1971) model suggested, subsequent research has continuously identified two types of problem orientations, positive and negative, that function orthogonally (Nezu, 2004).

A positive problem orientation involves the tendency for individuals to

a. Appraise problems as challenges
b. Be optimistic in believing that problems are solvable
c. Have a strong sense of self-efficacy regarding their ability to cope with problems
d. Understand that successful problem solving involves time and effort
e. View negative emotions as an integral part of the overall problem-solving process that can ultimately be helpful in coping with stressful problems

A negative problem orientation is one that involves the tendency to

a. View problems as threats
b. Expect problems to be unsolvable
c. Have doubts about one's ability to cope with problems successfully
d. Become particularly frustrated and upset when faced with problems or confronted with negative emotions

Because an individual's orientation can have a strong impact on his or her motivation and ability to actually engage in focused attempts to solve problems, the importance of assessing and addressing this dimension in treatment has always been significantly underscored (Nezu, 2004; Nezu & Perri, 1989). In support of this emphasis, two recent meta-analytic reviews of the extant literature of randomized controlled trials of PST found that exclusion of a specific focus on this orientation dimension led to significantly less efficacious outcomes across various populations (Bell & D'Zurilla, 2009b; Malouff et al., 2007).

Note that we are not suggesting that individuals can be characterized exclusively by either type of orientation across all life problems. Rather, each represents a general tendency to view a certain type or set of problems from a particular perspective. For example, it is very possible (and common in our clinical experience) for an individual to be characterized as holding a positive orientation when addressing achievement relevant problems (e.g., work, career), while additionally having a negative orientation when dealing with affiliation or interpersonal problems (e.g., dating, parenting issues). This is in keeping with Mischel and Shoda's (1995) cognitive-affective system theory of personality that accounts for individual differences in predictable patterns of behavioral variability across situations. For example, it is possible for stable situation–behavior relationships to exist, such that if a given person is confronted with situation A (e.g., representing relationship problems), then he or she is likely to approach it with a negative problem orientation. But if the same person experiences a situation representing a different class of problems (e.g., work- or career-related difficulties), then it is plausible that he or she can approach it with a positive problem orientation. As such, we believe assessing for these situation-behavior patterns is crucial to successful treatment (i.e., accurately identifying both strengths and weaknesses by type of situation).

Problem-Solving Styles

The second major SPS dimension, problem-solving style, refers to the set of cognitive-behavioral activities that people engage in when attempting to solve or cope with stressful problems. Our research has identified three differing styles: (a) rational problem solving (now referred to as planful problem solving, (b) avoidant problem solving, and (c) impulsive-careless problem solving (D'Zurilla, Nezu, & Maydeu-Olivares, 2002; D'Zurilla et al., 2004). Rational or planful problem solving is the constructive approach to coping with stressful problems that involves the systematic and thoughtful application of the following set of specific skills:

1. Problem definition (i.e., clarifying the nature of a problem, delineating a realistic problem-solving goal or set of goals, and identifying those obstacles that prevent one from reaching such goals)
2. Generation of alternatives (i.e., thinking of a range of possible solution strategies geared toward overcoming the identified obstacles)
3. Decision making (i.e., predicting the likely consequences of these various alternatives, conducting a cost-benefit analysis based on these identified outcomes, and developing a solution plan that is geared toward achieving the problem-solving goal)
4. Solution implementation and verification (i.e., carrying out the solution plan, monitoring and evaluating the consequences of the plan, and determining whether one's problem-solving efforts have been successful or need to continue)

We note here again that researchers at times have incorrectly equated rational problem solving with social problem solving, and tended to disregard the important clinical implications inherent in the more complex model that includes orientation variables presented in this chapter (Nezu, 2004).

In addition to planful problem solving, two styles have been further identified, both of which, in contrast, are dysfunctional or maladaptive in nature. In general, both styles are associated with ineffective problem solving. Moreover, people engaging in these styles tend to worsen existing problems and even create new ones.

An impulsive/careless style is the problem-solving approach whereby an individual engages in impulsive or careless attempts at problem resolution. Such attempts are narrow, hurried, and incomplete. A person characterized as frequently engaging in this type of response pattern typically considers only a few solution alternatives, often impulsively going with the first idea that comes to mind. In addition, he or she scans alternative solutions and consequences quickly, carelessly, and unsystematically and monitors solution outcomes carelessly and inadequately.

Avoidant style is another dysfunctional problem-solving pattern, this one characterized by procrastination, passivity, inaction, and dependency on others. This type of problem solver prefers to avoid problems rather than confronting them head on, puts off problem solving for as long as possible, waits for problems to resolve themselves, and attempts to shift the responsibility for solving his or her problems to other people.

PROBLEM-SOLVING THERAPY: TREATMENT OBJECTIVES

In order to achieve the treatment goals stated at the beginning of this chapter, the specific treatment objectives for PST can be thought of as

1. Enhancing positive problem orientation
2. Decreasing negative problem orientation
3. Fostering planful problem solving
4. Minimizing avoidant problem solving
5. Minimizing impulsive/careless problem solving

PROBLEM-SOLVING THERAPY: TREATMENT COMPONENTS

Conceptually, several major obstacles can exist for a given individual when attempting to reach these treatment goals. These include the existence of any or all of the following:

a. Cognitive overload, especially when under stress
b. Limited or deficient ability to engage in effective emotional regulation
c. Biased cognitive processing of various emotion-related information (e.g., negative automatic thoughts, poor self-efficacy beliefs, difficulties in disengaging from negative mood-congruent autobiographical memories)
d. Limited motivation due to feelings of hopelessness
e. An ineffective or maladaptive problem-solving style

In order to achieve these treatment goals and objectives, PST focuses on training clients in four major problem-solving toolkits. Students of PST will recognize several revisions and updates in this current description of contemporary PST, as compared to previous treatment manuals (e.g., D'Zurilla & Nezu, 2007; Nezu et al., 1998; Nezu et al., 1989).

The four toolkits include

1. Problem-Solving Multitasking
2. The Stop, Slow Down, Think, and Act (*SSTA*) method of approaching problems
3. Healthy Thinking and Imagery
4. Planful Problem Solving

Section III of this manual will describe these toolkits and provide for detailed clinical guidelines in order to effectively conduct PST.

SUMMARY

PST is a psychosocial intervention primarily geared toward enhancing one's ability to cope effectively with life stressors as a means of decreasing existing health and mental health difficulties as well as preventing future difficulties from occurring. Since the original model of D'Zurilla and Goldfried (1971) was published, multiple adaptations have occurred, addressing a wide range of clinical populations and problems. Moreover, this original model has been revised in accordance with research both directly addressing PST as well as from other related areas of psychology and neuroscience. Definitions of important concepts were provided in this chapter, including problem solving (i.e., the self-directed process of directing one's coping efforts at changing the nature of a situation such that it no longer represents a problem, one's maladaptive reactions to such a situation, or both), problem (i.e., a life situation that requires an adaptive response but for which no effective action is immediately apparent), and solution (i.e., a coping response that is the outcome of the problem-solving process when applied to a specific situation).

The revised model of SPS includes two major dimensions—problem orientation (i.e., a person's generalized beliefs, attitudes, and emotional reactions to problems in living and his or her ability to effectively cope with them) and problem-solving style (i.e., the cognitive and behavioral activities that are applied to solve or cope with problems in living). Research continuously identifies two orthogonal types of orientations—positive and negative—as well as three types of problem-solving styles (i.e., rational or planful problem solving, avoidant problem solving, and impulsive/careless problem solving).

Overarching PST treatment objectives include the following: (a) enhancing one's positive problem orientation as well as his or her planful problem solving and (b) minimizing one's negative problem orientation, avoidant problem solving, and impulsive/careless reactions. Major obstacles to achieving such objectives include the presence of (a) cognitive overload, (b) poor emotional regulation skills, (c) biased cognitive processing, (d) feelings of hopelessness, and/or (e) ineffective planful problem-solving skills. Given this context, PST trains individuals in a myriad of skills that fit into four toolkits, labeled: *Problem-Solving Multitasking, The SSTA Method, Healthy Thinking and Positive Imagery,* and *Planful Problem Solving.* Section III of this manual provides for detailed guidelines in teaching these skills.

The next chapter describes the underlying conceptual model upon which PST is based.

TWO

A Problem-Solving Approach to Understanding Psychopathology: A Diathesis-Stress Model

This chapter provides an overview of a conceptual model that attempts to explain the role that social problem solving (SPS) plays regarding adaptive versus maladaptive reactions to stressful life events, both major and minor in nature. It builds upon the relational/problem-solving model of stress described as part of our earlier work (e.g., D'Zurilla & Nezu, 2007; Nezu, 2004) but is more expansive in nature in order to place it within a larger biopsychosocial context. Specifically, it additionally takes into account more recent research that focuses on the interplay among certain psychosocial and neurobiological variables regarding stress, emotions, coping, and adjustment. Whereas multiple aspects of this model are associated with empirical support, others have yet to be well researched. As such, we offer this framework as a heuristic that can potentially inform both theory and treatment decisions, as well as providing clients with a worldview that can help them better understand how problem-solving therapy (PST) can potentially be of help.

Note that our problem-solving model of stress involves the interplay among various systems, each of which describes how certain psychosocial, neurological, and biological factors impact and interact with each other to produce negative or positive health and mental health outcomes. Each system represents a dynamic amongst certain variables that impact the next system. It is developmental in nature in that it describes distal, proximal, and immediate levels of analysis regarding how stress impacts health outcomes, as well as how problem solving serves as a potential moderator and mediator of these relationships. With specific relevance to PST, this model provides for a context in which to better understand how and why this approach can be effective across multiple clinical problems and difficulties.

A PROBLEM-SOLVING, SYSTEMS MODEL OF STRESS AND ADAPTATION

This model describes the interplay among three related systems, each of which provides for a level of analysis regarding stressful events, problem solving, and health/mental health outcomes. System I is a distal system and represents our first level of analysis that focuses on the relationship between certain genetic factors and early childhood life stress. This combination can lead to certain biological vulnerabilities regarding increased stress sensitization. System II, the proximal system, focuses on later life (adolescence and adulthood) and the interactions among major negative life events (e.g., divorce, combat trauma, loss of a loved one), daily stressors (e.g., chronic lack of resources, difficult problems with coworkers, marital or relationship problems), and various neurobiological systems that are etiologically related to extant distress. The third system, System III, is the more immediate level of analysis and represents a more microanalytic perspective that addresses the interactions among stressful stimuli, various brain components, and emotions. The role of problem solving is also described within each level of analysis. Note that System I is believed to set the stage for System II outcomes, whereas both these systems impact the outcome of System III, which, in turn, reciprocally impacts System II. The outcomes of each of these systems then predict health and mental health outcomes for a given individual at a given time.

System I: Genetic Influences, Early Life Stress, and Early Biological Vulnerabilities

Figure 2.1 is a graphic representation of System I. This depicts how one's genotype, in combination with early life stress, can produce certain biological vulnerabilities that influence one's reactivity to stress occurring later in adolescence and adulthood.

In essence, research has suggested that individuals who carry certain genotypes, if they experience stressful events early in life, are likely to suffer negative outcomes as an adolescent or adult, especially under conditions of further stress. For example, Gatt and colleagues (2010) found that two genetic factors, brain-derived neurotrophic factor (BDNF) valine 66 to methionine (Val66Met) and serotonin receptor gene 3a (HTR3A), if present

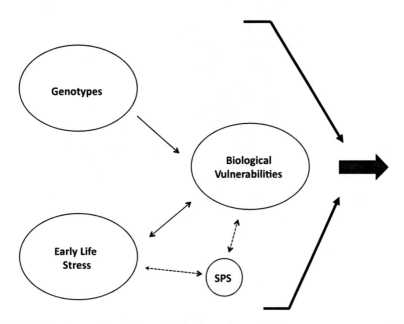

FIGURE 2.1 System I variables: relationships among early life stress, genotypes, social problem solving, and biological vulnerabilities.

and in combination with early life stress, significantly predict a variety of depression risk factors. These include electroencephalogram (EEG) asymmetry, emotion-elicited heart rate, and self-reported negativity bias (i.e., the tendency to see oneself and the world as negative) later in life. Animal models also provide evidence that early life stress enhances an organism's vulnerability to stress later in life via the activation of a gene-mediated transcription within the prefrontal cortex (Uchida et al., 2010).

In addition, Caspi and colleagues (2003) reported that adults with the short-form allele (SS) of a polymorphism of the serotonin transporter gene, 5-HTT, were more likely to develop major depression after experiencing a stressful event as compared to those adults possessing the long-form allele (LL). In essence, the short form of the allele is represented by reduced 5-HTT expression and serotonin uptake and has been shown to be associated with heightened activity in the amygdala, which is highly involved in emotional regulation. Additional research with twins suggest that further 5-HTT genetic variability moderates the negative impact of daily life stress and the risk of experiencing full-blown depression (Wichers et al., 2009). More specifically, these researchers found that the short/long variant of the allele appears to buffer the effects of daily stress, whereas the short/short and long/long variants were shown to increase the risk of depression.

Of particular interest to this model is a study by Wilhelm and colleagues (2007). The major goal of their study was to assess the problem-solving strategies people apply when coping with stress as a function of differing serotonin transporter genotypes. Ten years after a cohort of students participating in a longitudinal study completed a measure of coping with stress, they underwent genetic testing to determine their 5-HTT genotype. Results indicated that the short variant of the 5-HTT promoter polymorphism was associated with the use of fewer problem-solving strategies. This suggests that a possible genetic influence on later emotional difficulties involves a limited ability for individuals with the short variant to draw upon multiple problem-solving strategies when dealing with stressful events.

Whereas genetic factors can create a susceptibility to negative emotional states under stress, stress itself can impact negatively on certain biological systems, including the immune system. For example, Pace and colleagues (2006) reported that depressed patients with increased early life stress were found to exhibit enhanced inflammatory reactions to psychosocial stress. In addition, in a review of the literature regarding the role of childhood trauma on the neurobiology of later mood and anxiety disorders, Heim and Nemeroff (2001) concluded that the extant research strongly indicates that early life stress creates a chronic and persistent hyperactivity and sensitization of various neurotransmitter systems (e.g., corticotropin-releasing factor), which leads to increased endocrine, autonomic, and behavioral stress reactivity. Under conditions of continuous life stress, this vulnerability can result in adult depression and anxiety disorders.

Also depicted in Figure 2.1 is the relationship of SPS within this system. During this period of development, it is likely that children begin to learn how to cope with stress as a function of a combination of multiple sources, including observing how one's parents cope with stress, the rewards and punishments observed by the child regarding how others cope with stress, and the amount of stress the child actually experiences. Because children developmentally are not capable of abstract reasoning (i.e., their frontal lobes are not fully matured until later in life), opportunities to learn concrete coping skills are likely to be limited and very dependent on the specificity of role models imparting such lessons. In other words, unless parents, guardians, or a school system provides formal instruction in coping with life skills, it is likely that a child has minimal opportunities to gain expertise in such skills, especially in terms of which skills are ultimately the correct ones to learn (e.g., planful problem solving versus avoidant problem solving).

Early life stress can be minor, such as minor illnesses or continuous moves due to parental job changes, as well as being very traumatic, such as emotional and/or sexual abuse. Low socioeconomic status, racial discrimination, lack of physical resources, natural disasters, and being bullied constitute additional examples. How one, as a child, deals with these stressors not only impacts the quality of one's coping skills, including SPS, that will persist later in life, but can also serve to moderate the negative effects of such stress at that time. For example, it is possible that even if one has a particular genotype for heightened stress reactivity, if certain stressors are effectively handled, the negative biological impact on the immune system, for example, may be attenuated. However, because such coping reactions are still developing, especially given that the child's brain is also only developing, and is therefore very limited, the role of SPS in this capacity is likely to be also minimal (hence dotted lines connecting SPS within Figure 2.1 are used to denote a somewhat weaker relationship). Moreover, if the stressors are particularly intense (e.g., loss of a parent, sexual abuse), they are likely to overtax one's coping ability, leading to an increased risk for negative biological consequences as well as having a negative impact on one's coping ability (i.e., ineffective problem solving).

It is also worthwhile to note that some early life stress may be necessary to provide the opportunity for children to learn how to cope with adversity. For example, Seery (2011) recently found that some stress during childhood is related to better health outcomes as compared to a history of significant life stress but also in comparison to a history of no early adversity. This notion has generally been supported by research with both monkeys (e.g., Parker, Buckmaster, Schatzberg, & Lyons, 2004) as well as humans. Another example with humans is provided by Gunnar, Frenn, Wewerka, and Van Ryzin (2009), who found that those children with moderate levels of early life stress were characterized by lesser physiological stress reactions as compared to children with either lower or higher levels.

Somewhat related to the above, a last point worth noting addresses the influence that the caregiving style of one's parents or guardians can have on the development of a child's problem-solving and other coping skills. For example, if a given set of parents' style of handling difficult family issues is to minimize the amount of stress the child experiences (e.g., encouraging the child not to cry, being overprotective, being intolerant of the child's emotional life), it is likely that the child will not be able to learn effective problem solving due to the lack of opportunities to do so.

In sum, System I suggests that certain genotypes, in combination with early life stress, can predispose one to certain negative neurobiological vulnerabilities that under future stressful circumstances in adolescence or adulthood increase the likelihood of experiencing negative physical and psychological symptomatology. In fact, a recent review of the overall literature regarding gene-early life stress relationships concludes that there is a definite and significant support for the effects of such interactions regarding the risk for depressive and anxiety disorders later in life (Nugent, Tyrka, Carpenter, & Price, 2011). As such, we suggest that the major impact of System I on System II lies in the creation of both biological (i.e., heightened sensitivity to stress) and psychological (e.g., poor problem-solving ability) vulnerabilities. Within this context, it is important to assess these more distal variables when working with clients in order to obtain a fuller clinical picture (e.g., history of stress and coping).

System II: Major Negative Life Events, Daily Problems, and Neurobiological Reactions

Figure 2.2 depicts the reciprocal relationships among major negative life events, minor or daily problems, and the body's neurobiological reactions to such stressors. It also identifies the role that social problem solving (identified as SPS) plays regarding these factors. This system then has a major impact on one's immediate reactions to stressful triggers (System II), which ultimately predicts health outcomes (see Figure 2.3).

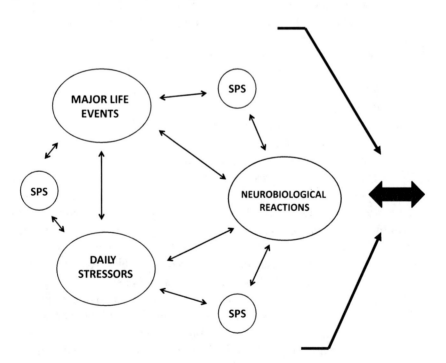

FIGURE 2.2 System II variables: relationships among major negative life events, daily problems, social problem solving, and neurobiological reactivity.

Overall, the first path identified by System II suggests that the experience of a major negative life event (e.g., divorce, loss of a loved one, spouse/partner diagnosed with a chronic illness) increases the likelihood of experiencing stressful daily problems or minor stressors (e.g., legal battles over custody issues, difficulties overcoming grief reactions, serving as a familial caregiver). In turn, experiencing continuing daily problems (e.g., problems with coworkers and/or a supervisor) can engender the occurrence of a major negative life event (e.g., getting fired). Moreover, *both* sources of stress independently and collectively serve to increase the likelihood of one being at a higher risk for experiencing clinical levels of distress, such as major depression and anxiety (Monroe, Slavich, & Georgiades, 2009; Nezu & Ronan, 1985). The relationship between these sources of stress (System II variables) and negative health outcome (the endpoint depicted in System III, as seen in Figure 2.3) are believed to be mediated, in part, by neurobiological kindling and behavioral sensitization, often referred to as *stress sensitization* (Post, 2007). This is depicted in Figure 2.2 by the arrows impacting neurobiological reactions, which then has a direct impact on System III in terms of ultimate negative health outcomes.

Decades of research have identified both direct and indirect effects of stress on health and psychological parameters. For example, work-related stress has been found to be a significant cause of a wide range of both physiological (e.g., pain, coronary heart disease, hypertension) and behavioral (e.g., burnout, aggression, depersonalization) consequences (Pandey, Quick, Rossi, Nelson, & Martin, 2011) as well as depression and anxiety (Melchior et al., 2007). Kendler, Karkowski, and Prescott (1999), for example, found that during a month in which one experienced a stressful life event, the odds ratio for eventually developing major depressive disorder increased more than fivefold. Research has also identified stressor-specific effects regarding stress sensitization. For example, Slavich, Monroe, and Gotlib (2011) found that individuals who experienced early parental loss or separation may be selectively sensitized to current stressors that involve interpersonal loss, even when they experienced overall lower levels of life stress at a given time in adulthood as compared to their less vulnerable counterparts (i.e., persons who did not experience early loss).

Whereas earlier research defined life stress in terms of major negative events (e.g., loss of a loved one, loss of a job), studies beginning in the 1980s (and continuing to date) focus further attention on the effects of daily life stress (often referred to as minor life events, chronic stress, hassles, or daily problems). Such research suggests that the accumulation of daily stressful problems over time can have a significant and independent impact on psychological, social, and health functioning beyond the experience of major negative events (e.g., Hammen, Kim, Eberhart, & Brennan, 2009; Monroe, Slavich, Torres, & Gotlib, 2007; Nezu & Ronan, 1985; Weinberger, Hiner, & Tierney, 1987).

Research focused on an attempt to better understand why individuals who suffer from a major depressive episode will also experience repeated recurrences of depression over their lifetime has identified chronic daily stress as a potential mediator of this relationship. More specifically, major negative life events tend to be associated with engendering the onset of a first depressive episode, but not recurrent episodes, whereas chronic stress (e.g., difficulty paying bills, infidelity, continuous spousal arguments) is associated with more frequent lifetime episodes but not related to the onset of an initial depressive episode (Monroe et al., 2007). Moreover, Monroe and colleagues (2006) demonstrated that, over time, if such daily stress remains chronic, progressively *less* severe forms of life stress are capable of triggering an episode of depression (i.e., stress sensitization).

Note that in Figure 2.2, System II is depicted as having a reciprocal relationship with the ultimate mental and physical health outcomes that are depicted in System III. In other words, the more negative health outcomes that are engendered by stress, the more likely that such diminished functioning will serve to increase stress (e.g., poor physical or emotional health leads to poorer work performance, which leads to increased problems at work, which leads to getting fired, and so forth). This process is often referred to as the stress generation hypothesis (i.e., poorer health leads to increased stress), which we suggest works in conjunction with the stress sensitization process. In other words, continuous daily stress can eventually lead to a lowered threshold that is necessary to trigger negative health outcomes (i.e., less stress is required to produce poor health over time, the stress sensitization hypothesis), whereas poor health can lead to or create additional sources of stress (e.g., increased daily problems and/or more severe chronic illness; the stress generation hypothesis).

Continuing within Figure 2.2, the arrows from both sources of stress impacting on neurobiological reactions refers to the basic biology of the stress response. This is the beneficial evolutionary response of one's physiological and biological systems in order to maximize a safe outcome in reaction to encountering a stressful stimulus. In essence, the body activates two separate, but interconnected, systems—the sympathoadrenal medullary (SAM) system and the hypothalamic-pituitary-adrenal (HPA) axis. The SAM system activates the "fight or flight" set of responses, which involves the release of epinephrine and norepinephrine. The HPA axis is one part of the central stress response system that is primarily defined by a neuropeptide, corticotropin-releasing factor (CHF), which serves as the critical mediator of the stress response.

Activation of both systems helps the body to prepare itself to ward off harm. However, too much activation can lead to harmful effects (Dallman, Bhatnagar, & Viau, 2000). Chronic stress can alter the regulation of the HPA axis by increasing production of glucocorticoid secretion (cortisol in humans), which can be generally deleterious. For example, decades of research support the notion that dysfunction of the HPA axis can lead to psychiatric disorders, particularly depression (Gutman & Nemeroff, 2011). The effects of severe early childhood stress, as suggested by System I, can potentially lead to abnormalities of this stress-response pattern by lowering the threshold or set point of the HPA axis to stressful events later in life (e.g., Heim, Mletzko, Purselle, Musselman, & Nemeroff, 2008). In addition, research suggests that hyperactivity of the HPA axis is a likely link between depression and one's increased risk for various medical conditions, such as diabetes, dementia, coronary heart disease, and osteoporosis (Stetler & Miller, 2011).

Another important biological system involved in the stress response is the immune system. For example, stress is known to increase one's vulnerability to both physical and psychological difficulties by its ability to suppress one's immune functioning, which generally organizes the body's responses to infections and other challenges (Dhabhar, 2011). Chronic stress can dysregulate the immune system and negatively affect health. For example, elevations in proinflammatory cytokines, such as interleukin-6 (IL-6) and C-reactive protein, serve a key role in increasing one's susceptibility to cardiovascular disease, type 2 diabetes, arthritis, Alzheimer's disease, cancer, and periodontal disease (Kiecolt-Glaser, McGuire, Robles, & Glaser, 2002). The cumulative effects of daily stressors have also been found to promote elevations in these inflammatory markers, explaining how chronic stress leads to poor health (Gouin, Glaser, Malarkey, Beversdorf, & Kiecolt-Glaser, 2012). Further, chronic stress can speed the rate of normal age-related immune dysregulation (Kiecolt-Glaser & Glaser, 2001). In keeping with the importance of understanding System I variables, early life stress is posited to also increase the likelihood of maladaptive immune responses to stress later in life as well as having negative effects on one's nervous system and physiology (Graham, Christian, & Kiecolt-Glaser, 2006; Pace et al., 2006).

Chronic stress has also been found to damage the hippocampus, which is the brain component that is part of the limbic system and plays an important role in the consolidation of information from short-term to long-term memory. However, the damage is not direct; rather, stress depletes hippocampal neurons of glucose (the major source of energy), thereby making them less capable of performing effectively, especially under times of stress (LeDoux, 2002). Because the hippocampus is responsible for regulating the release of cortisol, the major chemical responsible for increasing one's risk of depression, when impaired by chronic stress, allows cortisol levels to increase in the blood stream, thus potentially being unable to prevent problems of memory and depression that are related to this rise in stress hormones.

In the absence of any formal (e.g., medical or psychological therapies) or informal (e.g., increase in social support, change in physical or social environment) interventions or changes, this continuous reciprocal relationship between Systems II and III are likely to lead to continuous recurrence of emotional and psychological dysfunction. This is where SPS is hypothesized to play a significant role. In other words, one psychosocial factor that can account for human individual variability may be largely determined by a person's way of initially reacting to and then handling stress (Nezu, 2004; Olff, 1999). This leads to the hypothesis that SPS can serve as an important moderator and/or mediator of the relationship between stress and emotional distress. Research to date supports this contention and takes the form of two differing types of studies. First, one body of literature has addressed whether ineffective problem solving is related to psychological distress. The second group of studies directly asks the question of whether problem solving can serve as a buffer of the deleterious effects of stress.

If SPS is posited to be an important general coping strategy that can reduce or prevent the negative effects of stress, then it should be significantly related to a wide range of adaptive and maladaptive reactions and consequences. Because a detailed description of this literature is beyond the scope of this chapter, the reader is referred to several sources for an overview (Chang, D'Zurilla, & Sanna, 2004; D'Zurilla & Nezu, 2007; Nezu, 2004; Nezu, Wilkins, & Nezu, 2004). In general, this research, using differing measures of problem solving and focusing on a wide range of subject populations, strongly underscores the relationship between ineffective problem solving and the following: depression, anxiety, suicidal ideation and behaviors, severe mental illness, hopelessness, pessimism, anger proneness, alcoholism, substance abuse, criminal offending, low global self-esteem, attachment insecurity, work stress, nonsuicidal self-injury, and sexual offending.

Deficient problem solving has further been found to be present among a variety of depressed medical patient populations, including individuals suffering from heart failure, cancer, diabetes, stroke, chronic fatigue syndrome, and low vision. It is also predictive of depression, burnout, and emotional distress among various family caregiver populations, including those caring for individuals with cancer, spinal cord injuries, stroke, diabetes, traumatic brain injury, amyotrophic lateral sclerosis (ALS), and vision loss. It has also been found to be related to noncardiac chest pain, chronic low back pain, obsessive-compulsive disorder, post-traumatic stress disorder, and border-line personality disorder (see D'Zurilla & Nezu, 2007 for a review of this literature).

Alternatively, effective SPS has been found to be significantly related to more effective overall coping, higher levels of optimism, peer-judged inter-personal competence, social adjustment, better study habits among college students, effective parenting and caregiving behaviors, higher perceived con-trol, positive mood, positive trait affectivity, better life satisfaction, greater sense of self-mastery and hope, higher levels of empathy, higher levels of motivation, and positive subjective well-being (see D'Zurilla & Nezu, 2007 for a review of this literature).

In addition, problem solving has been found to be a better predictor of physical health than physical activity, alcohol consumption, and social support (Largo-Wight, Peterson, & Chen, 2005). It has also been found to mediate the relationship between executive functioning (i.e., reasoning, concept formation, cognitive flexibility) and social outcome among children experiencing a traumatic brain injury (Muscara, Catroppa, & Anderson, 2008). The perception of life problems as being threatening and unsolvable (high negative problem orientation) and an impulsive problem-solving style was further found to predispose elderly adults to commit suicide (Gibbs et al., 2009).

A second group of studies directly evaluated the hypothesis that SPS is a moderator and/or mediator of the relationship between stressful events and psychological and physical distress. An early example is represented by a study conducted by Nezu and Ronan (1985) with college students (and sub-sequently replicated with individuals diagnosed with major depressive disorder) that found support for the following associations: (a) major nega-tive life events increased the number of daily problems; (b) higher levels of daily problems were associated with higher levels of depressive symptoma-tology; and (c) problem solving served to mediate the relationship between daily stress and depression. Another type of study found that under simi-lar levels of high stress, college students characterized as effective problem solvers reported lower levels of depressive symptoms as compared to their ineffective problem-solving counterparts, suggesting that problem solving, by virtue of its moderating effect on stress, served to attenuate the negative effects of experiencing high levels of such stress (Nezu, Nezu, Saraydarian, Kalmar, & Ronan, 1986). These results were later replicated with regard to anxiety (Nezu, 1986b), within a longitudinal design (Nezu & Ronan, 1988), with regard to adults with major depressive disorder (Nezu, Perri, & Nezu, 1987), as well as adult cancer patients (Nezu, Nezu, Faddis, DelliCarpini, & Houts, 1995).

Additional investigators have found SPS to serve a similar stress-buffering function regarding, for example, interpersonal conflicts and anxiety (Londahl, Tverskoy, & D'Zurilla, 2005); suicidal behaviors and ideation among adolescents (Grover et al., 2009); depression and anxiety among middle-aged and elderly community residents (Kant, D'Zurilla, & Maydeu-Olivares, 1997); psychological well-being among middle-aged adults (Chang, D'Zurilla, & Sanna, 2009); adjustment in elementary school children (Dubow & Tisak, 1989); childhood abuse and suicidality among a juvenile delinquent sample (Esposito & Clum, 2002); daily stress and adjustment in college students (Bell & D'Zurilla, 2009a); perceived stress and noncardiac chest pain (Nezu, Nezu, & Jain, 2008); depression among female college students (Brack, LaClave, & Wyatt, 1992); perfectionism and depressive symptoms among Chinese adults (Cheng, 2001); depression in adolescent girls (Frye & Goodman, 2000); childhood depression (Goodman, Gravitt, & Kaslow, 1995); anxiety and anger (Miner & Dowd, 1996); hopelessness, depression, and suicidal ideation among college students (Priester & Clum, 1993; Yang & Clum, 1994); adjustment, health, and academic performance of British university students (Baker, 2003); suicide ideators and attempters (Rudd, Rajab, & Dahm, 1994); suicidality among college students (Clum & Febbraro, 1994); and adolescent depression (Spence, Sheffield, & Donovan, 2003).

Collectively, the above findings are consistent with the assumptions posited by our model that characterizes SPS as an important coping mechanism that can attenuate the negative effects of various sources of stress. As such, these results suggest that teaching individuals to better cope with stressful circumstances via PST can serve as an effective means of both attenuating extant pathology, increasing one's resilience to stress, and possibly preventing future health and mental health difficulties. In other words, learning to more effectively cope with stress can serve to decrease the experience of major negative life events and chronic daily problems as well as potentially attenuating the impact that such stress can have on one's immune functioning, physiology, and neurobiology.

It is interesting to note that sometimes the inability to tolerate the negative neurobiological effects of stress in and of itself is associated with poorer problem solving. For example, as described in Chapter 1, we characterized a negative problem orientation, in part, as involving difficulties with simply experiencing negative emotions. Further, an avoidant problem-solving style can be negatively reinforced if one successfully avoids feeling negative affect by either engaging in avoidant behavior (e.g., drinking) or impulsive behavior (e.g., quickly trying to deal with the problem in order to not have to experience the negative emotion). A particularly serious example of this scenario is presented by Nock and Mendes (2008), who found that adolescents who frequently engage in non-suicidal self-injury (NSSI; e.g., self-cutting) do so because (a) they experience heightened physiological arousal following a stressful event, (b) use NSSI to regulate this emotional distress, and (c) have deficits in their problem-solving skills, particularly with regard to decision making and having a negative problem orientation, that limit their ability to identify and engage in more adaptive social responses.

In sum, System II focuses on a global picture of how two sources of stress, major negative life events and chronic daily problems, serve to increase the likelihood of ultimately experiencing symptoms and problems on a clinical level, such as major depression. The means by which this occurs involves the impact of stress on various biological systems, including the SAM system, the HPA axis, and the immune system. Whereas the evolutionary benefit of having such alarm systems is to increase survival, that is, to have the body become better prepared to either "fight" a given threat or to "flee" it, overtaxing these systems can lead to harmful effects. Because the outcome of System I processes leads to increased stress sensitivity, then even normal levels of daily stress can trigger significant pathology. In addition, the experience of either major negative life events or chronic daily problems was shown to potentially serve as sources of stress generation. In other words, major negative life events can lead to multiple daily problems and, reciprocally, chronic daily problems can create a major negative life event. Having both processes (stress sensitization and stress generation) continue to occur in the absence of any formal or informal intervention or change is hypothesized to increase the probability of an individual experiencing a variety of both health and mental health difficulties.

System III: Stress, Emotions, the Brain, and Social Problem Solving

System III, as depicted in Figure 2.3, is not a system independent of System II. Rather, it is a more microanalytic and immediate representation of how components of the brain react to stress, both consciously and nonconsciously to produce emotional reactions, which, depending on their intensity and chronicity, may lead to poor health and psychological outcomes. As such, this analysis represents another major departure from our prior relational problem-solving model of stress in that we previously gave primacy to Lazarus's (1999) depiction of emotion as being primarily cognitive and conscious in nature. In the current model, we contend that physiologic arousal occurs within milliseconds, which often can engender negative emotional reactions in the absence of cognitive appraisals (Damasio, 1999; LeDoux, 1996). In fact, difficulties in solving real-life stressful problems can

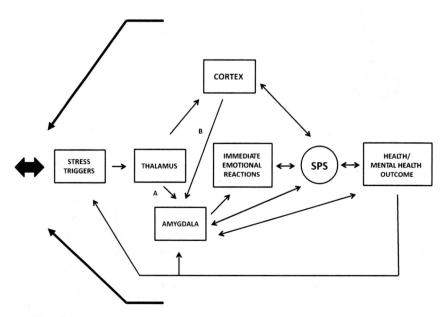

FIGURE 2.3 System III variables: relationships among stress, emotions, brain components, social problem solving, and health outcomes.

result from a person *not* knowing or being able to cognitively label an emotional response (e.g., as sadness, anger, anxiety), even though such a response directs both further emotional and behavioral reactions (e.g., feeling panicky in a crowd leads one to run away, pushing people while doing so, and experiencing significant physical anxiety symptoms in the absence of being able to label such a response as being a panic attack due to the similarity between certain stimulus cues felt in the crowd as compared to previous combat events). In other words, we often experience a feeling without even knowing that a feeling is taking place (Damasio, 1999).

This disconnect between one's immediate emotional response and subsequent behavior (especially attempts to solve or cope with stressful life problems), which can often be ineffective under stress, has substantial implications for treatment. For example, our therapy protocol for better handling immediate negative emotional responses has greatly expanded (see Chapter 8, "*The Stop, Slow Down, Think, and Act*" method of problem solving, to help individuals make better decisions regarding what strategies to employ in order to solve problems under stress, in part, by better understanding their emotional reactions.

Figure 2.3, in part, can be viewed as the microanalytic system that occurs with the neurobiological reactions box in System II with specific regard to brain functioning. In addition, the box labeled stress triggers represents the immediate stimuli, both external (e.g., loud noise, angry boss) and internal (e.g., physical sensations of pain, thoughts about an upcoming stressful business meeting), that can trigger an emotional reaction in a given individual. As depicted in Figure 2.3, information about such stressful or threatening stimuli directly reaches the amygdala by way of the sensory thalamus, as well as via an indirect path through the cortex. Before we continue, we need to remind the reader about these brain functions (note that because a detailed description of brain functions and their relations to emotions is far beyond the scope of this book, we refer the reader to several sources—Damasio, 1999; LeDoux, 1996, 2002).

The thalamus is that part of the brain, situated between the cerebral cortex and midbrain, that is responsible for relaying sensory and motor signals to other parts of the brain, particularly the cerebral cortex. It can be thought of as the brain's switchboard. The amygdala, part of the limbic system, are almond-shaped clusters of nuclei located deep within the brain's medial temporal lobe and is considered the neural structure most closely tied to the processing and memory of emotions. The cerebral cortex is the tissue outermost to the brain's cerebrum (one's grey matter) and plays a key role in the brain's higher level cognitive functioning processes, such as memory, attention, awareness, thought, language, and consciousness.

Relevant to this discussion, it is important to note that research has shown that damage to the amygdala is associated with impairment in decision making in both experimental tasks (e.g., Bechara, Damasio, Damasio, & Lee, 1999) as well as in real-life situations (Tranel & Hyman, 1990). To some degree, this additionally points to the importance of emotions in facilitating effective judgments (Damasio, 1999), which is an important aspect of PST, in that we believe both (i.e., reason and emotion) are important for effective coping and problem solving.

In part, Figure 2.3 depicts not only how emotional stimuli (i.e., stress triggers) are processed via these parts of the brain but, more importantly, how such processing can lead to one's immediate emotional responses. LeDoux (1996, 2002) refers to the path in Figure 2.3 (stimulus to the thalamus to the amygdala, labeled "A") as the "low road," which is shorter and faster. Having this sensory input occur so quickly allows us to react to threats in a timely manner for survival value. However, this low road, because it is so fast (milliseconds), unfortunately provides the amygdala with less complete and accurate information about the threat. The second path (thalamus to cortex to amygdala, labeled "B" in Figure 2.3) is slower, but because it travels through the cortex, allows for a more accurate representation of the emotional stimulus. LeDoux refers to this as the "high road."

To better understand the implications of these two pathways to emotions, LeDoux (1996) provides for an illustration suggesting that we imagine ourselves walking in the woods when we hear a crackling noise. The noise represents the incoming stimulus, which is received by the thalamus and goes straight to the amygdala (the low road). Based on previous experiences, the amygdala may interpret this sound as that of a rattlesnake shaking its tail. However, the noise stimulus also travels from the thalamus to the cortex (the high road), which may ultimately recognize the noise to be that of a dry twig being snapped as we walk through the woods. But as LeDoux continues to explain—" . . . by the time the cortex has figured this out, the amygdala is already starting to defend against the snake. The information received from the thalamus is unfiltered and biased toward evoking responses. The cortex's job is to prevent the inappropriate response rather than to produce the appropriate one" (p. 165). Note that this analysis is not implying that the high road is actually the conscious path to the amygdala. The amygdala only engages in implicit processing, regardless of which route the sensory information travels (LeDoux, 2002). The emotional stimulus only reaches our consciousness when we process the information through brain networks involved in working memory.

As such, it is this nonconscious emotional reactivity that can direct behavior, for better or for worse. As noted in LeDoux's (1996) example, one's nonconscious reaction to a noise can result at times in fear (if processed as a snake via the low road) or nonchalant neutrality (if processed as a twig snap via the high road). In order for the person to correctly appraise the true nature of the threat (e.g., is it a snake, a dry twig, or a wolf stepping on a dry twig?), the emotional stimulus needs to be processed more consciously. In essence, as Pessoa (2010) contends, the amygdala can be viewed as the brain structure that attempts to answer two questions: (a) "What is it?" (i.e., what is this emotional stimulus, e.g., a snake or a twig?) and (b) "What's to be done?" (i.e., should I fight the snake, run away because it is too scary and ferocious, or do nothing because it's just a twig?). In trying to answer these questions, the amygdala serves to mobilize the organism to obtain additional information from the environment. From a PST perspective, this implies that it may be important to help individuals to (a) better understand how their emotional reactions may or may not be appropriate or effective given the emotional stimulus that initially triggered off the response; and (b) if, in general, such reactions are *not* effective (i.e., the problem does not get solved), to help them to discover, invent, or identify more effective ways of coping with stressful difficulties (i.e., to become better problem solvers). In other words, it is important to help direct the amygdala to choose a more effective response, especially since emotional stimuli can frequently impair cognitive performance, such as disrupting goal-attainment behavior (Dolcos & McCarthy, 2006).

It should also be emphasized that chronic daily stress represents a much larger impact on the brain and the body as compared to a singular encounter with a "snake/twig sound." Continuous daily stress (e.g., marital distress, poor work environment, lack of financial resources) leads to continuous activation of the amygdala, which can negatively impact on one's ability to engage in more high-road processing unless provided with the opportunity to stop and think. In the event that environmental (e.g., demanding boss at work) and/or internal (e.g., negative ruminative thinking) emotional stimuli continuously activate the amygdala, immediate emotional reactions to such stimuli can be difficult to handle in the absence of effective coping strategies.

Of additional significant relevance to this aspect of the model is research by Davidson and his colleagues (summary provided in Davidson & Begley, 2012) regarding resilience. In essence, Davidson suggests that people who have significant difficulty bouncing back from adversity are characterized by having fewer signals traveling from the prefrontal cortex to the amygdala. This can be caused by low activity in the cortex itself or from a lack of actual neural connections between the left prefrontal cortex and the amygdala. People characterized as being particularly resilient have been found to have the opposite—strong left prefrontal cortex activation in response to adversity and strong connections between the cortex and the amygdala. The implications of this process are significant—"By damping down the amygdala, the prefrontal cortex is able to quiet signals associated with negative emotions, enabling the brain to plan and act effectively without being distracted by negative emotion . . ." (p. 72).

Although they do not map onto each other 100% (remember that LeDoux [2002] emphasizes that the high road is not a conscious pathway), it is interesting to note that various decision-making researchers have also proposed dual-system models, albeit not necessarily biological in nature, that differentiate between more implicit and explicit pathways to human judgment. For example, Stanovich and West (2000) propose two systems of cognitive functioning that provide for a remarkably similar model to that of LeDoux. These decision-making researchers differentiate between two differing systems. System I refers to one's intuitive system, characterized as being fast, automatic, effortless, implicit, and emotional (similar to LeDoux's low road). System II, on the other hand, reflects the reasoning pathway that is slower, conscious, effortful, explicit, and logical (at least in function, somewhat similar to LeDoux's high road).

Also similar to LeDoux's (2002) description of the brain pathways, Stanovich and West (2000) suggest that both these systems can be involved in making a given choice or decision. Further, System II can improve upon the product of an impulsive, System I judgment and make a better decision (this function parallels that of the high road improving upon the accuracy of recognizing the exact nature of the emotional stimulus or trigger). However, if the person making the decision is under pressure or stress, or if System II functioning is overtaxed, then it is likely that System I will take precedence.

In addition, similar to the notion that at times low road information can be very important (i.e., to alert the individual that a threat or aversive stimulus may be present, such as the snake), System I thinking can also be helpful to survival. For example, not having enough time to decide if the noise was a snake or not, the choice to flee the area is probably a good one, even if it was only a twig breaking, as the cost-benefit payoff of avoiding danger is much lower than the loss of staying in one place for a longer time, regardless if that part of the woods was perceived as beautiful or peaceful immediately before the noise was heard.

Collectively, the research described above from both neuroscience and decision theory appear to underscore the importance of including information from two differing systems in order to maximize the success of one's attempts at problem solving real-life stressful difficulties.

Getting back to Figure 2.3, in the absence of any formal or informal changes or interventions, we suggest that the cumulative processes of Systems I, II, and III can ultimately lead to negative health and mental health outcomes. The experience of such negative symptomatology, due to its reciprocal relationships with elements of System II, can further impact negatively, via stress generation and stress sensitivity, on other components of this model, including one's coping or problem-solving ability. As an example, Leykin, Roberts, and DeRubeis (2011) found that individuals characterized by high levels of depressive symptomatology sought less information that could be helpful in their attempts at problem solving, made use of fewer resources, were less likely to make decisions that would resolve ambiguous situations, and made poorer decisions overall. In addition, Keinan (1987) had found that individuals under stress, regardless of how controllable that stress was perceived to be, were more likely to make impulsive decisions and to not consider a wide range of alternatives that could have resulted in better decision making.

On the other hand, according to our model, if one is an effective problem solver, it is possible that he or she can respond to stressful situations in ways that can attenuate the negative effects of stress (i.e., effectively solve stressful problems), as supported by research described previously (e.g., Bell & D'Zurilla, 2009a; Nezu et al., 2008).

SUMMARY

This chapter presented a problem-solving model of stress in which three systems were identified: one being distal in nature (early childhood), the second system being more proximal (current stress), and the third more immediate and microanalytic. This model is offered as a heuristic framework that explains (a) how early life stress, in combination with certain genotypes, can negatively impact later reactivity to negative life events and daily problems during adolescence and adulthood by increasing one's stress sensitivity; (b) how two sources of stress (major events and daily problems) reciprocally interact with each other via a stress generation process (i.e., major events can create or generate daily problems and daily problems can engender major life events); (c) how such stress impacts various neurobiological systems that serve to increase one's survival potential under normal conditions (i.e., prepare the body to fight or flee from a negative emotional stimulus), but if overtaxed (i.e., either via the experience of significant stress in the form of major trauma or chronic daily stress or both, or if one's coping ability is insufficient to effectively handle such stress) can lead to harmful negative health outcomes (e.g., depression, anxiety, chronic medical illness); (d) how emotional stimuli are processed in dual systems (the low road and the high road), both of which involve implicit processing by the amygdala, and can lead to variable behavioral and emotional reactions; and (e) how SPS can serve to moderate these relationships such that effective problem solving can potentially attenuate the negative effects of stress on well-being at multiple levels throughout the three systems. Whereas aspects of this model have yet to be empirically supported (e.g., does problem solving have any direct impact on neurobiological parameters?), on the molar level of focusing on the moderating role of problem solving regarding major and minor stressful events, substantial research does point to the buffering aptitude of effective problem solving, hence supporting the rationale for viewing PST as an efficacious intervention.

THREE

Problem-Solving Therapy: Empirical Support and Flexibility of Applications

This chapter first provides a brief overview of the empirical support underscoring the efficacy of problem-solving therapy (PST). As indicated previously, this type of information, while not usually offered to a client in detail, can be important for the therapist to convey as a means of instilling confidence that this approach is scientifically grounded. A second goal of this chapter is to demonstrate how PST can be flexible in terms of its multiple applications across clinical problems and populations as well as with regard to the methods or venues by which it can be implemented.

EMPIRICAL SUPPORT FOR PROBLEM-SOLVING THERAPY

Since the initial publication of the D'Zurilla and Goldfried (1971) training model, clinical researchers have applied and evaluated PST, both as a singular intervention strategy, or as part of a larger treatment package, with regard to a wide variety of adult patient populations and problems. In part, Table 3.1 provides for a listing of such studies by participant group. Because the details of such studies are beyond the scope of this manual, the reader is encouraged to review those studies of interest as well as peruse a more comprehensive description of this literature in D'Zurilla and Nezu (2007). More importantly, as described in the next section, recent meta-analyses of this literature provide for a general summary and set of conclusions regarding the efficacy of PST.

TABLE 3.1 Problem-Solving Therapy Outcome Studies for Adults by Diagnosis/Problem Area

Alzheimer's Disease (Comorbid with Depression)
- Teri, Logsdon, Uomoto, & McCurry (1997)

Arthritis
- DeVellis, Blalock, Hahn, DeVellis, & Hockbaum (1987)
- Lin et al. (2003)

Cancer Patients
- Allen et al. (2002)
- Audrain et al. (1999)
- Doorenbos et al. (2005)
- Fawzy et al. (1990)
- Given et al. (2004)
- Mishel et al. (2002)
- Nezu, Nezu, Felgoise, McClure, & Houts (2003)

Caregivers (of)
- Berry, Elliott, Grant, Edwards, & Fine (2012): adults with severe disabilities (TBI, stroke, cerebral palsy)
- Cameron, Shin, Williams, & Stewart (2004): adults with advanced cancer
- Demeris et al. (2012): hospice residents
- Elliott, Brossart, Berry, & Fine (2008): spinal cord injured adults
- Gallagher-Thompson et al. (2000): physically/cognitively impaired elderly
- Gendron, Poitras, Dastoor, & Pérodeau (1996): dementia patients
- Grant, Elliott, Weaver, Bartolucci, & Giger (2002): stroke patients
- Rivera, Elliott, Berry, & Grant (2008): traumatic brain-injured patients
- Sahler et al. (2002): pediatric cancer patients
- Wade, Wolfe, Brown, & Pestian (2005): children with traumatic brain injury

Depression
- Dowrick et al. (2000)
- Lynch, Tamburrino, & Nagel (1997)
- Nezu (1986b)
- Nezu & Perri (1989)
- Robinson et al. (2008)
- Warmerdam, van Straten, Twisk, Riper, & Cuijpers (2008)

Depression/Anxiety/Work-Related Stress
- van Straten, Cuijpers, & Smits (2008)

Depression (Collaborative Care Model)
- Ell et al. (2010): comorbid with diabetes
- Ell et al. (2008): comorbid with cancer
- Katon et al. (2004): comorbid with diabetes
- Unützer et al. (2001)
- Williams et al. (2000)
- Williams et al. (2004): comorbid with diabetes

Depression Comorbid With Cardiovascular Disease
- Gellis & Bruce (2010)

(continued)

TABLE 3.1   Problem-Solving Therapy Outcome Studies for Adults by Diagnosis/Problem Area (*continued*)

Depression (Elderly)
- Alexopoulos, Raue, & Areán (2003)
- Areán et al. (1993)
- Areán, Hegel, Vannoy, Fan, & Unuzter (2008)
- Areán et al. (2010)
- Ciechanowski et al. (2004)
- Gellis, McGinty, Horowitz, Bruce, & Misener (2007)
- Williams et al. (2000)

Depression Prevention
- Feinberg et al. (2012)
- Rovner, Casten, Hegel, Leiby, & Tasman (2007)

Diabetes Patients
- Anderson et al. (1995)
- Glasgow, Toobert, & Hampson (1996)
- Halford, Goodall, & Nicholson (1997)
- Toobert, Strycker, Glasgow, Barrera, & Bagdade (2002)

Generalized Anxiety Disorder
- Dugas et al. (2003)
- Ladouceur et al. (2000)
- Provencher, Dugas, & Ladoucher (2004)

Hypertension
- García-Vera, Labrador, & Sanz (1997)

Marital/Couples Therapy
- Jacobson & Follette (1985)
- Kaiser, Hahlweg, Fehm-Wolfsdorf, & Groth (1998)

Mental Retardation/Intellectual Disabilities
- Benson, Rice, & Miranti (1986)
- Castles & Glass (1986)
- Loumidis & Hill (1997)
- Nezu, Nezu, & Areán (1991)
- Tymchuk, Andron, & Rahbar (1988)

Neuroticism
- Stillmaker & Kasser (2012)

Obesity
- Black (1987)
- Black & Threlfall (1986)
- Murawski et al. (2009)
- Perri et al. (1987)
- Perri et al. (2001)

Offenders
- McGuire (2005)
- Nezu, Fiore, & Nezu (2006)
- Ross, Fabiano, & Ewles (1988)

Pain
- van den Hout, Vlaeyen, Heuts, Zijlema, & Wijen (2003)

(continued)

TABLE 3.1 Problem-Solving Therapy Outcome Studies for Adults by Diagnosis/Problem Area (*continued*)

Personality Disorders
- Huband, McMurran, Evans, & Duggan (2007)

Posttraumatic Stress Disorder
- McDonagh et al. (2005)

Primary Care Patients (Depressed)
- Barrett et al. (1999)
- Barrett et al. (2001)
- Katon et al. (2002)
- Mynors-Wallis, Gath, Day, & Baker (2000)
- Mynors-Wallis, Gath, Lloyd-Thomas, & Tomlinson (1995)

Primary Care Patients (Mixed Anxiety/Depression)
- Catalan, Gath, Bond, Day, & Hall (1991)
- Hassink-Franke et al. (2011)
- Kendrick et al. (2005)
- Lang, Norman, & Casmar (2006)
- Mynors-Wallis, Davies, Gray, Barbour, & Gath (1997)
- Schreuders et al. (2007)

Psychosis/Schizophrenia
- Bradshaw (1993)
- Falloon et al. (1982)
- Glynn et al. (2002)
- Hansen, St. Lawrence, & Christoff (1985)
- Liberman, Eckman, & Marder (2001)
- Liberman, Falloon, & Aitchison (1984)
- Liberman, Wallace, Falloon, & Vaughn (1981)
- Marder et al. (1996)
- Tarrier et al. (1998)
- Wallace & Liberman (1985)

Social Anxiety
- DiGiuseppe, Simon, McGowan, & Gardner (1990)

Traumatic Brain Injury
- Rath, Simon, Langenbahn, Sherr, & Diller (2003)
- Wade et al. (2011)

Suicide and Self-Harm
- Biggam & Power (2002)
- Fitzpatrick, Witte, & Schmidt (2005)
- Lerner & Clum (1990)
- McLeavey, Daly, Ludgate, & Murray (1994)
- Salkovskis, Atha, & Storer (1990)

Traumatic Brain Injury
- Rath, Simon, Langenbahn, Sherr, & Diller (2003)
- Wade et al. (2011)

Unexplained Medical/Physical Symptoms
- Wilkinson & Mynors-Wallis (1994)

Results of Meta-Analyses

The first published major meta-analysis regarding PST was conducted by Malouff, Thorsteinsson, and Schutte (2007) and contained 32 studies encompassing 2895 participants. It included randomized controlled trials (RCTs) that evaluated the efficacy of PST across a variety of mental and physical health problems. Results of this meta-analysis found that although there was a trend in favor of PST when compared to other bona fide interventions, that difference was not significant. In other words, PST was found to be equally effective as compared to other legitimate forms of psychotherapy. Further, PST was found to be more effective than no treatment, attention placebo conditions, and treatment as usual. These results strongly suggest that PST is an efficacious clinical intervention. In addition to these main effects, the authors also tested the relevance of various moderators of outcome. Significant moderators included whether the PST protocol being evaluated included training in the problem-orientation component, whether homework was assigned, or whether a developer of PST (i.e., Nezu) was a coauthor of a particular study.

Although a trend in favor of a higher number of hours of treatment was associated with greater effect sizes, this was not significant. Additional analyses indicated that the following variables were also not significantly associated with outcome: whether treatment was provided in a group setting or individually; whether the participants had been identified before the study as having a clinical problem; whether that problem involved depression; whether the investigation used self-report, objective, or both types of measures; and the length of the follow-up assessment.

A second meta-analysis published the same year focused exclusively on PST for depression studies (Cuijpers, van Straten, & Warmerdam, 2007). Their analysis included 13 RCTs evaluating PST for depression (total $N = 1133$ participants). This analysis found that the majority of studies assessed identified favorable results for PST. The overall effect indicated moderate to large effects of PST on depression, although the effects tended to vary among studies. In this analysis, in contrast to the Malouff et al. (2007) meta-analysis, Cuijpers and colleagues identified a stronger outcome for group interventions as compared to individual interventions. Similar to that earlier meta-analysis, these authors also found that those investigations that included training in problem orientation had larger effect sizes than those studies that did not. They further concluded that although additional research is necessary, especially in light of the variability in outcome across the included studies, PST is an effective approach for the treatment of depression.

A second meta-analysis that also focused exclusively on PST investigations for depression that included seven additional studies beyond that encompassing the pool in the Cuijpers et al. (2007) meta-analysis yielded a similar conclusion (Bell & D'Zurilla, 2009b), that is, PST is an effective treatment for depression. In addition, PST was found to be equally as effective as both alternative psychosocial therapies and pharmacological treatments, but more effective than supportive therapy and attention control groups. Moreover, significant moderators of treatment outcome included whether the PST program included problem-orientation training, whether all four problem-solving skills (i.e., problem definition, generating alternatives, decision making, and solution implementation and verification) were included, and whether all five components were included (i.e., problem orientation and the four problem-solving skills). Another moderator of outcome that approached significance was whether a measure of social problem solving was included.

A fourth meta-analysis of interest did not focus exclusively on PST. Rather, Cape, Whittington, Buszewicz, Wallace, and Underwood (2010) conducted a meta-analysis and meta-regression regarding brief psychological therapies (i.e., less than 10 sessions) for anxiety and depression in primary care. The majority of these 34 studies fell under three categories: cognitive behavior therapy (CBT), counseling, and PST. In essence, all three types of interventions were found to be effective, and equally so, for treating anxiety and depression in primary care settings.

These four meta-analyses collectively provide substantial evidence supporting the efficacy of PST for a variety of physical and mental health problems, particularly depression. Of particular importance is the finding across the three PST meta-analyses that assessed this issue, that excluding training in the problem-orientation component served to decrease its impact and efficacy. Note that this specific hypothesis was tested directly in a study with clinically depressed adults and yielded results in keeping with these meta-analytic conclusions (Nezu & Perri, 1989). Given these overall findings, therapists providing PST to a client can be confident that the basics of PST are scientifically grounded.

FLEXIBILITY OF PROBLEM-SOLVING THERAPY

In addition to its efficacy, we also wanted to illustrate how flexible PST can be with regard to its adaptability across client populations and means of implementation. Table 3.1 already provides a sense that PST can be adapted to treat problems of individuals ranging in intensity of mental illness (e.g., individuals with schizophrenia), intellectual functioning (e.g., adults with mental retardation/developmental disabilities), and physical limitations (e.g., patients suffering from stroke, traumatic brain injury, executive functioning deficits). It has also been applied to patients themselves, family caregivers, and couples.

PST has also been found to be adaptable regarding varying types of modes of implementation. Following is a brief overview highlighting these various populations and venues.

Group Problem-Solving Therapy

An example of PST applied in a group format is an outcome study that evaluated the efficacy of PST for adults reliably diagnosed with unipolar depression (Nezu, 1986a). Specifically, depressed adults in a community outpatient setting were randomly assigned to one of three conditions: (a) PST; (b) problem-focused therapy (PFT); or (c) waiting-list control (WLC). Both therapy conditions were conducted in a group setting over 8 weekly sessions lasting from 1.5 to 2 hours. The PFT protocol involved therapeutic discussions of patients' current life problems but did not include systematic training in problem-solving skills per se. Both traditional statistical analyses and an analysis of the clinical significance of the results indicated substantial reductions in depression in the PST group as compared to both the PFT and WLC conditions. These results were maintained over a 6-month follow-up period. Further analyses revealed that PST participants increased significantly more than the other two groups in problem-solving effectiveness and also improved significantly in locus-of-control orientation (i.e., from external to internal). These improvements were also maintained at the 6-month follow-up. Overall, these results provide support for the basic assumption that PST produces its effects by increasing problem-solving ability and strengthening personal control expectations.

Problem-Solving Therapy for Individuals and Significant Others

Conceptualizing the stress associated with adjusting to cancer and its treatment as a series of problems (Nezu, Nezu, Houts, Friedman, & Faddis, 1999), PST has been applied as a means of improving the quality of life of adult cancer patients (Nezu, Nezu, Felgoise, McClure, & Houts, 2003). As with most chronic medical conditions, the diagnosis and treatment of cancer can serve as a major stressor and, consequently, can increase the likelihood that such patients will experience heightened levels of psychological distress (Nezu, Nezu, Felgoise, & Zwick, 2003). This study, known as Project Genesis, represents how PST can be applied on an individual and couples basis. In this project, adult cancer patients with clinically meaningful elevated scores on measures of depression and psychological distress were randomly assigned to one of three conditions: (a) PST (10 individual sessions), (b) PST-plus (10 sessions of PST provided to both the patient and a patient-selected significant other in order to evaluate the effects of including a caregiver as a problem-solving coach), and (c) a WLC. Results of pre/post analyses across multiple measures that included self-reports, clinician evaluations, and collateral ratings, provide strong evidence underscoring the efficacy of PST in general for this population. Moreover, these results were maintained at 6-month and 1-year follow-ups. Additional analyses provided evidence that including a significant other in treatment serves to enhance positive treatment effects beyond that attributable to receiving PST by oneself. More specifically, at the two follow-up assessment points, patients in the PST-plus condition, on several of the outcome measures, were found to continue to experience significant improvement as compared to individuals in the PST condition.

Problem-Solving Therapy as Part of a Larger Treatment Package

PST has also often been included as an important component of a larger cognitive behavioral treatment package. As an example, García-Vera, Labrador, and Sanz (1997) combined PST with education and relaxation training for the treatment of essential hypertension. Overall, compared to participants comprising a WLC, treated patients were found at posttreatment to have significantly lowered blood pressure. These positive results were further found to be maintained at a 4-month follow-up assessment. Whereas studies evaluating the efficacy of a treatment package cannot provide data specific to any of the included intervention components, a subsequent analysis of their outcome data (García-Vera, Sanz, & Labrador, 1998) revealed that reductions in both systolic and diastolic blood pressure were significantly correlated with improvements in problem solving. Moreover, problem solving was found to mediate the anti-hypertensive effects of their overall stress management protocol, suggesting that PST was at the very least an important and active treatment ingredient.

Problem-Solving Therapy for Caregivers

In addition to the effects on patients themselves, chronic illness and its treatment can have a significant impact on the lives of a patient's family members, in particular, a primary caregiver (Houts, Nezu, Nezu, & Bucher, 1996). The impact of the role of caregiver involves increased distress, physical symptoms, and feelings of burden. In this context, several researchers have applied PST as a means of improving the quality of life of caregivers themselves across a range of medical patient problems (C. M. Nezu, Palmatiere, & Nezu, 2004). For example, Sahler et al. (2002) evaluated the efficacy of PST for mothers of newly diagnosed pediatric cancer patients. After an 8-week intervention, mothers in the treatment condition were found to have significantly enhanced problem-solving skills, which was associated with significant decreases in negative affectivity. Similarly, Grant, Elliott, Weaver, Bartolucci, and Giger (2002) found PST provided to caregivers of stroke patients to be effective in decreasing caregiver depression as well as enhancing their problem-solving ability and caregiver preparedness.

Problem-Solving Therapy as a Means to Foster Adherence

Beyond applying PST as the major treatment modality to decrease psychological distress and improve functioning, it has also been used as an adjunct to foster the effectiveness of other cognitive and behavioral intervention strategies. For example, Perri et al. (2001) hypothesized that PST would be an effective means by which to foster improved adherence to a behavioral weight loss intervention by helping individuals to overcome various barriers to adherence, such as scheduling difficulties, completing homework assignments, or the interference of psychological distress. More specifically, after completing 20 weekly group sessions of standard behavioral treatment for obesity, 80 women were randomly assigned to one of three conditions: (a) no further contact (BT only), (b) relapse prevention training, and (c) PST. At the end of 17 months, no differences in overall weight loss were observed between women assigned to the relapse prevention and BT-only groups, or between those assigned to the relapse prevention and PST groups. However, PST participants had significantly greater long-term weight reductions than BT-only participants, and a significantly larger percentage of PST participants achieved clinically significant losses of 10% or more in body weight than did BT-only members (approximately 35% versus 6%). As such, these findings further highlight the flexible applicability of PST for a variety of clinical goals. In another study that focused on women who participated in a lifestyle intervention for obesity, improvements in problem solving were found to mediate the relationship between treatment adherence and weight loss outcome (Murawski et al., 2009). In addition, women experiencing reductions in body mass index $\geq$ 10% were found to demonstrate significantly greater improvements in problem solving than those participants with reductions < 5%.

Problem-Solving Therapy as a Secondary Prevention Strategy

Research has identified a strong association between problem-orientation variables and levels of functional disability among persons experiencing low back pain (LBP). For example, van den Hout, Vlaeyen, Heuts, Stillen, and Willen (2001) found that a negative orientation toward problems was associated with higher levels of functional disability in persons with LBP. In addition, Shaw, Feuerstein, Haufler, Berkowitz, & Lopez (2001) found low positive orientation and both high impulsivity and avoidance to be correlated with functional loss in LBP patients. Based on such findings, van den Hout, Vlaeyen, Heuts, Zijlema, and Wijen (2003) evaluated whether PST provided a significant supplemental value to a behavioral graded activity protocol in treating patients with nonspecific LBP regarding work-related disability. Their results indicated that in the second half-year after the intervention, patients receiving both graded activity and problem solving (GAPS) had significantly fewer days of sick leave than their counterparts who received graded activity plus group education. Further, work status was more favorable for the GAPS participants in that more employees had a 100% return-to-work record and fewer patients received disability pensions one-year posttreatment. These results point to the potential efficacy of PST as a secondary prevention strategy.

Problem-Solving Therapy as Part of a Collaborative Care Approach

PST has frequently been evaluated as part of an overall collaborative care model of treatment. This type of program had been originally developed to better meet the needs of patients being treated for depression in primary care settings (Katon et al., 1997) and more recently been applied to individuals suffering from a medical disease comorbid with depression. Essentially, individuals identified as being depressed follow a particular algorithm in part based on patient choice. For example, in a study by Ell and colleagues (2010) that focused on treating major depression among low-income, predominantly Hispanic patients with diabetes, such individuals were initially provided a choice of either PST or antidepressant medication (Weeks 1-8). During Weeks 9 through 12, patients with a partial or nonresponse to this initial protocol were offered a different antidepressant medication, the addition of an antidepressant medication, or PST. During the third phase, patients who remitted were moved to a monthly maintenance/relapse prevention telephone monitoring protocol, whereas nonresponsive individuals were considered for additional PST, additional medications for insomnia, or referral to specialty mental health. The research protocol compared this collaborative care approach to enhanced usual care. Although results did not identify a significant impact of treatment on blood glucose levels, individuals in the collaborative care program were found to experience significantly lowered depression, anxiety, diabetes symptoms, and other psychosocial variables.

Problem-Solving Therapy and Telephone Counseling

At times, access to university or hospital-based intervention programs can be limited for people living in rural or sparsely populated areas. In addition, due to other responsibilities and commitments such as child care, many medical patients may not have the ability to travel to a university or major medical center where such research is taking place. As such, we need to be able to identify additional means by which to reach such individuals and increase the clinical applicability of such interventions. One approach has been the use of the telephone to administer psychosocial protocols. Allen et al. (2002) conducted a study where PST was delivered over the telephone as a means of empowering women with breast carcinoma to cope with a range of difficulties when diagnosed in midlife. Specifically, six PST sessions were provided to 87 women with breast cancer—two were in person and the middle four were provided by a nurse over the phone. Whereas PST was found generally to be an effective approach, results were not as supportive of the efficacy of this method of providing PST *across all subjects*. More specifically, relative to the control group, patients receiving PST who were characterized as poor problem solvers at baseline experienced no changes in the number and severity of cancer-related difficulties. However, patients with average or good problem-solving skills at baseline were found to have improved mental health as compared to controls as a function of the intervention. Collectively, these results provide partial support for this method of PST but suggest that a more intensive form of this intervention (e.g., more sessions, more face-to-face contact) may be required for individuals with premorbid ineffective coping ability. The Grant et al. (2002) study involving PST for caregivers of stroke patients noted previously also used a telephone counseling approach, providing further support for this mode of PST implementation.

Problem-Solving Therapy Over the Internet

Another means of enhancing accessibility to treatment is via the Internet. Warmerdam, van Straten, Twisk, Riper, and Cuijpers (2008) compared two intervention approaches, Internet-based CBT and Internet-based PST, with a WLC among community adults with elevated depression scores. The CBT program included 8 weekly lessons and contained education, exercises, and audiovisual aids with examples of people applying the CBT principles. Although PST did not include audiovisual aids, it did involve information, exercises, and examples of people applying the principles of PST provided over 5 weekly lessons. At a 12-week assessment point, both conditions were represented by clinically significant drops in depressive symptom severity as compared to the WLC. No differences in efficacy were identified between CBT and PST; however, the effects of PST were realized more quickly.

Problem-Solving Therapy Using Videoconferencing/Videophones

Videoconferencing and videophones represent a third means by which researchers have attempted to provide PST as a means of enhancing accessibility to treatment. For example, Elliott, Brossart, Berry, and Fine (2008) delivered individualized PST to family caregivers of persons living with a spinal cord injury. The initial session involved a 2- to 3-hour face-to-face meeting with the caregiver in their residence. Subsequent sessions were conducted in monthly videoconferencing meetings over the course of one year. Results indicated that, as compared to an education-only condition, caregivers receiving PST treatment were found to experience less depression, while their care recipients reported significant gains in social functioning. More recently, Demeris and colleagues (2012) conducted a noninferiority trial of PST for hospice caregivers wherein a videophone condition was compared to PST in person. Members of both conditions received three PST sessions either face-to-face or by video calls. Results from 126 caregiver participants indicated that there were no differences in outcome between experimental arms; that is, caregiver quality of life improved and anxiety decreased under both conditions. These two studies strongly support the notion that this form of treatment implementation (i.e., videoconferencing) can be an effective means of providing PST, thus, helping to overcome accessibility barriers.

Problem-Solving Therapy as a Prevention Strategy

More recently, we have been collaborating with the Department of Veterans Affairs to develop a prevention program applying PST-based principles in order to help Veterans who are experiencing challenges in adjusting from active duty to civilian life (Nezu, Nezu, Tenhula, Karlin, & Beaudreau, 2012; Tenhula, 2010). The focus of this pilot program is on prevention and early intervention among Veterans of the conflicts in Iraq and Afghanistan who may be experiencing distress. The PST training has been designed to promote psychological resilience and prevent a worsening of mental health symptoms (Nezu, 2009; Nezu & Nezu, 2010b). In part, as a means of minimizing any stigma associated with mental health treatment, this program is provided in classroom settings and promoted as life skills training. Evaluation of this program, termed *Moving Forward*, is currently underway. However, preliminary results of the program evaluation analysis including close to 170 veterans indicate very high levels of attendance and treatment acceptability as well as significant improvements in depression, overall distress, problem solving ability, and resilience.

SUMMARY

Since the publication of the D'Zurilla and Goldfried (1971) training model, multiple efforts have been geared to apply PST to a wide variety of adult populations and clinical programs. Three major meta-analyses of this literature, two of which specifically focused on PST for depression, provide significant support of characterizing PST as an evidenced-based intervention. Of particular significance are findings that PST is equally effective as other psychosocial (e.g., CBT) and medical (e.g., antidepressants) treatments. An additional meta-analysis evaluating various brief forms of psychotherapy for depression and anxiety among primary care patients also found PST to be an effective intervention. This chapter further demonstrated how flexible PST can be in terms of applying it to various clinical disorders, as well as with regard to the mode of treatment delivery. For example, it has been found to be efficacious when applied individually, in groups, with caregivers, and in primary care settings, as a means of enhancing adherence to other treatments, conducted over the telephone, using videoconferencing, or over the Internet.

SECTION II

Assessment, Treatment Planning, and General Clinical Considerations

FOUR

Assessment and Treatment Planning Issues

This chapter first focuses on practical assessment issues related to the effective implementation of problem-solving therapy (PST). Readers who are interested in broader conceptual, theoretical, and/or research issues related to the assessment and evaluation of the construct of social problem solving (SPS) are referred to other sources (D'Zurilla & Maydeu-Olivares, 1995; D'Zurilla & Nezu, 1990, 2007). Secondly, this chapter provides for treatment guidelines to help the reader best determine what form or version of PST (e.g., full-blown PST versus problem-solving skills training) should be implemented with a given individual.

PROBLEM-SOLVING ASSESSMENT

The three basic categories of clinical assessment of problem solving include

1. Assessment of problem-solving abilities and attitudes
2. Assessment of current problem-solving activities
3. Assessment of problems experienced by a given client or client population

Assessment of Problem-Solving Abilities and Attitudes

This type of evaluation can be useful for three general purposes:

1. Determining whether PST would be a useful intervention for a given individual

2. Obtaining a detailed clinical picture of a person's overall and specific problem-solving abilities and beliefs in order to determine his or her strengths and weaknesses

3. Assessing changes in problem-solving abilities as a function of engaging in PST or other forms of therapy

Social Problem-Solving Inventory-Revised

A measure that we developed to address the above goals is the Social Problem-Solving Inventory-Revised (SPSI-R; D'Zurilla, Nezu, Maydeu-Olivares, 2002). This is a subsequent version of the original 70-item, theory-driven Social Problem Solving Inventory (SPSI; D'Zurilla & Nezu, 1990) that was revised based on a series of factor-analytic studies (Maydeu-Olivares & D'Zurilla, 1995, 1996). The SPSI-R contains 52 items and is a Likert-type inventory that provides for a total score as well as scale scores for the following five major scales that map onto the two problem orientation dimensions and the three problem-solving styles previously described in Chapter 1:

- Positive Problem Orientation Scale (PPO; 5 items; e.g., "Whenever I have a problem, I believe it can be solved.")
- Negative Problem Orientation Scale (NPO; 10 items; e.g., "Difficult problems make me very upset.")
- Rational Problem-Solving Scale (RPS; 20 items; e.g., "Before I try to solve a problem, I set a specific goal so that I know exactly what I want to accomplish.")
- Impulsivity/Carelessness Style Scale (ICS; 10 items; e.g., "When I am attempting to solve a problem, I act on the first idea that comes to mind.")
- Avoidance Style Scale (AS; 7 items; e.g., "I wait to see if a problem will resolve itself first before trying to solve it myself.")

Further, the items of the RPS Scale are divided into four subscales (each with five items) corresponding to the four planful problem-solving skills:

- Problem Definition and Formulation (PDF)
- Generation of Alternatives (GOA)
- Decision Making (DM)
- Solution Implementation and Verification (SIV)

The SPSI-R has strong psychometric properties (see SPSI-R test manual; D'Zurilla et al., 2002). For example, estimates of internal consistency across multiple samples ($N > 1800$) for the total SPSI-R score range from .85 to .96. Test–retest reliability has been estimated to be .87 for the total score. In addition, studies have demonstrated the SPSI-R to have strong structural, concurrent, predictive, convergent, and discriminant validity properties. It is also sensitive to the effects of PST interventions and is not correlated with general measures of intelligence. Normative data is available for both men and women older than 13 years of age and divided into four normal samples: adolescents, young adults, middle-aged adults, and elderly adults. In addition, normative data is provided for select distressed populations, including psychiatric adults, psychiatric adolescents, adult distressed cancer patients, depressed outpatients, and suicidal adult inpatients.

In addition to the SPSI-R, a 25-item short form of this measure is also available (the SPSI-R:S), which measures the five major dimensions but does not measure the specific skills within the RPS scale. This short form is recommended for research purposes or for circumstances where length of testing time is an issue. The 52-item version generally requires about 15 to 20 minutes to complete, whereas the short form can be completed in about 10 minutes.

Note that the SPSI-R has been translated into Spanish (Maydeu-Olivares, Rodríguez-Fornells, Gómez-Benito, & D'Zurilla, 2000), Chinese (Siu & Shek, 2005), German (Graf, 2003), and Japanese (Sato et al., 2006). In each such case, the 5-factor model was cross-validated, providing support for the universal existence of this model of SPS. Moreover, other researchers have validated this model focusing on additional select populations, including a sample of 325 Spanish-speaking North American Hispanic adults (De La Torre, Morera, & Wood, 2010), 219 Australian university students (Hawkins, Sofronoff & Sheffield, 2009), and 499 adult male sexual offenders in the United Kingdom (Wakeling, 2007).

When comparing an individual's SPSI-R scores with the normative data provided in the manual (D'Zurilla et al., 2002), raw scores are converted to standard scores such that the total SPSI-R score as well as each of the five major scale and four subscale scores have a mean of 100 with a standard deviation of 15. In that manner, one can determine a client's particular problem-solving strengths or weaknesses (e.g., one standard deviation above or below the mean in the appropriate direction). For example, if a patient has a score of 120 on the NPO scale (higher scores on NPO indicate more dysfunctional or poorer problem-solving attitudes), then it can be said that he or she is above the normed group average, suggesting a potential problem-solving weakness or area in need of focused intervention. Scores more than two standard deviations from one's group norms are indicative of a *definite* weakness. On the other hand, a score of 132, for example, on the RPS scale, represents a particular strength for a given individual, in that it is two standard deviations beyond the mean of his or her comparison group.

Converting raw scores into standard scores clinically helps to identify areas of relative strengths and weaknesses that might affect a person's current and/or future functioning. It also can help determine the presence of vulnerabilities that may suggest the need for differential levels of treatment. For example, in the absence of any known psychopathology or intense extant emotional distress, average total SPSI-R scores would not trigger decisions to recommend that the person enter PST or other forms of therapy. However, SPSI-R total scores close to two standard deviations below the group mean, in combination with the presence of complaints of emotional or functional difficulties, would support a recommendation for entering PST.

The SPSI-R can also be applied as a means of assessing progress (or lack thereof) for an individual receiving PST or other forms of related psychotherapy where changes in problem-solving abilities and skills would be predicted if the person is getting better. From an evidenced-based perspective, one would expect improvements in problem solving to *precede* improvements in a targeted outcome, such as depression. As such, assessing changes (or lack thereof) in SPSI-R scores can be helpful in determining the success of the intervention at various points during treatment. For example, after several months of PST, if either the ultimate outcome (e.g., depressive symptoms) or problem-solving abilities (e.g., SPSI-R scores) do not improve, then the clinician may need to reassess the appropriateness of this approach.

Problem-Solving Test

A similar measure we developed, called the Problem-Solving Test, was originally intended to be used as a self-help guide for individuals to be able to obtain a ballpark estimate of their real-life problem-solving abilities (Nezu, Nezu, & D'Zurilla, 2007). Whereas it is based to some degree on the SPSI-R, it has not been subjected to any psychometric scrutiny or evaluation to date. This self-help test contains 25 items, shown in Table 4.1. In situations where a therapist believes asking a client to complete this test might be beneficial, the scoring key and brief explanation of the test scores are contained in Appendix I. However, clinicians should remember that this test has unknown psychometric properties and should only be used with caution when attempting to interpret the scores.

TABLE 4.1 **Problem-Solving Test**

1. I feel afraid when I have an important problem to solve.
2. When making decisions, I think carefully about my many options.
3. I get nervous and unsure of myself when I have to make an important decision.
4. When my first efforts to solve a problem fail, I give up quickly, because finding a solution is too difficult.
5. Sometimes, even difficult problems can have a way of moving my life forward in positive ways.
6. If I avoid problems, they will generally take care of themselves.
7. When I am unsuccessful at solving a problem, I get very frustrated.
8. If I work at it, I can learn to solve difficult problems effectively.
9. When faced with a problem, before deciding what to do, I carefully try to understand why it is a problem by sorting it out, breaking it down, and defining it.
10. I try to do anything I can in order to avoid problems in my life.
11. Difficult problems make me very emotional.
12. When I have a decision to make, I take the time to try and predict the positive and negative consequences of each possible option before I act.
13. When I am trying to solve a problem, I often rely on instinct with the first good idea that comes to mind.
14. When I am upset, I just want to run away and be left alone.
15. I can make important decisions on my own.
16. I frequently react before I have all the facts about a problem.
17. After coming up with an idea of how to solve a problem, I work out a plan to carry it out successfully.
18. I am very creative about coming up with ideas when solving problems.
19. I spend more time worrying about problems than actually solving them.
20. My goal for solving problems is to stop negative feelings as quickly as I can.
21. I try to avoid any trouble with others in order to keep problems to a minimum.
22. As soon as someone upsets me or hurts my feelings, I always react the same way.
23. When I am trying to figure out a problem, it helps me to stick to the facts of the situation.
24. In my opinion, being systematic and planful with personal problems seems too cold or "business-like."
25. I understand that emotions, even bad ones, can actually be helpful to my efforts at problem solving.

1 = *Not at all true of me*
2 = *Somewhat true of me*
3 = *Moderately true of me*
4 = *True of me*
5 = *Very true of me*

Assessment of Current Problem-Solving Activities

In addition to the SPSI-R, another form of assessing extant problem-solving abilities and attitudes, prior to conducting PST, can involve a self-description of the actual activities in which an individual engages when attempting to handle or solve a real-life problem. During the initial intake or evaluation period, the clinician can request that clients complete a Problem-Solving Self-Monitoring (PSSM) form that provides for a self-description in response to the following questions regarding a particular real-life problem. A copy of this worksheet is included in Appendix II as a Patient Handout.

- *What was the problem?* Requests clients to provide a brief description of the problem situation, specifically asking who was involved, why they considered this situation to be a problem, as well as to state their goals and objectives for this situation.
- *What was your emotional reaction to the problem?* Asks individuals to describe their initial feelings when the problem first occurred as well as their emotions throughout the episode. Also requests people to note if their emotions changed.
- *What did you do to handle the problem?* Asks people to describe what they did to handle or cope with the problem. In addition, requests that they be as specific as possible while describing their thoughts and actions while in the situation.
- *What was the outcome?* Requests clients to describe the outcome of their problem-solving efforts and to specify their emotional reactions to this outcome. Also asks people to note if they were satisfied with the outcome and to note if they believed the problem was solved or not.

This information, in combination with the person's SPSI-R results, can provide the therapist with important information about a given individual's overall and specific problem-solving attitudes and reactions to a specific problem. It would also be noteworthy to compare individuals' actual problem-solving actions regarding a specific problem to their responses to the SPSI-R, in an attempt to determine how close their self-report matches their actual attempts in real life.

Another important assessment issue would be to request a person to complete more than one PSSM form, specifically requesting him or her to select different types of problems. As noted in Chapter 1, we suggested that it is possible that an individual may be characterized as holding a positive (for example) orientation when dealing with certain types of problems (e.g., achievement-oriented situations such as those involving work, career, or school), while additionally having the opposite type of orientation when reacting to other types of problems (e.g., interpersonally oriented situations, such as those involving romantic relationships, friendships, or social interactions). As such, having the individual complete at least two differing PSSM forms, one for an achievement-oriented problem and one for an interpersonal or relationship-oriented problem, can provide insight into a given client's problem-specific, problem-solving strengths and weaknesses.

Assessment of Current Problems

A third area of assessment involves obtaining a clinical picture of the type of problems a client is currently experiencing. Whereas such information can be obtained via a semistructured interview, at times it is helpful to use various problem checklists or inventories. For example, four differing versions of the Mooney Problem Checklist (Mooney & Gordon, 1950) exist that contain a myriad of age-specific problems (i.e., junior high school, high school, college, and adults) that can be helpful as a quick means of gathering initial intake information.

If the referral problem is specific (e.g., distressed cancer patient), or if PST is being provided to a group that was constituted around a common diagnosis (e.g., depressed heart failure patients or distressed caregivers of patients with traumatic brain injury), other checklists may exist or can be developed that include common problems related to that diagnosis or group theme. Examples of such checklists can be found in Table 4.2 (general problem checklist), Table 4.3 (work-related problem checklist), Table 4.4 (cancer-related problem checklist adapted from our work with adult cancer patients; Nezu, Nezu, Felgoise, McClure, & Houts, 2003), and Table 4.5 (heart failure-related problem checklist adapted from our work with adults diagnosed with heart failure; Nezu et al., 2011).

Requesting that clients complete such brief checklists not only can provide the therapist with important intake information in a timely manner, but can also help to foster a patient's awareness and relief that other people also experience similar types of problems (i.e., normalizing and validating the experience of problems).

PROBLEM-SOLVING THERAPY:
TREATMENT PLANNING CONSIDERATIONS

In order to foster effective treatment planning and clinical decision making specific to PST, this next section provides for a series of "FAQs" (frequently asked questions) for therapists unfamiliar with this approach.

TABLE 4.2 General Problem Checklist

Job or career problem
Drug problem
Marriage problem
Time-management problem
Problem with children or adolescents
Self-discipline problem
Low self-esteem
Academic problem
Emotional problem
Conflict between job and family responsibilities
Moral conflict
Religious problem
Conflict between academic and family responsibilities
Legal problem
Lack of recreation or leisure activities
Housekeeping or home maintenance problem
Transportation problem
Problem with parents or other relatives
Concern about the neighborhood
Concern about the community
Lack of social relationships
Concern about the environment
Interpersonal conflicts
Problems with business products or services
Sexual problem
Sleep problem
Problem with professional services
Financial problem
Illness or disability problem
Problem with social or government services
Lack of exercise
Weight problem
Concern about world problems
Drinking or drug problem

Is PST appropriate for my patient?

When attempting to answer this question, the following issues should be considered:

- Has PST been found to be effective for the types of problems (e.g., depression, generalized anxiety, back pain) that *this* client is presenting?
- Does *this* individual find PST to be acceptable?
- Is *this* person experiencing a significant health or mental health problem?

TABLE 4.3 **Work-Related Problem Checklist**

Problem finding a job
Not enough job autonomy
Job interview problem
Limited opportunity for advancement
Inadequate job performance
Absenteeism or tardiness
Unsafe practices
Poor communication with superiors
Too much work
Too little work
Work not challenging enough
Poor communication with subordinates
Work too difficult or complex
Ambiguous job demands
Poor relationship with peers
Ambiguous job goals
Interpersonal disputes
Conflicting job demands
Ineffective delegation or lack of assertiveness
Too much responsibility
Too little responsibility
Lack of recognition
Lack of opportunity to participate in decision making, which affects job
Aversive or unhealthy work environment
Inadequate pay or benefits
Procrastination
Poor job security
Unproductive meetings
Commuting problems
Wasting time
Too much traveling for the job

Chapter 3 provides for support that PST has been found to be effective for a wide range of psychological problems (see Table 3.1). Moreover, research has suggested that PST is well received as an acceptable intervention approach to treat emotional problems (e.g., Kasckow et al., 2010). As such, affirmative answers to the above questions for a particular patient suggests that PST would be an appropriate intervention for that individual.

What form of PST should I conduct?

Taking a case formulation approach to clinical decision making (i.e., where results of an individualized assessment inform treatment planning decisions)

TABLE 4.4 Cancer-Related Problem Checklist

Physical
- I have trouble walking
- I have difficulty with household chores
- I can't engage in recreational activities anymore
- I'm losing weight
- I'm having problems working
- I have lots of pain

Psychological Distress
- I'm ashamed of the way my body looks
- I worry more than ever now
- I can't seem to think straight
- I have problems making decisions
- I have difficulty talking to my friends
- Most of my friends shun me
- I feel sad all the time
- I have trouble sleeping

Marital and Family
- We aren't talking a lot lately
- Too little affection between us
- My family won't leave me alone
- Change in family roles

Interactions with Health Care Team
- I can't get the information I want
- I can't seem to communicate with the medical team
- I don't like feeling out of control
- I get nervous asking questions
- I get very angry waiting for so long to talk to the doctor for just a few minutes
- I feel like I'm just a patient, not a real person

Sexual
- I lost interest in sex
- Sex is difficult for me
- My partner doesn't want to have sex with me anymore
- I feel so unattractive
- Sex is now very painful
- I can't let my husband see my surgical scars

in addressing this question suggests that the following three dimensions need to be considered:

- The client's overall problem-solving strengths and needs
- The intensity of his or her predominant symptomatology (e.g., depression, anxiety, anger)
- Presence of recent major negative life events or trauma

TABLE 4.5   **Heart Failure–Related Problem Checklist**

I feel tired all the time.
I have difficulty asking questions of my doctors.
I have difficulty doing things around the house.
I feel dizzy a lot.
I don't like the way I look since my heart problems.
I am bothered by the side effects of the medications.
I have difficulty understanding what the health care team tells me.
I find that doctors don't explain things that well to me.
I cannot go to places or travel like I used to.
I have difficulty getting around physically.
I worry about my heart problems all the time.
I feel helpless because of my heart condition.
I feel angry a lot of the time.
I have difficulty sleeping.
I feel sad a lot of the time.
I worry that I will die.
I do not feel sexually attractive.
I have memory difficulties.
I do not feel good about myself.
I have financial problems.
I have problems sticking to a healthy diet.
I have difficulty talking with friends/family members about my health.
I find that friends/family members ignore or avoid me since being diagnosed.
I don't feel that people really understand my situation.
I feel my life has changed for the worse.
I do not feel interested in having sex any more.
I don't get along with people, including family, as well as I used to.
I have difficulty asking people for help.
I feel like a burden to my family and friends.
I often forget to take my medications.
I find it difficult to exercise.

According to Figure 4.1, the more significant the client's problem-solving deficits or the greater the severity of his or her emotional distress or functional problems, the more likely that one should implement a more comprehensive version of PST. The one exception would be the situation where although the individual might not be experiencing emotional distress at clinically significant levels at the present time, he or she has recently experienced a major negative life stressor (e.g., diagnosis of a significant medical illness, divorce, losing a job, losing a close friend or family member) that can increase his or her vulnerability to experience such significant distress in the near future.

An example of this latter approach involves Moving Forward, a 4-session, classroom-like protocol developed by Nezu and Nezu (2012) specifically for veterans of the recent campaigns overseas (i.e., Operation Enduring Freedom,

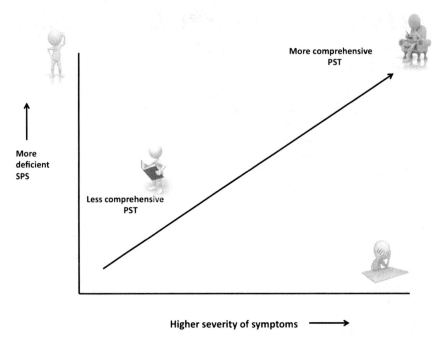

FIGURE 4.1 The relationship between client characteristics and decisions regarding the form of problem-solving therapy to implement with a given client.

Operation Iraqi Freedom, Operation New Dawn). This program is based on selected problem-solving principles and implemented as a prevention approach. More specifically, it is geared to help Veterans better readjust to civilian life by dealing with stressful problems using problem-solving strategies. The goal is to decrease the likelihood that such individuals would eventually experience significant psychological problems and require less medical and psychiatric care.

Less comprehensive forms of PST might entail bibliotherapy (e.g., self-help manuals and handouts, such as those provided within the Moving Forward program or a book based on an earlier version of PST written for the lay public [Nezu, Nezu, & D'Zurilla, 2007]), problem-solving skills training (less emphasis on the orientation treatment components), or a PST workshop (e.g., classroom setting). These types of approaches may be particularly appropriate for primary care or other medical settings, whereby initial PST-based psychoeducational materials can be provided to aid medical patients to (a) better adjust to the experience of a chronic illness (e.g., diabetes, heart disease) and (b) improve their ability to adhere to certain medical treatment regimens, such as complex medication prescriptions.

Last, if time is an issue, depending on results from a more formal assessment of an individual's problem-solving strengths and weaknesses (e.g., SPSI-R findings plus clinical interviews), PST can be tailored to emphasize those areas where deficits are identified while de-emphasizing training in those areas that represent his or her problem-solving strengths.

Can I conduct PST in a group format?

As noted in Chapter 3, PST has successfully been applied in group settings (e.g., Nezu & Perri, 1989). Group treatment can be preferable in those situations where multiple clients are able to serve as sources of feedback to each other regarding both problem-solving skill acquisition and implementation. In addition, group members can share ideas and experiences as well as serve as models and sources of social support and reinforcement. This approach can be particularly effective if structured around a specific clinical population or client problem in order to foster a sense of normalization. Conducting PST in a group format can also serve as a more efficient use of therapists or facilitators. It can also provide for a meaningful analogue to everyday life (i.e., representing numerous interpersonal interactions) in which new ways of coping can be encouraged.

How much time will PST take?

Similar to many other forms of directive psychotherapy, there is little research that directly answers this type of question. RCTs evaluating PST represented by good outcome have included a range of 8 to 20 sessions. Many of these sessions have been between 1 to 1.5 hours in length. Clinically, it would seem fair to suggest that the more intense the negative symptomatology (e.g., moderate versus severe depression), the more likely that PST will take longer. Certain patient populations (e.g., those with chronic illness, traumatic brain injury, or developmental disabilities) may also require more lengthy treatment. In most outpatient settings, the overall length of treatment may be dictated more by insurance considerations, as compared to clinical issues. Given that PST has been found to be effective across multiple settings and venues, it is likely that the basic therapy process can be tailored to fit the needs of a patient population within the restraints of various provider care limitations in most circumstances.

My patient is asking if his spouse can be included in PST, although there are no marital problems. Is this a good idea?

We believe that if both members of a dyad (e.g., married couples, same sex couples, couples living with each other) are willing, having both individuals included can potentially enhance treatment efficacy. This recommendation is directly supported by a study we conducted with adults coping with cancer, entitled Project Genesis (Nezu et al., 2003), where the inclusion of a significant other or support person led to a clinically significant improvement beyond that which was achieved by having only the cancer patient himself or herself receive PST. In certain situations, we believe that such an invitation can also be extended to other family members or adult friends as well.

The significant other can serve as a problem-solving coach and cheerleader. In such a role, such individuals can help motivate, guide, and support the patient. He or she can reinforce the identified client when he or she is actively using a skill and can suggest the use of specific skills (i.e., reminders) when this individual is experiencing distress and not utilizing the skills effectively.

Whereas the primary focus would be for the significant other to be a support person, it is important to provide these individuals with a personal benefit from PST as well. As such, caution should be exercised never to ignore the personal needs of the family members or support person. In addition, some patients may come to treatment experiencing guilt and a sense of burden to their families as a function of the difficulties he or she has been experiencing. Significant others, caregivers, and other family members may also feel particularly guilty or hesitant to talk about their feelings of burden. Caregivers or individuals engaged as coaches may feel additionally burdened by homework assignments or other requirements of the PST intervention. As such, it is important to communicate to the support person that his or her participation in PST can help improve one's own quality of life as well. At times, the problems addressed in treatment may well focus on improving family relationships and communication patterns.

My patient is having severe anxiety and depression problems. I want to apply PST, but I also think it would be a good idea to use other cognitive and behavioral strategies as well. Is this okay?

The astute cognitive behavior therapist will easily note that various overlaps exist among PST and other cognitive behavior therapy (CBT) interventions. As such, there exists a strong compatibility among these therapies regarding philosophy, common features, and at times, specific strategies. As such, PST can easily be combined in conjunction with multiple other types of CBT approaches within a more comprehensive overall treatment plan. For example, PST and various behavioral stress management strategies can be effective in treating a variety of stress and anxiety-related disorders, where PST is included to help an individual better cope with extant stressful problems and events, and stress management techniques are geared to aid in reducing an individual's negative physiological arousal occurring in reaction to such stressors. As another example, PST and behavioral activation strategies can be a powerful means of treating clinical depression by simultaneously addressing two critical depression-related difficulties (i.e., coping with stress and difficulties eliciting and enjoying positive events in one's life). Many of the studies supporting the efficacy of PST have, in fact, combined it with other treatment components in order to maximize the efficacy of a larger treatment package.

I work with a lot of Latina/Latino clients as well as African Americans and Black persons. Has PST been found to be effective for them as well?

Similar to many other evidence-based psychosocial interventions, PST has not been extensively validated with individuals of diverse ethnic backgrounds. However, it has been found to be effective in several studies when provided to Hispanic and Black individuals (Ell et al., 2010; Nezu et al., 2011). As such, although substantial research has not yet been conducted with individuals of a variety of diverse backgrounds, the extant research does underscore the potential applicability and efficacy of PST with such individuals.

Some of the planful problem-solving strategies reminds me of what I do as a therapist in trying to develop treatment plans for various clients. Is there a way that I can use these principles in this way more formally?

We have previously developed a model of clinical decision making and case formulation for cognitive and behavioral therapies that is based on various problem-solving principles (Nezu, Nezu & Cos, 2007; Nezu, Nezu, & Lombardo, 2004). For example, various principles and activities related to helping individuals better define a social problem can easily be thought of as relevant to conducting a comprehensive assessment in order to develop an individualized case formulation model of a given client's problems. The GOA process can foster the assessment (e.g., identifying alternative ways of obtaining clinical information), treatment planning (e.g., identifying alternative treatment strategies to help reach a goal), and evaluation (e.g., identifying alternative means of determining whether treatment is working) phases of therapy. The decision-making set of tasks taught to a client can also be used by a clinician, such as predicting the possible outcomes if a particular cognitive and/or behavioral strategy is implemented, conducting a cost–benefit analysis among the various identified treatment alternatives in order to determine which ones to carry out, and developing an overall treatment plan based on such decisions. The SIV steps would involve the clinician determining whether treatment was being optimally conducted as well as assessing whether it is leading to its predicted outcome.

The relevance for using such problem-solving steps in case formulation and treatment planning increases with the complexity of a given case. Because all patients experiencing the same problem (e.g., depression) are "not created equal," such an approach is highly recommended. In other words, multiple individual difference variables, as well as environmental and social context dimensions, are likely to exist and significantly distinguish among such individuals, thus leading to the need for the therapist to explore how he or she can optimally personalize or tailor PST treatment to a specific client. Readers interested in learning more about the use of problem-solving principles in this context are directed to the above references.

SUMMARY

This chapter first described three major assessment tasks that can help guide PST: assessment of problem-solving abilities and attitudes, assessment of current problem-solving activities, and assessment of problems the individual is currently experiencing. Various inventories and questionnaires were identified to help the therapist conduct such assessments, including the SPSI-R, the Problem-Solving Test, the PSSM form, various Mooney Problem Checklists, and a variety of problem-specific checklists. A second goal of this chapter was to help the clinician to better identify whether PST is an appropriate approach for a given client, as well as to address a variety of additional questions regarding treatment planning issues. These were presented as answers to several FAQs that a therapist beginning to learn this approach might ask.

Before presenting the "nuts and bolts" of PST in Section III, the next chapter addresses a variety of general clinical considerations and training issues.

FIVE

General Clinical Considerations

This chapter addresses a variety of general clinical and therapy issues regarding the effective implementation of problem-solving therapy (PST). First, we briefly discuss the ideal problem-solving therapist and emphasize the importance of the therapist–client relationship. Next, we describe a variety of adjunctive therapy strategies and instructional guidelines that can be used by the clinician to enhance a client's overall problem-solving learning and skill acquisition. We realize that the experienced clinician is likely to find some of this material rather basic, but believe it should be included to remind beginning therapists of the importance of such basics. The third and last topic provides a list of "do's and don'ts" specifically related to the effective implementation of PST.

THE PROBLEM-SOLVING THERAPIST AND THE THERAPIST–PATIENT RELATIONSHIP

Therapist Characteristics

It is likely that most clinicians would argue that, in general, it is important for therapists to be perceived by their clients as warm, empathetic, trustworthy, and genuine. Such is the case with PST. However, these types of characteristics, within the context of PST, should be viewed as representing minimally required, but not sufficient, therapist skill areas. Because the PST clinician is attempting to change long-term patterns of unsuccessful attempts at coping with stress, it is possible that clients may perceive the therapist's attempts to do so as an attack upon their personality (i.e., that it is their poor problem solving that is at fault). As such, it is essential that the PST clinician communicate an acceptance and respect for the individual, while simultaneously explaining why certain habits or patterns may actually be working against his or her goals. Therapists must also realize that when attempting to change such well-learned behaviors, many people may experience fear, frustration, and anger. Such reactions can be directed toward the therapist and the therapy approach itself. In practicing the philosophy of PST, the clinician needs to remain objective in observing, understanding, and analyzing these types of reactions (i.e., effective and appropriate problem definition techniques).

It is also important for the PST therapist to be well-versed in the areas of social problem solving, stress, emotional regulation, brain–behavior relationships, and the various details of a variety of health and mental health problems. A reasonable amount of preparation and understanding of these areas is required in order to convey to the patient a sense of expertise and competence. This also helps the client to better understand how he or she "got to this place in time" (i.e., why the individual currently is having these types of difficulties). As noted in Chapter 2, providing a context or etiological framework within which patients can better understand the nature and cause of their problems can foster clarity regarding therapy goals and the means by which to achieve them. Snyder and colleagues (2002) define hope as the belief that people can find pathways to their desired goals and become motivated to use such pathways. Within this context, providing the client with a brief overview of the problem-solving model of stress not only can suggest which pathways led him or her to the current state of distress, but, more importantly, can create hope by outlining how he or she can identify more effective pathways to reach more positive goals.

In addition, we suggest that the best therapists for this approach are those who tend to use problem-solving strategies in their own lives as a means of coping with stressful situations. This is especially valid if the stressful situation actually involves conducting PST for the first time. For example, we have frequently observed beginning therapists demonstrate a predictable naiveté in their initial approach when addressing certain problem-orientation variables. Armed with a plethora of information concerning the types of selective thinking processes and negative appraisals and attributions associated with disorders such as depression and anxiety, student therapists often report surprise and frustration when patients resist changing these beliefs. They wonder why their clients are so stubborn or resistive. These students, however, are often wrestling with their own self-evaluations of competency and desire to be helpful and successful. Using the PST perspective allows the novice therapist to see how these fears are predictable problems in their own training that need to be solved.

Finally, we further suggest that the best problem-solving therapist is one who also uses these strategies and principles as a guide to his or her clinical decision making and judgment. As introduced in the prior chapter, we have previously developed a comprehensive model of clinical decision making based on a problem-solving formulation (e.g., Nezu & Nezu, 1989; Nezu et al., 2011). In essence, this model posits that a therapist needs to be flexible about developing individualized client treatment plans as well as being aware of the types of biases inherent in all human judgment. Use of the various problem-solving strategies, such as brainstorming a list of treatment strategies for a given patient with a given set of symptoms, rather than engaging in a knee-jerk prescription based on the (possibly false) similarity between this patient and others experiencing similar symptoms, can increase the likelihood that treatment will be ultimately effective.

The Problem-Solving Therapy Therapist–Patient Relationship

As in other forms of psychotherapy, the therapist–patient relationship is also important to a problem-solving approach. Although PST can be thought of as consisting of various training modules, ignoring the importance of the therapist–patient relationship can have a severe impact on the overall effectiveness of this approach. Particularly when individuals are fearful of being independent due to poor self-esteem, they may have difficulties learning strategies that would increase their self-efficacy and help them to function more independently. There may be less anxiety, initially, for such an individual to engage in a counseling approach that relies more on the therapist's problem-solving abilities that provides for a strong sense of social support. The approach that we believe communicates the most respect for a patient is one where the therapist approaches the case with confidence as a scientist to observe, question, test, and synthesize information, and *not* to fix everything.

In addition, the PST clinician should attempt to strike a meaningful balance between being an active and directive practitioner and conveying a sense of collaboration with the client. Because of the inherent psychoeducational flavor of PST, we often present our role of the PST therapist as a teacher, coach, or educator. Moreover, analogies such as becoming a team of investigative reporters, detectives, or personal scientists are often useful in characterizing this collaborative relationship. In other words, they help convey a sense of mutual exploration into the nature of a patient's problems and experience of distress by creating a framework of being active members of a team working toward a mutual goal of getting to the bottom of the story, solving a mystery, or testing certain scientific hypotheses.

Building a Positive and Collaborative Training Relationship

Below are some general guidelines that we have found helpful in developing a positive therapist–patient relationship.

Display Warmth, Empathy, and Genuineness
Whereas many psychotherapies incorporate these positive therapeutic characteristics, there are certain applications to PST interventions that may be particularly important. In addition to showing that one cares about a participant's well-being, expressing warmth by way of a kind, gentle, and patient guidance through this new and uncertain way of coping can do much to reduce the tendency for the client to reject a new learning experience because it may represent unchartered territory. Empathy expressed through careful listening when clients describe their problems and concerns, recognizing their feelings, and communicating one's understanding of such problems and concerns can serve as important steps toward increasing hopefulness that learning these problem-solving skills will be relevant and effective for them. It is also important for the PST clinician to identify a given patient's strengths and to convey that these strengths will serve as "building blocks" upon which to build further skills. One should show genuineness by being a real person in the relationship; using self-disclosure, if and when appropriate (i.e., one's own problem-solving mistakes and successes); and answering a client's questions and concerns honestly and respectfully without being patronizing or condescending. It is important to be genuine regarding the realistic ways in which problem solving may help the person's life. For example, if coping somewhat more flexibly and creatively can improve one's life satisfaction by 10%, 20%, or 50% (versus perfectly), the philosophy to instill is as follows—"Why reject the opportunity to improve your well-being?"

Convey Enthusiasm and Belief in the Intervention
In order to maximize feelings of hope and expectations of benefit in participants, it is important to emphasize the relevance and effectiveness of problem-solving training for a given individual's life. As such, it is helpful if the PST therapist is somewhat familiar with the relevant PST outcome literature. In addition, conveying confidence in this approach is often best communicated by therapists who actually use and have personal confidence in problem solving. The clinician should explain that this approach will help them cope more effectively with stressful daily problems and reduce the negative impact of stress on their emotional and physical well-being in order to better achieve one's life goals. It is important to convey to the client that

PST is *not* just for people who are poor problem solvers. In other words, one should emphasize the fact that it helps good problem solvers to become even *better* problem solvers, as well as better teachers of problem solving (e.g., teaching their children to become effective problem solvers), and that it helps people learn how to apply their problem-solving strengths (e.g., those applied to a work situation) to new (e.g., those required to improve a relationship) problems.

Encourage Participation

Although much didactics do occur in this approach, the therapist needs to conduct PST in an interactive manner that encourages as much participation by the individual as possible. The major training methods for encouraging participation include rehearsal and homework assignments. Rehearsal involves guided practice in solving hypothetical and real problems in the training sessions, and homework assignments involve supervised practice in applying problem solving to real current problems in the natural environment. Note the old Chinese adage regarding the most effective teaching approach:

> *Tell me, and I will probably forget.*
> *Show me, and I might remember.*
> *Involve me, and I will understand.*

ADJUNCTIVE THERAPY/TRAINING STRATEGIES

Similar to many other directive forms of psychotherapy or counseling, in particular those under a cognitive-behavioral umbrella, the success of PST to a large degree depends on the effectiveness of the manner in which it is actually implemented. Therefore, in this section, we describe several general instructional or training principles regarding how to optimally conduct PST.

Psychoeducation/Didactics

PST involves imparting substantial psychoeducational knowledge, using verbal instructions and written materials, while also making use of the Socratic approach to instruction, which emphasizes questions and discussions that encourage individuals to think for themselves and formulate their own conclusions, deductions, and elaborations. Such instruction is consistent with the overall problem-solving goal of facilitating independent productive thinking.

Coaching

Coaching primarily involves verbal prompting, such as asking leading questions, providing suggestions, and offering instructions. For example, the PST therapist can prompt an individual during a brainstorming exercise to begin the process of generating alternative solutions or ask the patient about times when he or she applied a given problem-solving skill during a stressful situation.

Modeling

This includes written and verbal problem-solving examples and demonstrations conducted by the therapist, using hypothetical as well as real problems, presented by the client. This can be done in vivo, through filmed or pictorial presentation, or through role-plays. Occasionally, PST clinicians have found it helpful in group settings to use brief movie or film clips that illustrate how certain characters engage in effective and/or ineffective problem-solving attempts. To facilitate learning and to help individuals discriminate more effectively, it is important at times to model both correct *and* incorrect ways of applying various problem-solving principles.

Shaping

This can involve specific training in the problem-solving process in progressive steps, with each new step being contingent on successful performance in the previous step. In addition, it can be useful to develop a hierarchy of a client's problems, based on the dimensions of severity or complexity, such that less intense or difficult problems may then be used as relevant examples early in treatment. Once the individual has mastered certain prerequisite problem-solving skills, more difficult problems can then be addressed. Shaping can also refer to the therapist providing more guidance in the beginning of the intervention and then requiring the patient to become more involved in a given task, such as generating alternative solutions to a problem.

Rehearsal and Practice

These techniques involve problem-solving practice exercises and homework assignments. In addition to written exercises and assignments, rehearsal may involve role-playing, practice in imagination (covert rehearsal), and practice with real-life problematic situations. The use of visualization, one of the foundational multitasking skills in PST, can be very useful when applied to rehearsing newly learned skills. In addition, homework assignments are a particularly important feature of any skill acquisition. Without practice, the ability to actually implement problem-solving skills in real- ife can be compromised.

Performance Feedback

Feedback about a client's in-session and outside-of-session activities should be provided on an ongoing basis. These include activities documented in their self-monitoring and self-evaluation forms, including homework or practice forms.

Positive Reinforcement

This includes the therapist's praise for trying to apply various problem-solving skills in general as well as specific reinforcement of a given act, even if not perfect. For example, although individuals may continue to react to a problem with worry or a high degree of emotional distress (i.e., negative problem orientation), they may also be simultaneously attempting to brainstorm creative solutions. The specific act of generating alternatives should be reinforced and accompanied with feedback that a more positive orientation could further enhance the benefits of applying that specific skill.

Use of Analogies and Metaphors

Using analogies and metaphors (where appropriate) can be helpful as a means of better illustrating various points or ideas. For example, the therapist can use various skills or knowledge bases (e.g., sports, cooking, driving, hobbies) as a means of explaining the concept that skills, such as problem solving, often take time to learn and that practice is usually required before someone becomes competent or expert in that skill.

PROBLEM-SOLVING THERAPY "DO'S AND DON'TS"

The following list of PST "Do's and Don'ts" are offered as important considerations based on decades of conducting PST, both in clinical and research settings, regarding how to optimally and effectively conduct this approach to treatment.

1. *DO NOT present PST in a mechanistic manner*—PST should be as interactive as possible. Consider this type of therapy as an opportunity for individuals to discover, share, learn, and grow. "Dryly" teaching the various problem-solving skills is likely to be received poorly—although PST is a learning experience, it should not be purely academic.

2. *DO make PST relevant to a particular client or group*—training examples should be specific and relevant to the people at hand. Do not deliver a canned treatment that does not incorporate relevant life experiences of a given individual or group. This is why it is important to conduct a sufficiently comprehensive assessment early during therapy. For example, when initially explaining the problem-solving approach, it is very helpful to elicit personal and relevant examples from the client's life. This should be conducted in an atmosphere of respecting the client's values.

3. *DO include opportunities for practicing the skills in session and between sessions*—as mentioned previously, practice is an important component of PST; clients should be encouraged to practice as much as possible between PST sessions. However, note that with certain individuals, the term homework can be negatively associated with tedious school assignments. Terms such as opportunities to practice, personal missions, or assignments (or other creative terms) will likely garner a better reception.

4. *DO focus on the patient as well as the treatment itself*—although correctly implementing PST is important to ensure its effectiveness, the patient himself or herself should always be the primary focus of attention. Consistently demonstrate respect for patients' feelings and foster the idea that they can use these negative emotions as important information that can help them clarify what is important to their lives.

5. *DO NOT focus only on superficial problems*—the therapist needs to use his or her own clinical decision-making skills to assess whether the problems being discussed are in fact the most crucial for a given client; otherwise, the effectiveness of treatment will be limited. For example, a superficial problem might involve helping a patient to get more dates, when the more important or core issue might entail coping with the fear of committing to an intimate relationship.

6. *DO remember that even creative and effective solution ideas require a solid action plan that needs to be carried out*—the client should be encouraged to implement the solution plan (or parts thereof) in order to obtain the best feedback possible (i.e., problem resolution).

7. *DO NOT equate problem-focused coping with problem-solving coping*—we define *problem-solving coping* as the more general process of dealing with stressful situations. Problem-solving coping entails both *problem-focused* coping (i.e., strategies to change the nature of the situation such that it no longer represents a problem) as well as *emotion-focused* coping (i.e., strategies geared to minimize emotional distress related to the problem and enhance emotional regulation). Individuals should be encouraged to be aware of their emotions as useful information concerning their goals and important values. In addition, the therapist needs to convey to clients that both forms of coping are advisable depending upon the nature of the situation. For instance, if a problem is perceived as unchangeable (e.g., the other person involved in an interpersonal problem is unwilling to change), then a potentially viable and effective solution alternative might be understanding that the situation will not change and to foster one's acceptance of that perspective. Often, problems require both types of problem-solving strategies. For example, the individual who is experiencing problems with a difficult coworker may need to identify several goals, such as (a) acknowledging and managing one's own emotional reactions, (b) changing one's current interpretations that the fellow employee is "out to get me," and (c) brainstorming ways to change the nature of their interpersonal interactions.

8. *DO use handouts as adjuncts to training*—written handouts help clients to remember and practice the skills between sessions. Often it may be useful to encourage the participants to purchase a loose-leaf-type notebook in which to store the handouts for current and future reference. Again, it would be important to adapt such handouts to be relevant to a given target population. We have found handouts to be an extremely useful and effective training tool in both our research and clinical work. Note that there are multiple patient handouts contained in Appendices II and III.

9. *Do conduct an adequate assessment of an individual's problem-solving strengths and weaknesses*—do not assume that "all patients are equal" and conduct PST accordingly (unless if required as part of a controlled clinical research study).

10. *BE SURE to address each participant's concerns if conducting PST in a group format*—it is possible that there may be one or two individuals within the group who tend to monopolize the session. Others may be very quiet and hesitant to participate. Be sure to manage the group such that all members can benefit equally from a group venue. Encourage all members to participate and limit those who tend to dominate.

SUMMARY

We began this chapter with a brief discussion of the characteristics of the "ideal" problem-solving therapist as well as underscoring the importance of the therapist–client relationship. Next, we provided a number of adjunctive instructional strategies and guidelines that can be used to enhance clients' overall learning and skill acquisition. Last, based on our research and clinical practice involving PST, we provided a list of "do's and don'ts" that we believe greatly enhances the efficacy of this approach.

SECTION III

Problem-Solving Therapy: Specific Treatment Guidelines

Overview of the Problem-Solving Therapy Process, Introductory Sessions, and the Case of "Megan"

This chapter begins this section of the therapy manual detailing the specific treatment guidelines encompassing problem-solving therapy (PST). We begin by delineating the components of the overall problem-solving therapy process, followed by a description of the introductory session(s) that include the provision of a rationale for applying PST with a given individual. Last, we provide a brief clinical summary of "Megan," a 27-year-old patient whom we will follow throughout the manual in order to illustrate a variety of training strategies and tools comprising PST.

In addition, beginning with this chapter, and continuing throughout the remainder of this manual, we will refer to numerous patient handouts that we have used in a variety of research and clinical settings. Copies of these handouts are included in the Patient Handouts sections of Appendices II and III. These materials can be useful as adjuncts to the verbal presentations of the various PST training strategies provided during a session. In addition, they can be offered to clients as materials that can be reviewed at home in order to reinforce the philosophy that effective learning and skill acquisition require active between-session activities and effort.

THE PROBLEM-SOLVING THERAPY PROCESS

PST encompasses the following major intervention components across the overall course of treatment:

1. Assessment and Treatment Planning
2. Introductory Session(s)

3. Training in Toolkit #1: Problem-Solving Multitasking—Overcoming Cognitive Overload
4. Training in Toolkit #2: The *SSTA* Method of Problem Solving Under Stress—Overcoming Emotional Dysregulation and Ineffective Problem-Solving Coping
5. Training in Toolkit #3: Healthy Thinking and Positive Imagery—Overcoming Negative Thinking and Low Motivation
6. Training in Toolkit #4: Planful Problem Solving—Fostering Effective Problem Solving
7. Guided Practice
8. Future Forecasting and Termination

As noted in Chapter 4, we suggest that the therapist engage in three types of PST-specific assessments in order to (a) help determine whether PST would be a useful intervention for a given individual, (b) obtain a detailed clinical picture of a person's overall and specific problem-solving abilities and beliefs in order to determine his or her strengths and weaknesses, and (c) assess changes in problem-solving abilities if PST is undertaken. These assessment areas include

1. Assessment of problem-solving abilities and attitudes
2. Assessment of current problem-solving activities
3. Assessment of problems experienced by a given client or client population

Based on the results of this assessment process, in conjunction with findings from the usual evaluation of additional standard demographic and clinical areas (e.g., presence and intensity of a person's emotional distress, daily functioning, treatment goals), the clinician can begin to determine whether PST is an appropriate treatment option for a given individual (see Chapter 4 for PST-related treatment planning considerations). Assuming this assessment leads the therapist to recommend PST to the individual, and assuming the patient agrees to this, the next step in treatment involves providing him or her with a more complete rationale for PST, while establishing a positive rapport.

INTRODUCTORY SESSIONS

Introductory Sessions: Therapeutic Goals

The goals of the introductory session (or sessions) in PST include the following:

- To establish a positive relationship
- To present an overview and rationale of PST
- To encourage optimism

Establishing a Positive Relationship

Using the guidelines presented in the previous chapter, it is important during the initial sessions with a new client to develop a positive therapeutic relationship. Therapists should begin by introducing themselves (e.g., one's professional background and current role regarding this patient's overall treatment) and presenting a brief overview of anticipated activities (e.g., "you and I will be working together to try to reduce some of the distress that you are currently experiencing"). A useful initial starting point is to ask the client about his or her story. In other words, what is currently occurring in the person's life that has led him or her to seek help. We have found it helpful in the beginning sessions to ask the following set of questions—"What do you hope to see happen by coming here?" (i.e., global goals), and "What is currently happening in your life that prevents or makes it difficult for you to get there without a therapist's help?" (i.e., extant obstacles to such goals). This provides for a context that will be repeated throughout PST; that is, conceptualizing the overall therapy process as a mutual effort to "solve the person's problem(s)."

Another area of early inquiry involves identifying recent major stressors that the individual may have experienced (e.g., divorce, rape, traffic accident, loss of job, chronic illness). If the individual was referred by a medical team due to psychosocial complications (e.g., depression, pain) related to a physical illness, it is important to ask the individual about his or her subjective experience (e.g., "Tell me about your experiences—how has [e.g., cancer] affected your life thus far?" versus "Give me the specifics of your medical treatment"). This approach has been reported by patients as comforting because of the relief that someone is willing to discuss the impact of an illness, such as cancer or heart failure, when so many friends and family members may have been avoidant and fearful of discussing such topics.

In addition, when discussing the patient's experience of a major stressor, it is important to ask questions regarding how his or her life has changed (e.g., what are his or her predominant reactions, the reactions of the family, or the effects on his or her job and friends). This information can be augmented by data gleaned from previously completed questionnaires or inventories, especially those addressing the nature and type of problems that the individual is currently experiencing (e.g., problem checklists). It is helpful at this stage to elicit from the person whether and how the major stressful event, such as loss of a job, has exacerbated negative emotional reactions to existing daily stressors (e.g., traffic jams, long lines at the grocery store, or minor arguments with family members) as well as creating new stressful problems (e.g., reduced resources for the family, inability to pay rent, or negative image of self).

During a patient's responses to these types of inquiries, it is important to apply counseling strategies geared to enhance the therapist–patient relationship (e.g., reflection of content and feeling—"It sounds like you felt your whole world fell apart when this happened"). Finally, as in almost all treatment approaches, it is critical for any therapeutic relationship that the clinician display warmth, support, genuine interest, and a sense of commitment to the patient.

If the client also has a comorbid medical illness, it is likely that such an individual may be reluctant to see the need for a "mental health professional" when the perception is that he or she only has a physical illness. As such, it may be helpful to emphasize one's role as a teacher or coach (i.e., to help clients sort through this experience and acquire new skills in order to foster their ability to cope with the illness), as compared to conducting intensive psychotherapy or analysis. In addition, the therapist should underscore the notion of teamwork and mutual respect (e.g., "You will help me to understand how your life has changed and the new problems you have encountered, and I will teach you how people can learn to become more effective at solving many of these types of problems created by this medical illness").

Presenting the Rationale

Upon obtaining a brief version of the client's story, it becomes important early in treatment to provide an overview of PST that includes a rationale for why it is relevant to, and potentially effective for, *this* individual. Providing a rationale increases the likelihood that both the therapist and client be "on the same page" (i.e., where the client understands and agrees with the underlying precepts and philosophy of PST) and, thus, can enhance the likelihood that this treatment will be successful. In doing so, the rationale should be presented in "lay terms," where the clinician is mindful of avoiding jargon and being a "talking head" lecturer. Instead, the information about PST and its potential effectiveness needs to be conveyed within a therapeutic context and with many examples drawn from the real world (e.g., other patients) as well as *this* patient's real world (i.e., using examples previously provided by the individual to illustrate various points, such as how major life events can create additional problems). Moreover, it is important for the therapist to appropriately adapt wording and language in concert with the client's developmental, educational, and cultural background.

We believe the following to be concepts and issues that are critical to include in the rationale provided to all clients. How much time is devoted to any one topic is heavily dependent on the relevance for a particular individual. The reader is directed to Chapters 1 through 3 for more specific information.

1. The impact of early life stress on current reactions to difficult problems (emphasize the *stress sensitization* hypothesis)
2. The negative effects of stressful events, both major negative life changes, as well as chronic daily stressors, on one's health and mental health (emphasize the *stress generation* hypothesis)
3. How the body is evolutionarily geared to react to stress (i.e., threats to one's well-being) with a "fight or flight" (or at times dazed) reaction, but few threats exist in one's current life that are life-threatening
4. How continuous stress, if left unchecked, can have significant negative effects on several parts of *everyone's* body and brain (i.e., emphasize the ubiquity of such responses), such that the ultimate reaction is likely to be clinical levels of distress (e.g., depression, anxiety)
5. How our brains are hardwired to react to emotional stimuli in such a way that at times results in misperceived threats
6. How the brain can be rewired via new learning experiences in order to become more resilient to stress
7. How improving one's coping ability (i.e., problem-solving skills) can decrease the negative impact of life stress
8. How research has demonstrated that PST, as a means of improving one's coping ability, has a strong scientific support base
9. That the skills taught in this intervention are similar to other types of skills (e.g., driving, sports, music, cooking) in that, similar to other skills, beginners are likely to feel awkward, nervous, and potentially skeptical. In addition, in order to become competent (and even expert) at such skills, one needs to practice

An example of a therapist's rationale follows. Note that this description should always include multiple pauses to provide for frequent opportunities for the client to ask questions or render reactions. However, note that this sample is not meant to imply that the therapist memorize a script. Rather, it provides for a sample flow of how to present information important to the rationale. The handout in the Patient Handouts section of Appendix II, titled "Stress, Heart Failure, and Depression," taken from our work with depressed heart failure patients, is an example of a potentially useful take-home handout that can augment the verbal presentation provided by the therapist in session. Clinicians are encouraged to adapt this handout to various patient populations for whom they frequently provide treatment.

This approach, called problem-solving therapy, or PST, is based on the idea that one major reason why people experience long-lasting depression, anxiety, anger, and other forms of emotional distress is usually related to the overwhelming effects of stress on one's physical and emotional health. Lots of research has demonstrated that stress has very significant and specific effects on one's body, brain, and emotional well-being.

Stress can take the form of major events, such as a recent job loss (*if possible, insert here a major negative life event that the individual has actually experienced*), as well as daily hassles that can collectively add up to become a much larger source of stress. Often such major events actually create new daily problems; for instance, the loss of a job can lead to many additional problems, such as loss of income, negative self-esteem, needing to obtain a new job, and so forth.

On the other hand, someone experiencing many daily problems, such as arguments with a spouse, financial difficulties, and parent-child relationship difficulties, can eventually experience a major negative life event, such as getting a divorce (*Again, if possible, the therapist should try to illustrate these points using examples directly from the patient's life*).

Let's think about divorce as another example. Not only is this a difficult major life change, which is stressful in-and-of itself, but frequently creates additional stressful problems, including the possibility of having to move one's home, potentially having to find new schools for one's children, having to find new resources (e.g., bank, grocery store, drug store), feeling lonely and wanting companionship, and so forth. Further, emotions are often mixed and involve multiple people. Problems with finances and extended family members are also common. These can all be very stressful!

Unfortunately, such stress leads to more distress. Moreover, increases in distress will lead to increases in stressful problems. For example, being upset with a divorce can lead to inappropriate parenting behaviors, which can then lead to additional parent-child relationship problems. This stress-distress downward spiral can eventually lead to despair and hopelessness. As an ancient Persian proverb suggests—"If fortune turns against you, even jelly can break your teeth."

Bottom line, stress can lead to more stress, as well as more distress. This is called "stress generation." Unfortunately, when we have difficulty handling or coping with such stress in an effective way, more stressful problems can occur (*If relevant, include the following:* This is especially true if the major event is the onset and treatment of a serious medical illness, such as cancer, heart disease, or diabetes, as they usually lead to multiple stressful problems).

Moreover, depending upon how much stress we may have had earlier in our lives while growing up, our bodies and brains can react in a way that becomes more sensitive to further stress. For example, sometimes having a bruise or broken leg makes that area of the body more sensitive to the touch or additional trauma. In that way, it takes less stress to make us upset, tense, annoyed, or uptight as compared to not having the bruise or broken leg from the beginning.

This is called "stress sensitivity." In other words, if we experienced a lot of stress earlier in our lives, it can make our bodies and brains more sensitive to stress later on, and, consequently, we react more strongly to even less intense levels of stress that we are experiencing now. In other words, early stress can make our bodies and brains more vulnerable and it takes less stress to get us upset (*If relevant, the therapist should illustrate these points using examples from the patient's earlier experiences*).

Does this mean you are crazy or weak or stupid? Of course not! At times, for a variety of reasons, the amount of stress we experience can be so great that it overwhelms us and we are unable to know exactly what to do. Sometimes we want to run away and hide or at other times we try to "attack" the source of stress in an impulsive way just to make it go away. This is common across people.

Specifically, when our brains become aware of a threat, our bodies react in a way that alerts us to the threat in an extremely fast manner, and begins to undergo various changes as a means of helping us to get ready to deal with the threat. This is called the fight or flight response. In other words, our bodies are getting ready to either fight the threat or run away to get out of harm's way.

Specifically, the heart begins to pump faster in order to get the blood flowing throughout the body, our immune system sends out certain types of cells to be prepared for an enemy's (e.g., germs) attack, and our breathing gets faster and more shallow because our lungs are trying to get in more oxygen to supply the body. Unfortunately, most often, the threats in everyday life are not combat warfare, or tigers, or dinosaurs trying to eat us. Rather, they often represent psychological and emotional threats, such as frustration from being in a bad traffic jam, not having enough money to pay this month's rent or mortgage, having to listen to a supervisor yell at us for a mistake we made, or having constant arguments with a co-worker, family member, or spouse.

Despite the differences in the objective nature of the threats, our bodies, nevertheless, react the same. When the stress is continuous, the body's reaction is also continuous. Unfortunately, our bodies are not made to sustain such constant stress reactions. Continuous stress puts a major strain on our bodies and brains. If nothing significant changes this situation, negative consequences can occur, including health problems, such as heart disease, and emotional problems, such as depression and anxiety.

So, what can we do? What we need is to "re-wire" our brains to be able to become more resistant to stress. We need to be able to become better able to cope with stress so that it no longer leads to emotional difficulties or physical problems. The good news is that this is possible! In other words, research has shown that through different learning experiences, we can actually re-wire our brains in order to become more resilient to stress!

What can help reduce this stress? There are many things that can help reduce, minimize, or prevent stress turning into distress. These can include the types of resources we have access to. For example, having family and friends can provide for a strong source of social support to help us handle the stress. A second very significant factor is the manner in which we cope with stress. Different people find various coping strategies to be helpful. These can include prayer, humor, exercise, and relaxation exercises.

Note: We have found Figures 6.1 and 6.2 to be helpful as visual tools to illustrate the negative effects of stress. This can be accompanied by the following explanation:

Let me illustrate what I've been talking about up to now *(give copy of Figure 6.1, titled* Stress, *to the individual)*. Let's look at the top figure of this handout, labeled #1. Think of the tabletop, or "B," as a person, including his or her ability to cope with stress. Think of "A" as the source of stress, and "C" as representing the person's external resources, such as family, friends, money, and so forth. The top figure, #1, represents "normal" levels of stress, where one's basic coping ability, combined with one's resources, is handling or coping with this stress fairly well. As such, there are no "cracks" in the tabletop. Now look at the

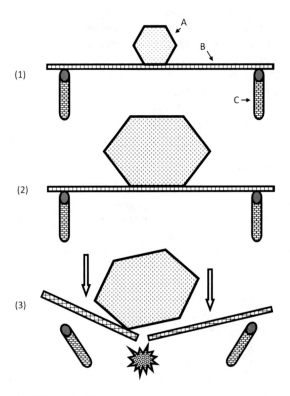

FIGURE 6.1   Stress.

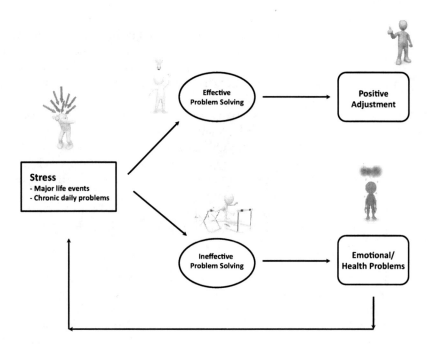

FIGURE 6.2 Problem-solving model of stress.

middle figure—where stress has gotten much bigger! If this continues, then the results can be illustrated by picture #3—where the "tabletop" cracks.

In other words, there is a negative effect on the person (depression, anxiety, pain, anger), as well as on his or her basic ability to cope. Remember—this is not just about our feelings, but about our body's general reactions to stress, including how the brain works.

What this suggests is that we need to find a way to stop this process from continuing—that is, the more stress, the more distress; the more distress, the more stress (in the form of difficult problems to solve). So, what to do? One strategy is to increase resources, that is, "strengthen the legs supporting the tabletop." Strong family and interpersonal relationships are an important source of help. However, sometimes interpersonal relationships are the problem and can be stressful themselves! So, a second strategy is to strengthen the tabletop, that is, one's ability to cope with stress. That's where problem solving comes into play. Your problem solving! Let me give you another handout. At this point, let me pause in order to let you know that I will be giving you multiple handouts throughout our time together so you have the ability to refresh your memory between sessions about important things we discussed.

This new figure basically suggests that stress, in the form of both major life events (**Note**: *Try to tie in the individual's life experiences here; i.e., if he or she recently was diagnosed with a medical disease or if the person experienced a* *traumatic event, either recently or in the past, discuss this figure incorporating his or her specific experiences)* and continuous daily problems, can ultimately lead to either positive adjustment, or to emotional problems, such as depression, anxiety, anger, relationship difficulties, and so forth, as well as a variety of physical health problems. Did you know that substantial research has shown that stress can lead to various medical problems, such as heart disease, diabetes, stroke, periodontitis, osteoporosis, and dementia? At the very least, stress can make existing medical conditions worse!

According to the figure, the path to positive adjustment is through effective problem solving (that is the top path), whereas the path to psychological and physical health problems involves ineffective problem solving (the bottom pathway). So, what do we mean by problem solving?

It is at this point that the "presentation" can now focus on a description of social problem solving:

Problem solving can be thought of as a set of skills or tools that people use to handle, cope with, or resolve difficult situations encountered in daily living. The type of problem solving I am talking about here is often referred to as social problem solving, to highlight the notion that there are different skills involved in attempting to solve stressful problems in real life versus the kinds of intellectual or purely academic problems that we had to solve on tests in school. That's because real-life problems that are stressful usually are connected to strong emotions. The parts of the brain needed to solve stressful problems can differ from the parts of the brain needed to solve arithmetic or crossword puzzle problems.

Research has demonstrated that social problem solving is comprised of two major components. The first is called problem orientation. This involves people's beliefs and attitudes about stressful problems and their ability to deal with them. In a way, think of it as one's worldview about problems or the type of glasses one sees through when looking at the world and thinking about problems. There are two types of orientations—one is positive in nature and one is negative. The second major component is referred to as one's problem-solving style. This involves the general way that people attempt to deal with stressful problems. The most effective style is called planful problem solving, where the approach is mainly thoughtful and systematic in nature, basically *planful*. Two other general styles have been identified—both being maladaptive and usually leading to unsuccessful problem solving—an avoidant style and an impulsive or careless style.

The therapist can describe the two different types of orientations (see Table 6.1) at this point, as well as the three types of problem-solving styles (see Table 6.2).

Alternatively, the therapist can describe the difference between an overall "effective" problem solver (i.e., one who has a positive orientation and

TABLE 6.1   **Characteristics of a Positive and Negative Problem Orientation**

Positive Orientation (the "Optimist")
Involves the tendency for individuals to
- Appraise problems as challenges
- Be optimistic in believing that problems are solvable
- Have a strong sense of self-efficacy regarding their ability to cope with problems
- Understand that successful problem solving involves time and effort
- View negative emotions as an integral part of the overall problem-solving process that can ultimately be helpful in coping with stressful problems

Negative Orientation (the "Pessimist")
Involves the tendency for individuals to
- View problems as threats
- Expect problems to be unsolvable
- Have doubts about one's ability to cope with problems successfully
- Become particularly frustrated and upset when faced with problems or confronted with negative emotions

TABLE 6.2   **Characteristics of the Three Problem-Solving Styles**

Planful Problem Solving (the "planful problem solver")
The constructive problem-solving style that involves systematic and thoughtful application of the following set of specific skills:
- *Problem definition* (clarifying the nature of a problem, setting realistic goals, identifying those obstacles that prevent one from reaching such goals)
- *Generation of alternatives* (thinking of a range of possible solution strategies geared to overcome the identified obstacles)
- *Decision making* (predicting the likely consequences of these various alternatives, conducting a cost-benefit analysis based on these identified outcomes, and developing a solution plan that is geared to achieve the problem-solving goals)
- *Solution implementation and verification* (carrying out the solution plan, monitoring and evaluating the consequences of the plan, determining whether one's problem-solving efforts have been successful or need to continue)

Impulsive/Careless Style (the "quick fixer")
The maladaptive problem-solving approach that involves impulsive or careless attempts at problem resolution. Such attempts are narrow, hurried, and incomplete. Such a person typically considers only a few solution alternatives, often impulsively going with the first idea that comes to mind. In addition, he or she scans alternative solutions and consequences quickly, carelessly, and unsystematically, and monitors solution outcomes carelessly and inadequately.

Avoidant Style (the "avoider")
This dysfunctional pattern is characterized by procrastination, passivity, inaction, and dependency on others. This type of problem solver prefers to avoid problems rather than confronting them head on, puts off problem solving for as long as possible, waits for problems to resolve themselves, and attempts to shift the responsibility for solving his or her problems to other people.

primarily uses a planful problem-solving approach) versus an overall "ineffective" problem solver (i.e., one who is represented by a negative problem orientation and uses either an impulsive problem-solving style, an avoidant style, or both). The handout, titled "What is Effective Problem Solving?" included in Appendix III, can be given to the client at this point and used as an adjunct to this type of presentation. In either approach, the major point is to begin to describe the major components of social problem solving, how they are related to negative health and mental health problems, and how they can be translated into training modules all geared toward improving the individual's ability to cope more effectively with stress as a means of decreasing extant emotional and health problems. The following is a sample therapist presentation:

> The importance of focusing on one's social problem-solving skills and abilities can be especially understood when looking at the research about differences between effective problem solvers and ineffective problem solvers. Basically, ineffective problem solving has been found to be strongly associated with high levels of depression, anxiety, suicidal thinking and attempts, hopelessness, pessimism, anger proneness, substance abuse, criminal activities, poor self-esteem, work stress, pain, and worsening of medical symptoms.
>
> On the other hand, effective problem solving has been linked to more effective overall coping, higher levels of optimism, social adjustment, positive mood, better life satisfaction, higher levels of hope, more motivation, and better overall well-being.
>
> Given these findings, I am suggesting that you and I work together to help you become a better problem solver and to more effectively manage all the stress in your life. We will start by looking at how you react to problems and understand your own emotions. In general, PST can help you to learn how to do the following: how to think of problems as challenges rather than aversive threats; how to approach problems in an adaptive manner (that is, a head-on approach versus avoidance); how to improve your problem-solving style (that is, planful versus impulsive and avoidant); how to define problems and set goals; how to understand why the situation is a problem; how to accurately identify major obstacles; how to set realistic goals; how to invent and to create new solutions to problems; how to make effective decisions; how to carry out a solution or action plan; and how to validate the outcome of the solution.
>
> I view these skills as an important way of successfully approaching and solving life's problems. In essence, you will learn a set of skills that can be applied to all types of problems—those that you are currently experiencing and those that you might encounter in the future. To a large extent, it's like the old saying—"Give a person a fish, he eats for a day . . . teach a person to fish, he eats for a lifetime." In other words, PST is like learning to fish—you will be able to use these skills throughout your lifetime.

What Kind of Problem Solver Are You?

At this point, it can be helpful for the therapist to engage in a discussion that basically asks the client to self-identify which orientation and style he or she believes matches his or her own past and current beliefs and actions, as well as to note any situation-behavior variability (i.e., differences in one's orientation or style depending on the situation). This can help individuals better understand these concepts, as well as to begin to discover their own means of coping with stressful problems. During this discussion, it is important to highlight the following:

- Identifying one's orientation and style at this point is helpful to better understand one's strengths and areas in need of improvement. We advocate using the expression that "knowledge is power" (Francis Bacon) as a means of underscoring the importance of this form of self-evaluation.
- Some people have differing orientations and/or styles depending on the nature of the problem—one aspect of PST can be geared toward helping the individual "transfer" his or her effective coping strategies to other areas of one's life.
- Having emotional and/or psychosocial difficulties at present does not imply that a person is or has always been an ineffective problem solver; rather, sometimes the stress is so overwhelming or the problem is very new or complex such that additional teaching, training, and practice in how to cope with such stress becomes necessary.
- One's problem orientation and/or style(s) do not represent personality traits. Rather, they represent long-standing patterns of coping that can be changed and improved.

In conducting such a discussion, the therapist can refer to the Patient Handout titled "What is Effective Problem Solving," introduced previously as an instructional aid. For example, in helping clients to self-identify their orientation and style, they are guided to think about a recent problem as a means of "matching" attitudes and actions to these problem-solving dimensions.

One activity that can be helpful here is to ask the client to describe how differing types of problem solvers might react to a variety of different hypothetical situations (see sample problems below). This type of discussion can lead to additional insight into the patient's understanding of these concepts as well as to provide for further learning opportunities.

Sample problems (the therapist is encouraged to think of additional sample problems, especially those that are relevant to a given client):

- *Football:* A team with a rather weak offense is currently in the "red zone" and the score is tied. The other team is known to have a very strong offense. It's the 4th quarter, 3rd down, and time is running out.
- *Traffic:* A counselor, Jane, lives 90 minutes away from the medical center. She is stuck in traffic because of a serious car accident that just happened and is at least an hour away from work. Traffic is totally stopped. She has an 8:00 am appointment with a seriously ill patient.
- *Rent:* John's rent is due tomorrow, but he has no means of paying for it. This isn't the first time, and he is worried that he may be evicted. While walking outside, he finds a wallet with $150 in it as well as the person's ID.

In addition, results from any formal assessments previously conducted, such as a completed PSSM form, the Social Problem-Solving Inventory-Revised, or the Problem-Solving Test, can augment this discussion. Of particular importance is to determine whether the client has accurately identified his or her correct orientation and style when compared to these more objective results. If there is a significant discrepancy, this should be pointed out with an ensuing discussion to determine why such a discrepancy occurred.

Overview of the Four Problem-Solving "Toolkits"

Part of the rationale should include a brief overview of the four problem-solving toolkits. We use the phrase toolkit or toolbox to underscore the notion that we are teaching a set of skills and providing individuals with a set of tools that can help them cope more effectively with stressful problems as a means of reducing extant negative symptoms. On the other hand, if the therapist feels more comfortable using other language (e.g., therapy components) or believes that the patient would be more accepting of differing language, we have no inherent reason to insist that such language be used.

In describing these toolkits for the first time, the therapist should provide a brief rationale for why these specific strategies are included. In essence, PST provides tools to help an individual reach a set of goals, including solving a variety of stressful problems. We conceptualize the four toolkits as means by which we can help people "overcome certain general obstacles that often prevent or make it difficult to reach such goals." Figure 6.3 (*Getting From "A" to "B": Obstacles to Effective Problem Solving*), as a patient handout,

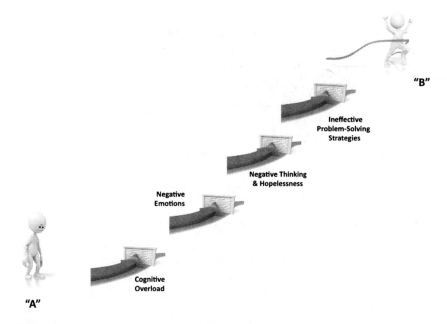

FIGURE 6.3 Getting from A to B: Obstacles to effective problem solving.

can be used to illustrate this point (contained in Appendix II). The four major sets of obstacles to reaching one's goals, which the four toolkits map onto, are as follows:

1. Cognitive overload (Toolkit #1: *Problem-Solving Multitasking*)
2. Emotional dysregulation under stress (Toolkit #2: *The* SSTA *Method of Problem Solving Under Stress*)
3. Negative thinking and low motivation (Toolkit #3: *Healthy Thinking and Positive Imagery*)
4. Ineffective problem solving (Toolkit #4: *Planful Problem Solving*)

As previously suggested in Chapter 4, whether all strategies in all toolkits are taught and emphasized is greatly dependent on the assessment of a client's problem-solving strengths and weaknesses as well as the therapist's clinical judgment regarding the relevance and importance of other related factors, such as the anticipated length of treatment, the severity of negative symptoms, and the subsequent progress (or lack of) being made by the individual. In other words, it is not mandatory to engage in all training activities across all four toolkits. Rather, the therapist should use assessment and outcome data to inform various treatment decisions.

In addition, for purposes of presentation, we describe each of the four toolkits in sequence. However, the PST therapist may wish to apply certain PST strategies out of sequence based on the specifics of a given case. For example, it is possible, based on material gleaned from the actual sessions (and possibly from standardized measures), that the client does not display appreciable tendencies to engage in negative thinking but does feel somewhat hopeless regarding the success of treatment. As such, the clinician may not need to engage in those aspects of Toolkit #3 pertaining to "negative thinking" barriers to effective problem solving. However, because the client voices strong feelings of hopelessness, the second part of Toolkit #3, "Positive Imagery," may be a particularly important treatment component to focus on earlier on in therapy.

The following is a sample presentation of these tools:

> Let me explain what PST will actually entail. Years of research and clinical experience have identified four major obstacles to successful problem solving in real-life, stressful situations. In other words, these are factors that make it difficult getting from point "A," which is where you are now, to point "B," which is where you would like to get to—in other words, reaching your goals. These include cognitive overload, negative feelings, negative thinking and feelings of hopelessness, and ineffective problem-solving strategies. PST has been developed to help you overcome these four obstacles by providing you with specific tools to deal with each factor. So, over the next several weeks, I will serve in many roles—teacher, coach, therapist, counselor, and problem-solving cheerleader. During this time, I will teach you a set of skills and strategies to help you overcome those obstacles. As noted before, PST has been shown, through rigorous science, to be effective for large numbers of people, experiencing a wide range of problems.

Encourage Optimism and a Sense of Control

During these initial sessions, it is also important to facilitate patients' sense of optimism and belief that they can regain control of their lives. Therapists should try to identify and point to examples of effective problem-solving attempts that clients have engaged in previously. It should be emphasized that our overall response to problems can either work *for* or *against* us; the goal of PST is to increase the chance that our problem-solving reactions will work *for* us.

In addition, it is important to reinforce a person's current competencies in various areas of living to enhance motivation for optimally engaging in PST. For example, the therapist can point out areas where the person is currently engaging in effective problem solving and coping as a means of highlighting various strengths. However, if the individual appears very pessimistic in the beginning, the therapist may wish to "go ahead" to Toolkit #3 and engage in the *Positive Visualization* activity as a means of enhancing motivation at this early stage of treatment.

Ground Rules and Therapy Expectations

A final point about the introductory sessions. Many individuals may not be familiar with a directive or skill development approach to psychotherapy and subsequently may be unaware of therapy expectations. As such, it is important to discuss with the patient several ground rules of the approach, along with other standard therapy issues, such as confidentiality and informed consent. We have found it useful to include such a discussion of session timing and frequency, as well as expectations of practice assignments between sessions, as part of PST ground rules. It can additionally be useful to obtain mutual agreement with patients concerning joint responsibilities. These include the following:

Therapist Responsibilities. The therapist should agree to draw upon all training, knowledge of the scientific literature, and clinical experience to best help the patient.

Patient Responsibilities. The patient needs to agree to "give it his or her best shot," to engage in-between session activities, practice skills, keep appointments, and let the therapist know of problems or disappointments with treatment.

THE CASE OF "MEGAN"

In this section, we present the case of "Megan" (all identifying information has been changed to protect her confidentiality, as well with regard to other cases described throughout this manual), a patient who underwent a PST approach to treatment with one of the authors (CMN), as a means of providing a context within which to provide for meaningful clinical illustrations and examples of how to apply various PST strategies. To begin with, we provide a summary of the initial assessment sessions and will revisit her throughout the remaining chapters in this manual.

Megan is a 27-year-old woman who approached psychotherapy stating, "I've reached a point in my life where I am reevaluating my lifestyle. I feel anxious and detached and I can't tell if it's me or due to my past alcohol abuse. Sometimes I wonder if I can't change my feelings of worry, depression, and detachment, or change my life for the better."

She stated that her problems began in high school and continued in college. Her college years were marked by a choice of an "easy" major (Italian Language) and weekends of heavy drinking and socializing. After college, she drifted from job to job and maintained a pattern of completing her required work duties during the week, followed by heavy drinking, eating, and socializing with friends who shared her interests. She had occasional brief sexual encounters when drinking, which usually occurred during an alcohol-induced blackout. She stated that she has had almost no "sober" sexual relationships, reported no history of sexual abuse or trauma, but described both sex and masturbatory activities as boring and not pleasant.

Approximately three months prior to her first appointment, she stopped drinking alcohol completely following a blackout, implementing a self-directed abstinence. The day after this blackout, she had experienced a sense of detachment, frightening sensory experiences (i.e., hypervigilance and seeing movement out of the corner of her eye), concentration difficulties, episodes of panic, a sense of detachment, and a fear of losing control of her thoughts. She attended a few Alcoholics Anonymous meetings but considered the organization a bad match for her. She committed to stop drinking on her own with the support of her sister and close friend. Over the three months prior to entering therapy, the episodes of panic and limited sensory hallucinatory experiences had diminished. However, her fears concerning loss of control, anhedonia, low motivation, and sense of detachment had remained particularly troublesome for her. She additionally experienced a fear of her roommate, due to this person's continued drinking, casual sexual encounters with men she brought home to the shared apartment, and the knowledge that her roommate owned a firearm (although Megan had never seen it or been threatened by her roommate in any way).

Megan was currently working as an administrative assistant for a biotechnology firm and performed her work duties well. She has no absenteeism and had recently received a promotion. She stated, however, that despite her recent successes, she experienced no joy or motivation for her work, and also felt detached from her coworkers, as well as those with whom she socialized. Her few friendships had remained the same and she indicated that there were times when she felt lonely because she no longer frequented the neighborhood bar where her familiar group of friends congregated on Friday evenings.

Megan reported few social supports. However, the individuals she did name as helpful provided her with a sense of safety and enjoyment. These included her older sister and one male friend. She described her family background and early home life as providing her and her siblings with a "good" upbringing, citing many activities and trips as a family. She initially described herself as a "basically happy kid" in her early years, without many challenges in school. However, the family home was described as having an undercurrent of tension between her parents. For example, when she was in high school, her parents separated and divorced, only to live in close proximity for several years and then remarry several years later. There was a family history of anxiety among Megan's two sisters, plus her older sister had been diagnosed with bipolar disorder.

Megan's initial assessment involved a comprehensive evaluation that included a series of clinical interviews, communicating with her primary care physician, completion of several diagnostic screening measures (for a range of clinical problems including bipolar disorder), psychological testing, symptom checklists, and the SPSI-R. In general, the results of this overall assessment protocol indicated that Megan met criteria for generalized anxiety disorder with a history of alcohol abuse, plus subclinical levels of depressive symptoms. In addition, she reported binge eating episodes and a significant alcohol abuse history. Her primary care physician reported her current health as generally good. However, she exhibited mild hypertension and smoked approximately one pack of cigarettes daily. She expressed a strong desire to reduce her symptoms and improve her life without the use of drugs.

With regard to standardized testing, Megan's scores confirmed a diagnosis of anxiety disorder and suggested that she did not meet criteria for a personality disorder. Her response to other self-report measures indicated life-long maladaptive schemas concerning hypervigilance and emotional inhibitions, suggesting that her home environment tended to place an emphasis on suppressing feelings, impulses, and choices. Further, her family tended to foster and support various rigid rules and expectations. Verbal reports of her early life were consistent with the self-report measures, as she reported an undercurrent of pessimism and worry in the home.

The SPSI-R revealed striking areas specific to her strengths and vulnerabilities in solving everyday problems. Specifically, her positive problem orientation responses were consistent with scores of individuals in the normative, nonpsychiatric group. This appeared to reflect her optimism and desire to seek help for the significant symptoms and fears that she was currently experiencing. However, the scores regarding her negative orientation were more than two standard deviations above the average normed score, reflecting her significant worry and intense fears of not coping well with life. Her concentration difficulties, feelings of detachment, experiences of depersonalization, and continual worry about her roommate's behavior when drinking all left her feeling hypervigilant and chronically anxious and tearful.

Megan's scores on the various components of planful problem solving (i.e., the *Rational Problem Solving* scale score; RPS) indicated that she had strengths regarding her ability to define problems clearly but revealed more limited abilities concerning flexibility and creativity in generating solutions, weighing alternatives, and following through on intended plans of thoughtful action. One example of the latter was her intention to eat better, organize her home, and exercise. She believed that if she could just "get started," she would follow through with what she needed to do. However, she reported her motivation to start as being very poor. Her total RPS scale score reflected the cumulative challenges she had with regard to her problem-solving ability and was fully within the area of scores more similar to those of psychiatric outpatient sample groups. Her scores with regard to impulsive/careless responding was a full standard deviation beyond the average nonpsychiatric patient. Finally, her scores with regard to avoidant responding were slightly, but nonsignificantly, above average. Overall, her total problem-solving score was two standard deviations *below* the average score for nonpsychiatric samples, indicating significant problem-solving deficits and limitations.

Consistent with our problem-solving philosophy of clinical decision making, Megan's therapist shared her case formulation with her. Rather than focus on the diagnostic labels or descriptions of her difficulties, her therapist presented this case formulation to provide an explanation of Megan's "life story." More specifically, how her early emotional learning experiences had contributed to the types of implicit emotional and cognitive responses that comprised her reactions to current stressors, as well as various explicit concerns, triggers, learned behavior, and desire for change. In addition, Megan's individual's strengths were underscored as one initial means of instilling hope and reinforcing constructive approaches to life problems. In sharing her understanding of Megan's "life story," the therapist also identified possible targets for change that would have the most significant impact on her current ultimate goals for treatment. These appeared to be improved management of anxiety, reduction of feelings of interpersonal detachment and sadness, and improved enjoyment in living.

Note that we have found that simultaneously sharing the case formulation with a patient, using a visual depiction of both the factors influencing his or her current level of distress, as well as highlighting how SPS is an important mediator of the stress–distress relationship (e.g., using a graphic such as Figure 6.2), is a useful way to underscore the relevance of PST for a given individual. In addition, this activity also provides an extra boost to the therapeutic alliance, as patients such as Megan have the opportunity to understand how the use of effective problem-solving skills, as well as other new learning experiences, can impact their effective management of life problems.

Megan responded very positively to hearing her case formulation shared in this manner; reporting that it provided a "different way" of looking at her current problems and symptoms. Moreover, she indicated that she felt "listened to and respected"; she felt the therapist understood how hard she was trying to manage her distress and to do the best she could. While discussing this case formulation, Megan volunteered additional information, describing that the tension and uncertainty in her childhood home regarding her parents' disagreements had given her the feeling that "something bad was going to happen" but not knowing what. As a function of this discussion, Megan began to understand that these early childhood stressful experiences had likely contributed to her current hypervigilance and reactivity when under stress (i.e., stress sensitization). Further, she was able to see how her current attempts at managing the current stress in her life, that is, heavy drinking, served to help her avoid, rather than confront, problems. Moreover, she realized that such "ineffective solutions" served only to engender further worries regarding her health and overall well-being and create new problems (i.e., stress generation). Her sense of hopelessness, inability to experience pleasure, and low motivation were some of the major symptoms of her subclinical depression. As part of the case formulation, it was explained to Megan that she had been drinking for so long that she had learned few other ways by which she could begin to challenge her worries and hypervigiliance, as well as her avoidance of feelings and social confrontation, and current concerns with regard to her roommate's behavior.

As suggested earlier, Megan was provided with an explanation of how problem-solving ability was related to stress. She was shown a diagram similar to Figure 6.2 with regard to her current major life stressors and daily problems and suggested how learning these skills might provide her with a new way of becoming more aware of and, consequently, more able to manage negative feelings, think planfully, and ultimately motivate herself to put more positive strategies into action. This would ultimately involve a new overall learning experience regarding her reactions to herself and others, and a different way of coping with life's problems.

Megan's initial reaction to this rationale was positive, indicating that she found this approach helpful, as it provided her with a view of herself as having certain reactive habits, albeit maladaptive, that were *learned* earlier in life, as compared to "it being in my DNA!" She also realized that by drinking, she missed multiple opportunities to learn how to cope more effectively with life's difficulties and that this approach can now provide such experiences. Moreover, she indicated that the case formulation convinced her that she had a future and that she was "not on the brink of a mental crash!"

One final note regarding Megan's initial case formulation: As part of providing a rationale for PST, her therapist also indicated that at times it might be prudent to incorporate additional empirically based strategies in her overall treatment plan. This was to underscore the point that a PST framework and PST-based intervention does not require an *exclusive* manual-driven implementation when applied in real-world settings. However, for the purposes of this manual, when we revisit Megan, we will only discuss case material specific to examples related to PST strategies and techniques.

SUMMARY

This chapter began with delineating the major intervention components of PST, which include (a) assessment and treatment planning, (b) introductory session(s), (c) training in Toolkit #1 (*Problem-Solving Multitasking*), (d) training in Toolkit #2 (*SSTA Method of Problem Solving Under Stress*), (e) training in Toolkit #3 (*Healthy Thinking and Positive Imagery*), (f) training in Toolkit #4 (*Planful Problem Solving*), (g) guided practice, and (h) "future forecasting" and termination. It was emphasized that ongoing clinical assessment of a client's problem-solving strengths and limitations, as well as improvement in symptoms and goal achievement (or lack thereof), should inform treatment planning, particularly with regard to the choice, emphasis, and timing of training in the various PST strategies and guidelines.

Goals of the initial introductory session(s) were described and involve (a) establishing a positive patient–therapist relationship; (b) providing an understandable overview and rationale of PST, particularly making it relevant to the specific individual; and (c) encouraging optimism.

Two graphic figures were presented as instructional aids when describing how stress, in the form of both major life events and chronic daily problems, can lead to negative health and emotional outcomes. In addition, these figures underscore the importance and relevance of effective problem solving as a major buffer of such negative consequences.

It was suggested that in describing PST, the therapist should provide an overview of the four PST toolkits, which involves specific skills and guidelines geared to help overcome four major barriers to effective problem solving: (a) cognitive overload; (b) emotional dysregulation; (c) negative thinking and feelings of hopelessness; and (d) ineffective problem-solving strategies. An instructional handout was provided that graphically depicts these four barriers. PST, then, as a treatment intervention, focuses on training individuals in these four toolkits.

Last, in order to provide an ongoing context to illustrate various PST exercises and strategies, we presented the case of "Megan," a 27-year-old woman suffering from multiple concerns, including anxiety, depression, fears of "going crazy," and prior alcohol abuse. In the following chapters, we will return to Megan to provide for relevant examples of certain PST training activities.

SEVEN

Toolkit #1—Problem-Solving Multitasking: Overcoming Cognitive Overload

This is the first of the four problem-solving therapy (PST) toolkits. Remember that all toolkits are presented to the client as sets of strategies geared to help them overcome a variety of common major obstacles to effective problem solving under stress. This particular toolkit addresses the challenges posed by the limited capacity of the human mind.

RATIONALE FOR TOOLKIT #1

We begin with an ancient Buddhist tale:

> A student of martial arts had a query for his teacher. "I wish to improve my skills in martial arts. Besides studying under you, I think I should practice with another teacher as well, so as to learn another style. Do you think that's a good idea? The master replied—"A hunter who tries to chase two rabbits at the same time will catch neither."

This lesson parallels research in cognitive psychology that consistently demonstrates that doing more than one task at a time, particularly if the tasks are complex, negatively affects accuracy and productivity (Rogers & Monsell, 1995). The conscious mind, unfortunately, is limited in the amount of activity that it can perform efficiently at any one time. In essence, the conscious mind engages in three important activities during problem solving: (a) receiving information from the environment (i.e., information is received and input from both external and internal sources), (b) displaying this information when needed (e.g., the mind attempts to remember information needed to address the problem), and (c) manipulating the various pieces of information that are remembered in an attempt to comprehend how the data fits together (e.g., combining different pieces of information, adding and subtracting information, and placing the differing pieces of information in a logical sequence).

However, the capacity of the conscious mind is quite limited in that it cannot perform all three activities efficiently at the same time, especially when the quantity and/or complexity of the information is significant. Trying to do two of the above activities at the same time without aid is very difficult. Often, one activity interferes with another. For example, attempting to remember all the important information about a problem can interfere with the manipulation of information that is involved in trying to comprehend or understand how they fit together.

In addition, the processing of information becomes increasingly difficult when a person is under stress. For example, remember in Chapter 2 we described LeDoux's concept of the high road versus the low road processing of emotional stimuli. In this context, consider the difference between the situation where the brain is attempting to process or interpret the differential danger of a given sound associated with either a snake or a twig being broken. Now consider how the brain likely reacts when a person is engaged in a very heated argument with a spouse or partner for *several minutes*, or the situation where an individual is being told that he or she is being laid off after recently purchasing a new home, or the circumstance where a person is told that he or she has cancer (i.e., continuous stimulation of the amygdala). When attempting to handle such complex situations, because the brain is not a "super computer" with unlimited memory and processing capabilities, productivity and accuracy can be severely compromised. In essence, the human brain is not designed to perform heavy-duty multitasking—people are not machines or computers. As such, we are unfortunately unable to go to the computer store and purchase a hard drive with more memory. If we require computers with low amounts of memory (i.e., our brains) to simultaneously process many requests involving many pieces of data, we can easily experience a "computer crash."

In addition, some research has shown that attempts to engage in *normal* multitasking (i.e., attempts to attend and respond to several sources of stimuli simultaneously) can actually produce negative effects on the immune system (i.e., increases in secretory immunoglobin A), suggesting that attempts to cope with stress in such a manner can ultimately have negative biological effects as well (Wetherell, Hyland, & Harris, 2004).

Given this limitation of the brain, additional tools become necessary to help people cope with problems, particularly if such problems are stressful and engender high levels of negative emotions. PST focuses on teaching individuals three multitasking strategies to address this concern. (Note that a Patient Handout, Problem-Solving Multitasking, is included in Appendix III as an instructional aid for clients to take with them.)

- Externalization
- Visualization
- Simplification

We conceptualize these three guidelines or strategies as fundamental tools necessary to engage in effective problem solving. Many people may already engage in one or all of these techniques for a variety of reasons. But we suggest that it becomes important for individuals to use these tools as often as possible, such that they become more habitual. The importance of these tools can be explained by using the analogy of teaching people who are interested in beginning to jog or run for exercise that correct stretching and breathing are fundamental activities required to run properly and without negative consequences.

Externalization

Externalization involves the display of information externally as often as possible (e.g., writing it down; drawing diagrams or maps to show relationships; recording information in one's computer, smartphone, or tablet; or using an audiotape recorder). This procedure relieves the conscious mind from having to actively display information being remembered, which allows one to concentrate more on other activities, such as better understanding the nature of a problem, creatively thinking and then writing down solutions on paper, and making decisions based on visually examining and comparing a list of pros versus cons.

In describing this strategy to patients, the therapist should ask for examples of when they use this tool (e.g., smartphones, to-do lists, post-it reminders, calendars, Blackberries) and how that helps their lives. Potentially, useful analogies include the notion that in building houses, blueprints are necessary, as are manuals when learning how to use a new camera, and the major reason why PST provides handouts—that is, externalization works!

As such, we encourage clients to purchase a small notebook or journal to use as aids while undergoing PST (or to use any electronic device they already have that has the capability to record information). A notebook can be useful to better record information learned in a given treatment session (in order to subsequently remember it) as well as to record responses when completing various practice or homework assignments given throughout the course of PST.

Note that this tool, in principle, is consistent with the effective intervention known as "expressive writing." James Pennebaker, a psychologist, pioneered this strategy in the 1980s. Specifically, this approach asks individuals to write about a traumatic experience that they have not shared with others and to "dig deep inside oneself" and put such information down on paper. The intervention recommends that one does this intensely three or four times over a one-week period. Research has demonstrated that such expressive writing has positive effects on one's immune functioning and overall well-being (Pennebaker, 2004). For certain patients, therapists may consider using this intervention as an adjunct to PST when and where appropriate.

Visualization

This tool emphasizes the use of visual imagery for a variety of purposes that can positively impact the problem-solving process. These include

- *Problem clarification*—One can visualize the problem in his or her "mind's eye" in order to separate differing parts of the problem in order to look at them one at a time, creatively generate new ideas for solutions, "map out" new pathways to get from "A" to "B," and/or draw imaginal diagrams or pictures to help describe the problem in a graphic format (see exercise in Chapter 10 regarding *Problem Definition*)
- *Imaginal rehearsal*—Sports figures frequently imagine engaging in various activities in order to enhance their success in a more time-efficient manner (e.g., a skier can visualize how one needs to bend his or her knees while going down a new slope; a basketball player visualizes how to throw the ball into the hoop when being chased down the court). This form of visualization can be useful when an individual is soon to carry out a solution plan but needs extra practice in how to carry it out
- *Stress management*—"Guided imagery" is a form of stress management that helps individuals reduce their stress and anxiety levels by "taking a vacation in their mind." A therapist provides detailed instructions that help an individual to better visualize taking a trip to a "safe place." Essentially, the individual is requested to use his or her "mind's eye" to vividly imagine a scene, one that represents a safe place, such as a favorite vacation spot. This activity can be taught to a patient as a general stress management strategy but also as one tool to help him or her to "slow down," a crucial PST concept that is part of Toolkit #2. A Patient Handout describing this stress management tool is provided in Appendix III with specific instructions on how to engage in this type of visualization

Any or all of these forms of visualization can be taught to clients as a means of enhancing their overall problem-solving ability. An additional form of visualization, we call *Positive Imagery*, is included in Toolkit #3 specifically to help individuals overcome feelings of hopelessness and to increase their motivation to continue "working" in treatment. Essentially, this approach asks individuals to visualize how they feel *after* a problem is solved but not to think about *how* they got to that point. It is similar to having a runner visualize "crossing the finish line" as a motivational tool.

Simplification

Simplification involves attempting to break down or simplify a large or complex problem in order to make it more manageable. To apply this strategy, clients are instructed to focus on the most relevant information; break down complex problems into more manageable subproblems; and translate complex, vague, and abstract concepts into more simple, specific, and concrete terms. It also refers to the process of identifying smaller steps to reach one's goals, as well as to specify these goals concretely. For example, rather than perceive graduating from high school (or college) as encompassing four long years, one can conceptualize completing one year (or one semester) at a time, which can make it appear less formidable (i.e., "What do I need to do to complete this semester?" versus "What do I need to do to graduate college?").

One method of helping the individual to translate vague ideas and concepts into more simple language is contained in the "Multitasking Patient Handout"; that is, to ask a friend to read one's written description of a problem in order to obtain feedback regarding its clarity.

REVISITING "MEGAN": PROBLEM-SOLVING MULTITASKING

Following a collaborative session in which the therapist shared Megan's case formulation with her, as well as providing a rationale for PST, initial treatment sessions introduced the concepts of the multitasking toolkit in order to provide her with a set of strategies that she would be able to apply throughout her treatment and thus improve her management of cognitive overload. This was extremely important to Megan in that her symptoms of "detachment" seemed to occur when she was overwhelmed with worry and ruminations about the possible health consequences of her heavy drinking history. Training in this toolkit provided an opportunity to work on better managing feelings of being overwhelmed that frequently fueled her avoidance of problems. The strategic use of externalization and simplification principles ultimately resulted in a significant decrease in her experience of interpersonal and emotional detachment.

After instructing her in the various ways in which she might better manage cognitive overload through the use of the problem-solving multitasking tools, she was given an opportunity to put them into practice by writing in a journal those experiences occurring during the week when she experienced herself as having thoughts and/or feelings that led to cognitive overload or feelings of being overwhelmed. She shared her notes with the therapist, which were discussed in an early treatment session. Below is an example of how her therapist demonstrated the process of simplification to help Megan begin to clarify her feelings and set reasonable and approachable targets for life change. The following is a brief dialogue between Megan (M) and her therapist (T) regarding this issue:

M: I decided to start writing when I was at work. I felt consumed with a sense of dread and worry that I had messed myself up and kept hearing the label "alcoholic" in my head. I started to shake, so I went to the bathroom and sat in a stall but tried to write this stuff down in my journal.

T: Can you share it with me here?

M: Okay. (Begins reading) "For some reason my mother comes to mind—she has no idea of what problems I have and I don't want to tell her. I'm going to visit my family in two weeks. It will be the first time that I'm not drinking. I can't imagine telling my mother that I stopped drinking. My aunt told her that she doesn't want her (my mother) to drink when she and her children are in her company, and my mother gets real nasty and sarcastic about it. She always plans to go out for drinks when we're together and has wine and beer in the house. I'm crying here (starts crying while reading) because I'm not there yet—I can't even think about telling her."

T: What do you expect will happen?

M: I don't know . . . I don't know (sobbing). She'll be disappointed, upset, and maybe be distant . . . (now laughing and crying) . . . I'm the favorite in the family. Wow. This is hard.

T: Stay with it Megan, lets break down your rush of feelings and worries here and see if we can simplify the goals a bit.

M: Okay.

T: You started to cry as you read about telling your mother that you had stopped drinking. I notice that you are less focused on the specific challenges of not drinking but more focused on what to say to your mother.

M: Yeah . . . that's true. That's what my parents do. Our family drinks . . . a lot. I'm afraid that if I tell them, they will be disappointed. Worse, they may blame themselves.

T: Why would that be so terrible?

M: Because I'm supposed to make everyone feel better! (Catches herself and laughs.) The weird thing is, my dad would probably be supportive, and my mother would eventually get over it. It's more me that's the problem.

T: Megan, I know this is hard for you. But let's see if we can make some sense of these big complicated issues. Looking at what you wrote, it seems that one problem is accepting and acknowledging your alcohol problem and developing new ways to cope with stress. Another part of your cognitive overload involves the worry and sadness you experience when you imagine sharing anything with someone you care about that you believe may disappoint them.

M: That's so true. It's like poison to me. I hate it. It makes me feel sick and queasy. But I think that these are two things I absolutely need to work on.

T: What you have done over this past week with your journal writing is an excellent example of how using the externalization and simplification tools can help move you forward with your goals for improving your life.

   Let's review. You were experiencing symptoms of detachment, worry, and a vague sense of dread. By writing down these experiences on paper and allowing yourself to get out the thoughts and feelings that you had, you were able to identify three important areas that we can work on in treatment: acceptance of your alcohol vulnerability, the need for new skills, and changing your over-magnified fear of disappointing others to more reasonable expectations. This is a very good start.

M: Sounds really hard but not so impossible. I like these tools.

T: I'm glad you found these helpful. Remember that they are important basic tools to apply throughout the problem-solving process.

SUMMARY

This chapter described the first Problem-Solving Toolkit, that of *Problem-Solving Multitasking*. As with the other toolkits, this first one is included in PST in order to help individuals to overcome ubiquitous barriers to effective problem solving. This set of tools specifically addresses the concern of the brain's inability to multitask efficiently, especially when addressing complex and/or emotionally laden problems. We suggested that to overcome this barrier, an individual should use three specific strategies: externalization, visualization, and simplification. Externalization involves placing information in an external format, such as lists, diagrams, maps, and audiotapes. Visualization, or the use of one's "mind's eye," is recommended for three important purposes: problem clarification, imaginal rehearsal, and stress management. Simplification involves breaking down complex problems into smaller ones; delineating a series of steps to goal achievement rather than one singular overall goal; and using simple, user-friendly language when describing problems and goals. We ended this chapter by revisiting Megan in order to illustrate certain points about problem-solving multitasking. As will be provided for each of the remaining toolkits, below are specific training guidelines, a list of patient handouts that can be used as instructional aids, and various recommended homework or practice assignments to be completed after training in these tools.

Key Training Points for Toolkit #1

1. Underscore the notion that the purpose of the toolkits in general is to help people to overcome common obstacles to goal attainment.
2. Provide rationale for Toolkit #1—that is, it helps teach people how to get their brain to deal with "cognitive overload" and how to continue to think effectively when experiencing negative feelings. Highlight the notion that when people are upset (e.g., sad, angry, scared, etc.), negative emotions frequently interfere with one's ability to think straight and problem-solve effectively.
3. Give out relevant patient handouts when appropriate.
4. Describe and discuss the three problem-solving strategies to "externalize," "visualize," and "simplify." Provide both generic and participant-relevant examples. Inquire about possible situations where individuals can actively use these techniques at the present time, particularly with regard to current problems. Emphasize that this set of tools is key to successful coping and should be consistently used throughout the program.
5. Practice in session the various multitasking exercises/strategies where relevant and appropriate.
6. Remind participants that this is one of four toolkits that will be taught.

Toolkit #1 Patient Handouts (contained in Appendix III)

- Problem-Solving MultiTasking
- Visualization—"Travel to a Safe Place"

Suggested Homework/Practice Assignments

▪ Complete at least one PSSM form to discuss during a subsequent session
▪ Practice the three multitasking strategies when attempting to complete a PSSM form
▪ Purchase a small notebook or journal to practice the externalization tool (can use smartphone, computer, tablet, etc. as alternative)
▪ Review handouts

EIGHT

Toolkit #2—The *SSTA* Method: Overcoming Emotional Dysregulation and Maladaptive Problem Solving Under Stress

The irony is this—our bodies react to stress in exactly the same way whether or not we have a good reason for being stressed. The body doesn't care if we're right or wrong.

—*D. Childre and H. Martin*

It's not stress that kills us, it is our reaction to it.

—*Hans Selye*

If you're having difficulty coming up with new ideas, then slow down. Creativity exists in the present moment. You can't find it anywhere else.

—*Natalie Goldberg*

As noted previously, a second potential barrier to effective problem solving involves difficulties in emotional regulation when attempting to cope with stressful problems. As such, this second Problem-Solving Toolkit focuses on helping individuals to better modulate their emotional reactions to stressful stimuli in order to prevent one's immediate negative emotional responses from becoming more intense as well as long-lasting. In essence, we describe this to clients as helping them to prevent the "train from leaving the station at an accelerating speed." Within contemporary problem-solving therapy (PST), doing so is important in order for individuals to

a. Become more aware and mindful of the actual nature of their emotional reactions (as compared to attempting to suppress or avoid such experiences)
b. Allow such emotions to better inform the problem-solving process (i.e., to better understand why they reacted to a given stimulus with a given emotion in order to eventually better understand why a given situation is actually a problem)
c. To ultimately process the stressful situation in a more thoughtful and "calm" manner via planful problem solving (e.g., "Can I do something about this situation?" "Should I do something about this problem?" "Can this problem be changed?" "Is my best solution to accept that this problem cannot be changed?")

If asked the question, "Is it usually a good time to make an important decision when you are upset?" it is likely you would quickly answer "no." Even though people frequently do make decisions or react to problems when upset, most individuals (if calm) would agree with your answer, suggesting that being angry, sad, disappointed, or tense can direct one's choices in ways that ultimately may be detrimental. As such, when we do have strong initial immediate reactions to problem situations, it is in our best interests to attempt to "regulate" such emotions so they no longer inadvertently "take over" or heavily influence our problem-solving efforts.

However, it is also important to point out that whereas there are ways in which our emotions can potentially *hurt* us, they can also *help* us, even the negative ones, such as sadness, tension, and anger. Emotions in general are important to (a) alert us to act a certain way, (b) fine tune decision making, (c) enhance our ability to remember certain events, and (d) foster interpersonal interactions (Gross & Thompson, 2007). Therefore, it becomes important to become more aware of our emotions and to actually experience them, rather than to engage in avoidant or impulsive problem-solving strategies that are geared to suppress, deny, or minimize our feelings. By becoming more mindful of our emotional life, we become more insightful about ourselves and our problem-solving orientations. These are important goals of contemporary PST.

RATIONALE FOR TOOLKIT #2

As explained in detail in our problem-solving stress model of psychopathology described in Chapter 2, encountering emotional stimuli triggers a multitude of neurobiological reactions in the body as well as cognitive interpretations of the source and nature of such stimuli. For example, stressful stimuli (e.g., getting stuck in a traffic jam, having a boss yell at you, being criticized, receiving a failing grade on a test, being rejected for a date, feeling someone behind you in a movie theatre continuously kick the back of your seat) are initially perceived by the brain's switchboard (i.e., the thalamus), which then sends the message to both the amygdala (the low road) as well as the cortex (the high road) within milliseconds. This information is then passed onto those parts of the brain representing working memory (i.e., frontal cortex, parietal cortex, anterior cingulate, and parts of the basal ganglia), which is the system that stores the information in order for the mind to engage in reasoning and comprehension (similar to a computer's hard drive). How this information is interpreted is a function of past experience and learning, the situational context, and one's appraisal of the current situation (similar to one's unique software programs).

However, because the amygdala is triggered within milliseconds, the body is likely to react more automatically based on past learning as compared to an attempt at reasoned understanding. If we do not have the time and ability to stop this process, and if the emotional stimuli is continuous (e.g., the traffic jam gets *worse*, your boss *continues* to yell at you) and/or we acknowledge that we are indeed being threatened, particularly if in a ruminative manner ("I'm always getting yelled at by my boss; I'm probably going to get fired, I'm not going to be able to get another job; I'm going to default on my mortgage and become homeless; I'm such a failure"), the amygdala also gets "bombarded" continuously and our emotional reactions are likely to become more intense. Experiencing such chronic stress can have significant negative effects on one's working memory, including actual architectural changes in the prefrontal cortex, such as dendrite atrophy and spine loss (Radley et al., 2006). These significant negative effects on both the structure (e.g., brain cell connectivity) and functioning (e.g., weakened ability to engage in the integration, processing, disposal, and retrieval of information) of the prefrontal cortex can significantly impact problem-solving effectiveness and is likely to be partially responsible for how stress leads to mental illness. In other words, stress sensitivity can lead to poor coping, which can then engender more stress and more distress (i.e., stress generation), and ultimately lead to poor adaptation and health outcomes.

Given the quickness by which a negative emotion can be triggered by a given stimulus, it becomes important to help an individual learn skills that can "stop and slow down" this process. In other words, because our goal is *not* to eradicate one's emotions (which would be analogous to cutting off someone's fingers to prevent him or her from ever getting burned by a hot cooking pot), we believe it is important to teach individuals to "stop and slow down" their immediate emotional reactions in order to allow their executive functioning processes to handle the problem situation in a more calm and thoughtful approach. In this manner, the negative effects of stress can be minimized and the likelihood that one's initial negative emotional reaction becoming more intense and long-lasting is attenuated. As suggested in the quote by Childre and Martin at the beginning of this chapter, it does not make a difference if the reason why someone is upset, angry, hurt, or disappointed is justified or correct (e.g., the boss made a mistake in yelling at you; you do not deserve to be in a traffic jam because you woke up early this morning to avoid such a jam but an accident caused it anyhow)—the negative effects will emerge nonetheless. This is why we believe that lowering one's stress reaction is important regardless of its source and potentially arbitrary nature and causality.

To help prevent intense and long-lasting emotional responses, PST provides individuals with a set of tools geared to help them "stop the train from leaving the station," or at least to help them decelerate its speed. In other words, PST is geared to help improve people's resilience to stress by helping them to "return back to their emotional baseline" (i.e., their emotional state prior to the amygdala being triggered) in order to more thoughtfully attempt to cope with the stressful problem that initially triggered the emotional reaction. However, before we describe this toolkit, titled *Stop, Slow Down, Think, and Act* (*SSTA*), in detail, we wish to place the concept of emotional regulation within a larger problem-solving context.

PROBLEM-SOLVING THERAPY AND EMOTIONAL REGULATION

According to Gross and Thompson (2007), five differing sets or categories of emotion regulation processes or strategies can be identified:

1. Situation Selection
2. Situation Modification
3. Attention Deployment
4. Cognitive Change
5. Response Modulation

Scrutiny of contemporary PST suggests that it actually includes treatment goals and specific strategies in *each* of these five categories, potentially enhancing its breadth, and ultimately, its robustness as an intervention. As such, therapists should highlight each of these five processes with clients as frameworks within which to learn how to better manage their emotional lives using these general strategies, especially within the context of solving real-life problems and attempting to adapt to stressful circumstances. In other words, an important tenet of contemporary PST is the notion of flexibility and choice. Providing a menu of various means to conceptualize and identify ways to better manage strong negative emotional reactions is in keeping with such a philosophy.

Situation Selection

These activities involve approaches to emotion regulation whereby a person engages in actions that make it more or less probable that he or she will ultimately be involved in situations that engender desirable or undesirable emotions. One goal of PST is to help individuals better understand the consequences of their behavior, particularly with regard to understanding the potential outcomes of a given solution or action plan in response to solving real-life problems (see Toolkit #4, *Planful Problem Solving*). More specifically, in addition to analyzing whether a given solution is likely to be effective, individuals are also taught to predict the consequences of that solution using the following additional criteria as guides: *personal* effects (e.g., emotional cost or gain, physical well-being, time and effort involved, consistency with one's values), *social* consequences (e.g., effects on one's spouse/partner, family, friends, coworkers, community), *short-term* effects, and *long-term* consequences.

Because PST teaches people to become more aware of their personal stress triggers as well as their emotional responses to such triggers (see this toolkit), in addition to becoming more adept at predicting the consequences of their action plans (Toolkit #4, *Decision Making* training), the combination of these strategies can be also be conceptualized and used as an emotion regulation strategy. An example of this type of process might involve the individual who is very unhappy with his current job. Considering the goal of becoming less unhappy (and possibly even fulfilled and satisfied), an emotion regulation strategy in this category might include changing jobs (within or outside of the present company or business) but doing so with a comprehensive self-understanding of what it is about various jobs and positions that makes him happy, as well as unhappy, and seeking employment in those specific contexts that are consistent with such criteria.

Situation Modification

The overarching goal regarding these types of emotional regulation strategies is to modify or change the nature of the situation such that it no longer engenders the type of emotional reactions one wishes to change. This is one of the major goals of PST, that is, to help individuals identify means by which to change a situation such that it is "no longer a problem" (i.e., resolving the problem). Getting back to our unhappy employee, one strategy in this family of emotional regulation approaches might involve identifying those aspects of his current job that are associated with negative emotions (e.g., low pay, too much or not enough responsibilities, physical work environment, lack of opportunities for growth and/or promotion, and so forth) and developing an overall solution plan that is geared to change some or all of these negative job dimensions.

Attentional Deployment

These include strategies that help individuals direct their attention in certain ways within a given situation as a means of influencing their emotions. One form of attentional deployment is *distraction*, where a person focuses his or her attention away from certain aspects of the situation or from the situation altogether. In the *SSTA* toolkit described in this chapter, several techniques are offered for individuals to help them "slow down" (i.e., attenuate the arousal) by directing their focus to other activities (e.g., counting down slowly from 20 to 1). Remember from Chapter 7 that the brain is incapable of multitasking (i.e., engaging in two activities at the same time without losing productivity); as such, teaching individuals to engage in distracting techniques can help them to refocus their attention on another task and not on the emotional stimuli. With regard to our unhappy employee, when various aspects of his current job trigger negative emotional reactions of hopelessness, frustration, or "burnout," focusing his attention on one of several "slowing down" activities can serve to attenuate the negative arousal and allow him to "use" these emotions to better inform the problem-solving process.

Cognitive Change

This fourth class of emotional regulation processes involves cognitive change strategies, including potentially changing how one thinks about the situation (e.g., appraisal of threat versus challenge) and/or about one's ability to meet the demands of the threat (e.g., "Can I adequately solve this problem?"). Many of the techniques inherent in various cognitive therapy approaches (e.g., Cognitive Therapy, Rational-Emotive Behavior Therapy) are examples of such strategies. Indeed, as noted previously, we suggested that a major barrier to effective problem solving under stress involves negative thinking, and as such, PST includes a variety of cognitive change strategies in Toolkit #3 (*Healthy Thinking and Positive Imagery*). Revisiting our unhappy employee, possible cognitive change strategies may involve reappraising his current position and focusing on the more positive aspects of this job in order to minimize negative arousal during the time remaining in this situation, while simultaneously attempting to solve the problem using planful problem solving.

Response Modulation

This family of regulation strategies includes attempts to directly impact the physiological, experiential, and/or behavioral responses comprising the emotional reaction itself. Examples might include relaxation, physical exercise, and guided imagery to attenuate a person's physiological arousal. As will be described in the next section, many of the activities included in the *SSTA* toolkit are specifically geared to help individuals decrease the intensity of their emotional reactions (as compared to suppressing or eradicating such reactions) in order to provide the opportunity to engage in planful problem solving within a less emotionally volatile context.

THE *SSTA* METHOD OF EMOTIONAL REGULATION AND PROBLEM SOLVING UNDER STRESS

The acronym *SSTA* represents

S = STOP
S = Slow Down
T = Think
A = Act

This toolkit encompasses the following components: (a) becoming more emotionally mindful, (b) identifying unique triggers, and (c) "slowing down." Although this toolkit focuses primarily on the "Stop and Slow Down" components of *SSTA*, we suggest introducing this acronym early in treatment to provide clients with the overarching guide of

1. *Stopping* when becoming aware of experiencing an emotional reaction that has the potential to "grow into a full blown negative response"
2. *Slowing down* one's emotional responding in order to

3. *Thinking* more planfully about what to do within the context of a lessened degree of interference from the triggered negative emotionality

4. Subsequently *acting* by carrying out a solution or action plan geared toward effectively coping with the stressful situation(s)

This acronym can serve as a mnemonic aid that can guide coping efforts, particularly under stress. A Patient Handout briefly describing the *SSTA* method of overcoming emotional dysregulation is contained in Appendix III as a Patient Handout.

Readers familiar with prior PST treatment manuals (e.g., D'Zurilla & Nezu, 2007; Nezu et al., 1998; Nezu, Nezu, Felgoise, McClure, & Houts, 2003) will note that the mnemonic aid previously recommended was the phrase "*STOP and THINK*." However, based on our clinical experience with a wide variety of patient populations, including those with more severe levels of distress, in combination with identifying a neurobiological explanation for why it may be so difficult to do so (i.e., to stop and then think in the face of continuous amygdala stimulation), we decided to add the component of "slowing down" to provide individuals with effective ways to do so. Adding the final "act" helps to underscore the notion that "ideas without actions are worthless" (a popular quote by H. Mackay) in terms of ultimate coping effectiveness.

As in previous manuals, PST continues to emphasize the notion that in order to effectively be able to "STOP," one needs to be aware of the types of affective, cognitive, physical, and behavioral reactions that uniquely constitute one's responses to stressful stimuli. By being aware, one can then identify the circumstances under which one needs to "STOP." Some individuals may be very aware of the types of reactions they have in response to stressful stimuli, whereas others may not. However, in addition to using such emotional reactions as "cues that a problem exists," becoming more aware of the nature of the emotions themselves and what they mean uniquely to a given individual becomes especially important later when attempting to define the problem accurately. Therefore, if relevant for a given individual, PST recommends training individuals to become more "mindful of their emotions."

Becoming More Emotionally Mindful

Training in this strategy is geared toward

a. Helping individuals to become more aware of their unique reactions to stressful stimuli in order to be able to identify when to "*STOP*"

b. Helping them to become more attuned to the meaning and nature of such emotional reactions (e.g., "Why am I so upset about this situation?")

In addition, by being more aware of such reactions, one can become better able to identify unique "triggers"; that is, those situations, events, people, internal thoughts, external stimuli (e.g., a song, visual image reminding one of a lost loved one) that stimulate the amygdala to produce potentially strong negative emotional reactions. In becoming better able to identify personal triggers, one can improve his or her ability to engage in "situation selection" types of emotional regulation (see above).

Below is an example of describing this activity to a client (remember to think of this script as one of *many* possible ways of presenting this material):

In this exercise, I want to talk about feelings. People experience upsetting feelings every day. However, emotions can be very tricky. Sometimes our feelings are a reaction to just one situation and they simply pass. At other times, we are bothered by upsetting feelings for longer periods of time. Problems like depression, anxiety, anger, and bereavement all involve distressful feelings. It is important for you to use this tool if you find that such feelings serve as an obstacle or barrier for you to adopt a positive orientation or if a strong emotional reaction hinders your ability to effectively resolve a particular problem.

It is very common for most people to need some help managing their negative feelings *(Note here, if relevant, that this might be the very reason why this person sought therapy. If not, continue as noted . . .)*. Emotional problems are often the reason why people seek help from counselors. The following guidelines are designed to give a step-by-step approach so you can use the power of feelings adaptively and to your advantage. By practicing these steps, you will be more aware of your negative feelings and be able to use them as signals or cues that a problem exists, rather than simply dwell on them, only to feel worse. In addition, this approach can help you deal better with such feelings, as well as with the problem that is causing your distress.

Consider the idea that negative emotions are one of nature's gifts to you. It is a mistake to view negative feelings as being all bad! Actually, negative emotions can be thought of as nature's way of telling you that something is wrong and that a problem exists. In this manner, they are helpful to our ultimate well-being, even though they may be unpleasant at the time.

Further, research has shown that trying to suppress negative feelings makes the situation worse—in fact, suppressing feelings actually increases their intensity! So, follow these steps in order to learn how to "Use Your Feelings as Cues."

Step 1. Throughout the day, any time when you begin to feel distressed or physically uncomfortable, stop to notice what you are feeling and how intense these feelings are. Try to put into words what emotion or feeling you notice first. Is it sadness? Boredom? Anger? Tension? Guilt? Write them down in your notebook, journal, laptop, or tablet. Remember to externalize. Externalizing can help you to remember, as well as to clarify what you are feeling.

Step 2. Now notice how you experience this feeling. Do you have any physical sensations, like your heart pounding, a lump in your throat, or your face flushing? Do you say things to yourself, like "I can't take this," "I don't need this," "I hate to feel this way," "I'll show him what it feels like," or "I give up?" What are you feeling? Sadness? Tension? Anger? What is your affect? Are you acting differently? Do you feel an urge to run away, fight someone, or shut down? As you begin to get familiar with how you experience your own emotions, consider all of these signs, that is, the physical sensations, the things you say to yourself, your affect or mood, and any changes in your behavior, such as cues, signals, or clues that "something is going on." In other words, "I'm upset about something— there's a problem that's occurring that I need to attend to!" Then go to Step 3 (*As an instructional aid, we include a worksheet, "Reactions to Stress," that individuals can use to write down this information. Note that it also requests clients to indicate the event that may have led to the change in emotions*).

Step 3. "STOP and Slow Down!" Imagine a stop sign or a flashing red traffic light as a way to help you stop. This step means stopping all action, almost like you would when you press the "pause" button on your DVD player or movie camera. You are going to stop all actions (even talking) for a few seconds to become more aware of your emotions. In this frozen moment in time, allow yourself to experience the emotion and then identify what you are feeling. Become more mindful of your experience. Inhibit the tendency to try to feel better before realizing what is truly going on or to deny the feeling in order to "make it go away." Let me show you this new figure (*Figure 8.1*)—it shows that

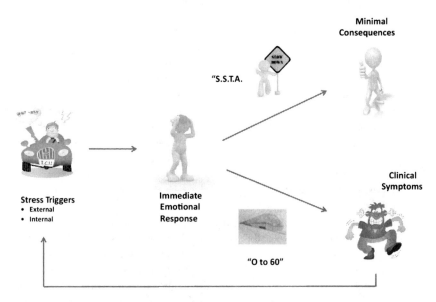

FIGURE 8.1 The *SSTA* method.

if an event like a traffic jam triggers someone's negative arousal, that person ultimately has 1 of 2 choices: to allow the train to continue to accelerate out of the station, or to engage in the *SSTA* method in order to give himself or herself the chance to "slow down."

Step 4. This step is geared to help you "Learn to be wise"—in other words, to be able to better understand what your emotions are "trying to tell you." When you react only with your feelings, it is difficult to listen to the logical or reasoned part of your mind. In such a case, you are likely to act impulsively with more feelings. For example, in reaction to something that has happened, you might get angry. However, for some people, getting angry leads to embarrassment, then embarrassment leads to fear, then fear leads to more anger. In this manner, one might never get away from these bad feelings and the original reason why you became angry (which may be natural and predictable) is lost!

On the other hand, if you think only with logic (for example, like "Dr. Spock" of *Star Trek* fame), you may disregard the important information that your emotions are telling you. For instance, suppose that you are feeling sad because you are lonely. Your logical thinking may lead you to discount or discredit your feelings ("I shouldn't be feeling this way, I'm okay!"), which may lead you to be unaware of the importance of seeking more support or friendship from others. What happens when we bring emotions and thinking together? In general, it takes both types of thinking to be wise—in other words, to be able to use your emotions to let you know what is "really going on." This can be hard work, because it means taking the time and effort to figure out what important information your feelings are providing you. With this new wisdom, however, you will be able to answer the question of what your emotions are telling you. Having this information allows you to decide what to do next.

Step 5. This next step helps you to answer the question—"What are my emotions telling me?" Remember one reason why you have emotions–to give you information! Your body is set up to react with certain feelings for very good reasons. Look at this table of emotions (see Table 8.1; also included as a Patient Handout in Appendix II). It contains the type of information you should be looking for when you are trying to identify what your feelings are "saying to you." We have also provided a few common examples of what the information may reveal.

Some of the information that a feeling "tells you" may point to an actual situation that you need to do something about it. It may also involve something that you are telling yourself or a situation that you are having difficulty accepting. Therefore, the information you receive from feelings can let you know what situation you need to focus on changing, self-statements that are irrational, exaggerated, or incorrect, and new situations or change that you must realistically confront.

Step 6. In order to achieve emotional balance in your life, it is important to work toward changing things that you can change, and becoming more realistic and accepting of things that you cannot. This is where true wisdom comes

TABLE 8.1   Listening to Feelings: What Your Emotions Might Be "Telling You"

EMOTION: FEAR/ANXIETY

Ways People Describe This Emotion: *Nervous, jittery, "on edge," scared, anxious, restless, uncomfortable, worried, panicked.*

Information to Look For: *Any sense of impending hurt, pain, threat, or danger. Anxious or nervous thoughts; sweating, dry mouth, upset stomach, dizziness, shallow breathing; urge to run away and hide, avoid situations.*

Examples of What the Information May Reveal:
- You fear physical or emotional injury for yourself or others.
- You fear that you are inferior to others and your sense of self-esteem is threatened (examples include fears about your intelligence, talents, physical skill, or outward appearance).

Why This Information Is Important:
- You can now work on better managing your fears, rather than trying to avoid them.
- You can examine the fears you have and see if they are realistic.
- You can face your fears and work on ways to reduce them. Similar to facing a schoolyard bully, facing your fears often leads to greater self-confidence, even if you sustain a bruise or two.

FEELING TYPE: ANGER

Ways People Describe This Emotion: *Frustrated, irritated, enraged, mad, "pissed off," angry, states a desire to break something or hurt someone.*

Information to Look For: *Being blocked from getting what you want—the block can be due to circumstances or specific people.*

Examples of What the Information May Reveal:
- You want success, achievement, or to be the best, but you see someone or something in the way.
- You want a relationship, but it seems like hard work, or you see the other person as creating problems.
- You want to be loved or admired, but others do not appreciate you.
- You want to be able to control circumstances or the reactions of others, but it is impossible to have that much control over situations or people.

Why the Information Is Important:
- You may discover that your anger is less about the other person and more about yourself, your pride, or what you want. Rather than focusing on your anger, you can direct your energies toward making your own life better.
- You may have unrealistic expectations regarding others or yourself. It may be time for you to "get real"—give yourself and others a break from such harsh standards.

FEELING TYPE: SADNESS

Ways People Describe This Emotion: *"Let down," disappointed, devastated, hurt, unhappy, depressed, drained, miserable, downcast, heartbroken.*

Information to Look For: *Losing something or holding the belief that you have lost something or someone important to you.*

Examples of What the Information May Reveal:
- You have lost a person (such as a friend, lover, or partner) in one of the following ways—a move, illness, death, disagreement, estrangement, or the person chooses to be with other people.

(continued)

TABLE 8.1   Listening to Feelings: What Your Emotions Might Be "Telling You" (*continued*)

- You have lost something other than a person. This may refer to something tangible (e.g., money, job, physical health, leisure time) or something intangible (e.g., a position or role in the family or work, respect from others).

Why the Information Is Important:

- You can begin to work on increasing pleasant or joyful moments in your life to help you heal from a loss.
- You may have the opportunity to see that your worth is more than the objects of loss. For example, your wealth is not a measure of your self-esteem; your physical strength is not equal to your spirit.

FEELING TYPE: EMBARRASSMENT

Ways People Describe This Emotion: *Humiliated, vulnerable, "feel like crawling in a hole," "self-conscious."*

Information to Look For: *You feel very vulnerable.*

Examples of What the Information May Reveal:

- You are concerned that others can see your imperfections, mistakes, and problems.

Why the Information Is Important:

- You can begin to focus less on imperfection and more on accepting yourself for the person you are.

FEELING TYPE: GUILT

Ways People Describe This Emotion: *Ashamed, "feel bad," "screwed up," failed.*

Information to Look For: *You regret something you did.*

Examples of What the Information May Reveal:

- You have hurt others through your own actions.
- You have not done anything wrong, but you or someone else is telling you that you were wrong and you have self-doubts.

Why the Information Is Important:

- You can work on ways to communicate your regret and make a plan for personal change for the better.
- In the case of self-doubt, you can begin to change your inner voice, such that you do not require the approval of others 100 percent of the time.

---

from— learning to actually "listen" to your emotions and then apply your logical thinking to decide what you need to do. In other words—STOP & Slow Down! Stopping and slowing down allows you to put the brakes on a potentially fast-moving train that is carrying negative emotions as baggage and determine your next move.

When you are in a calmer state, you can then attempt to go on to the next steps of *SSTA*—"think, and then act." The Nobel Peace Prize winner, Albert Schweitzer, once said—"Think first, then do." In other words, if we don't stop and slow down, we might allow our negative arousal to direct our actions. By slowing down, you can give yourself the chance to really think about what's the best course of action! I know "slowing down" is easier said than done—but I wanted to emphasize that this toolkit contains a variety of specific techniques and tools you can learn to do exactly that—"Stop and Slow Down."

Identifying Unique Triggers

By becoming more mindful and aware of their specific emotional reactions (i.e., affect, thoughts, physical sensations, behavioral changes), individuals can also become more aware of those types of situations, events, or stimuli that uniquely serve as triggers of such arousal. While completing the "Reactions to Stress" worksheet, clients are also asked to identify the event that occurred immediately prior to experiencing a negative emotion. By having such information available, the therapist can then engage the client in a discussion to better identify his or her unique triggers. We have also used the phrases "red switches" or "hot buttons" to denote the idea that certain stimuli can be responsible for engendering a negative emotional reaction (i.e., "pictures of your ex-wife, or women who physically resemble her, serve as 'switches' to turn on your feelings of sadness, regret, and remorse"; "because of your previous experiences, hearing your neighbor's dog barking actually pushes your anger button and makes you obsess over if the dog is actually on your lawn eating your beautiful flowers").

Table 8.2 provides for a list of categories of both personal and environmental stimuli that can serve as triggers. A form that allows individuals to externalize such information is also included as a Patient Handout in Appendix II ("Unique Triggers Worksheet"). Note that reactions to stress (e.g., affect, thoughts, physical sensations, and behavioral changes) can also serve as triggers for other reactions as well as increasing its own intensity (e.g., having a negative thought can lead to additional negative thoughts).

From a behavioral chaining perspective, these internal (or personal) stimuli are all part of a network of responses that comprise a larger (often

TABLE 8.2 Categories of Potential Unique Triggers

PERSONAL

Affect: sadness, anxiety, anger, guilt, embarrassment, concern, anger, etc.
Conflict: between emotions, thoughts, goals, values, beliefs, ideas, etc.
Cognitions: thoughts, flashbacks, memories, internal images, "hunches," etc.
Physical sensations: headache, pain, dizziness, stomachache, fatigue, sweating, etc.
Urge to act differently: "run away," fight, drink alcohol, sleep, overeat, take drugs, etc.

ENVIRONMENTAL/SOCIAL

Interpersonal: being criticized, yelled at, intimidated/bullied, rejected, ignored, etc.
Physical: noise, hot/cold weather, crowds, music, pictures, smells, etc.

implicit) emotional reaction that is likely to have been engendered by stimu-lating the thalamus → amygdala → cortex pathway. In other words, for exam-ple, the individual may become aware that he or she is experiencing anxiety only seconds or minutes after encountering an external stimulus (e.g., being criticized) that likely triggered such a response. As such, the affect itself may be experienced by the individual as the immediate trigger. Other internal stimuli can also serve as triggers, such as memories of a previous painful experience or thoughts about an upcoming anxiety-provoking meeting with one's boss.

External stimuli that are possible triggers are also important to identify, emanating both from the social as well as the physical envi-ronment. A variety of interpersonal events can serve to trigger negative emotional arousal, such as being the recipient of criticism, rejection, or aggression from another person. Possible physical environment triggers can include music, noise, bad weather, traffic, crowding, and so forth. Note how movies tend to be able manipulate our emotional responses simply by varying the type of music presented (e.g., think of your reaction to a horror movie that contained music usually associated with a comedy or romantic drama).

It is not so important to be able to have individuals identify the actual initial stimulus within the behavioral chain that ultimately led to increased negative arousal (i.e., "What started me feeling this way in the first place?"). Rather, it is more important that they understand that a multitude of stimuli can serve as triggers within a network of factors and to ultimately become better able to identify such triggers. Identifying one's unique buttons helps individuals to obtain increased clarity about their emotional experiences as well as to ultimately better identify *why* such stimuli tends to reliably trigger such reactions; that is, *why is this situation a problem for me?* As such, it can provide a fuller understanding and appreciation of how one can engage in a multitude of emotion regulation strategies across the five cat-egories previously described as a means of attenuating or preventing high levels of negative arousal. For example, knowing what types of situations typically have engendered, what types of negative emotional reactions in the past can allow one to decide whether to avoid such situations, become better prepared to deal with such events in a different coping manner (e.g., engage in various stress management strategies in order to enter the situa-tion with a "lowered level of stress"), to practice focusing on the more posi-tive aspects of the situation as compared to ruminating about the negative features, or attempt to change his or her thinking about such situations (e.g., try to be more accepting that such negative events are a part of life that's unavoidable).

In addition, such discussions can help the client to identify particular patterns, whereby various triggers appear to represent possible themes, such as fear of committing to relationships, sadness about being continuously rejected by people, anxiety about never "advancing in life," becoming angry when confronted with criticism, perceiving any disagreement as a threat to one's self-esteem, and so forth. Identifying patterns can be very helpful in later clarifying the nature of one's problem-solving styles in relation to specific types of situations. Further, it can provide for a mechanism of enhanced self-awareness of what types of problems particularly are troublesome for a given individual.

Clinical Dialogue: Identifying Unique Triggers

The following dialogue demonstrates the use of this strategy by a therapist (T) with Eva (E), a 38-year-old woman who described her emotional dysregulation as "going from 0 to 60 mph in three seconds," especially when it involved a disagreement with her husband or challenging behavior of her 10-year-old son, Sam.

E: I didn't like filling out this form, but I did it and it just shows once again that my husband Ben is so critical of me. This is one of those times that we are on completely different planets, and I don't think I can stand his tedious, analyzing way . . . it "drives me up a wall."

T: Okay. Sounds like something we can simplify and make some sense of. Let's look at what you wrote on the "Reaction to Stress" worksheet.

E: Okay. Here we go. The event—I went out with my friend to see this other friend's new house and Ben said he would make dinner for Sam and Becky, our children. Okay. That was nice, but then I got home and there was water all over the kitchen counter and a half of a cookie that was left on the counter that got all mushy. When I asked about it, Ben got real[ly] mad and critical of me and stormed off. My thoughts were, "you're such a jerk" . . . my physical sensations . . . I was just pissed off. I'm not sure what you wanted me to write here.

T: Let's see if I can help. Remember last week we talked about how feelings can arise so quickly because we have made some nonconscious connections that are so well learned, and that they occur so quickly that we don't actually remember a conscious experience until after the fact?

E: [Nods head]

T: That sounds like what happened here. In such a case, our bodies may provide us with some "expert information" so that we can recognize a negative feeling before it goes, to use your words, from "0 to 60."

E: I see. Okay . . . I was hot in my face, my fists were clenched, I wanted to fight, and I felt almost panicky. I think that when I first questioned Ben and said something like, "What's with all the water?" I didn't feel anything physical. But then he didn't seem concerned that it was dripping off the counter and there was this mushy cookie there—he acted like I was interrupting his playtime with Sam and Becky and embarrassing him by asking him about it in front of them. It really pissed me off—that's when I felt the physical stuff—the thoughts actually came after that because he tried to say that I always look at the negative side of things and what's wrong . . . not what's right. He said that he had done something nice, and that while I was out with my girlfriends, he was taking care of things at home. I can't take this anymore . . . I'm always the one who is "crazy" or "nuts"—he's the big hero. I wished he would just stick up for me once instead of caring about everybody else first. I was upset about the water, damn it, and he didn't care about my feelings. I was so tired, I just went to bed.

T: Do you see any pattern with situations like this, where the trigger for you is when Ben indicates that he views you as overreacting and disagrees with the way you handle things?

E: Of course. My mother always put me down, blamed me for everything, and acted like she was the one who knew everything.

T: So, maybe when Ben disagrees with you, or gives you even constructive feedback, you hear it as a put-down or criticism, before you even realize it?

E: I'll have to admit that's true. It's why I get so mad at Sam (oldest child) sometimes. He was diagnosed with attention deficit disorder and when I see him struggling, I think, that's so sad (starts crying), he's trying and he may not succeed. It makes me worried. It makes me feel like a bad mother. Our daughter Becky and I are totally different—she doesn't push my buttons.

T: How about using one of the stress reaction worksheets when you experience that trigger with Sam this week? Knowing your unique triggers can help you to know when to "Stop and Slow Down" like we previously discussed.

E: Sounds good.

Slowing Down: Specific Strategies

In teaching individuals to slow down, we suggest that a menu of several possible slowing down strategies be available that can be taught, some of which may be relevant and effective for a given individual, whereas others may not. The point here is to demonstrate that multiple choices are available and that it may be important for the client to try several of them in order to have a number of tools at his or her disposal to address differing circumstances and situations. In describing the various strategies, we strongly recommend that the therapist actually demonstrate how to apply those that appear "strange" (e.g., yawning) or novel (e.g., deep breathing) and have the client practice them in session. As the reader continues down the list presented here, he or she will note that some may be obvious choices, whereas others may not. Some, in fact (e.g., "fake smiling," "fake yawning," and gum chewing), the client may meet with laughter, which may indicate significant reluctance to engage in such activities. For those that appear "unusual," we provide scientific evidence in support of their efficacy and recommend that the therapist provide a professional and user-friendly explanation of their utility and effectiveness.

Many of the approaches listed are effective major stress management strategies in-and-of themselves. Note that we provide Patient Handouts in Appendix III for several of the listed approaches. In addition to those presented here, we urge the clinician to engage in a discussion with patients regarding additional ways they, themselves, may have used in the past to help "slow down" and "prevent the train from leaving the station."

Note that some of these approaches require more time than others, as well as more practical private space (e.g., we would not recommend that a client engage in a closed-eye guided imagery exercise in response to becoming very angry in a traffic jam while driving). In discussing these techniques, the PST clinician should ultimately help the client to determine which may be effective and appropriate for him or her, and under what circumstances.

The following are recommended "slow down" strategies:

1. Counting
2. Deep Breathing
3. Guided Imagery/Visualization
4. "Fake" Smiling
5. "Fake" Yawning
6. Mindful Meditation
7. Deep Muscle Relaxation Exercises
8. Exercise/Mindful Walking
9. Talking to Someone
10. Gum Chewing
11. Prayer
12. Others

Counting

Slowly counting up from "1" to "20" or down from "20" to "1" and attempting to visualize the numbers changing is a brief and simple method of "slowing down." It can be considered one form of an attentional deployment strategy of emotion regulation in that it helps distract the individual by focusing away from both the emotional stimulus and one's reaction to the stimulus.

Deep Breathing

Diaphragmatic or deep breathing is a common stress management tool that helps individuals to lower their arousal (McCraty, Atkinson, Tiller, Rein, & Watkins, 2003). This tool requires an individual to engage in slow, deep, and rhythmic breathing to counteract symptoms of tension and negative arousal (e.g., irregular, rapid, and shallow breathing). Practicing this strategy when one is in a calm state ultimately fosters skill acquisition and being proficient in applying it under stress. When able to engage in deep breathing, it can be a very powerful means to "slow down," especially since it requires little time to apply. Specific instructions to learn this technique are contained in Appendix III.

Guided Imagery

Using one's "mind's eye" to go to a safe place or to take a vacation in one's mind is another highly effective stress management tool (Nezu, Nezu, & Lombardo, 2001). This was initially presented in Chapter 7, and a Patient Handout teaching individuals how to apply it is contained in Appendix III. This strategy would be most useful when individuals have the time and privacy to engage in the visualization.

"Fake" Smiling

The facial feedback hypothesis suggests that facial movements can influence one's emotional experience. For example, if one is asked to smile while watching a boring television program, he or she will actually come to find the program more of an enjoyable experience. While controversial, more recent research by Havas, Glenberg, Gutowski, Lucareli, and Davidson (2010) does provide support for a strong association between facial muscles and emotional experiences. Suggesting this strategy to an individual can engender skepticism; however, our point in offering this alternative is not to make someone "happy" when he or she is feeling sad; rather, to serve as one possible "slow down" technique to help the individual begin to better manage his or her initial negative arousal. By engaging in "fake smiling" to themselves, people can attempt to slow down and "stop the train from leaving the station." Our major goal is to help individuals *reverse* the direction of the experience of negative arousal (from accelerating to decelerating). Engaging in fake smiling, perhaps in combination with other "slow-down" strategies (e.g., visualization), can facilitate this process. In describing this technique to an individual, the therapist should physically demonstrate what a "fake smile" may look and feel like. For some clients, an added note of caution may be appropriate regarding how "silly or funny" it may first appear, but with practice, and applying it in private (i.e., not to fake smile in front of someone), this strategy can be very effective.

"Fake" Yawning

Yawning is a human reflex involving simultaneous taking in of air and stretching of the eardrums, followed by exhaling of breath. It is socially contagious (i.e., seeing someone yawn can elicit a yawn) in humans as well as chimpanzees and dogs. The major reason why it is included as a "slow down" technique is due to its highly positive effects on the brain and body. More specifically, recent neuroscience research indicates that yawning simultaneously both relaxes and energizes the body; influences brain chemistry in a positive manner; decreases the temperature of the brain; improves focus; and enhances awareness, compassion, and communication (e.g., Newberg & Waldman, 2009; Walusinski, 2006). Once again, suggesting this strategy to individuals can be easily met with skepticism. However, in addition to telling them about the neuroscience research that has identified yawning's powerful positive effects, the therapist can also inform them that this is a common strategy used in voice therapy to relax the throat and reduce anxiety and to enhance focus and improve relaxation among sharpshooters and paratroopers in the military and among high-level athletes. A prime example is Apolo Ohno, a speed skater who won eight Olympic medals during the course of his career, who was frequently observed yawning right before the beginning of a race.

Because real yawning is usually not possible "on demand," we recommend that individuals engage in "fake yawning"; that is, to fake a yawn and stretch their arms widely if possible (the combination of simultaneously yawning and stretching is known as *pandiculation*) about 6 to 8 times in a row. For most people, doing so will actually begin to elicit real yawns. As with the fake smiling technique, the therapist should demonstrate this strategy and possibly underscore the notion that whereas it may seem "silly" at first, practicing this activity and applying it in appropriate contexts can be very effective as a means of "slowing down."

Mindful Meditation

The concept of *mindfulness* refers to a centuries-old meditative practice that has been an integral aspect of spiritual training in various Eastern religious faiths such as Buddhism. It can be described as a conscious state of nonjudgmental awareness, that is, the ability of one to be fully aware of a situation (or emotion reaction), without judging what one is experiencing. Practicing this strategy allows one to more fully experience what is happening "in the present moment" (e.g., one's breathing, physical sensations, movements) "without getting caught up in thoughts or emotional reactions." As such, mindfulness meditation can help individuals slow down by approaching a situation "mindfully," that is, to simply experience the situation rather than allowing one's emotional reactions to escalate. Mindful meditation has been scientifically found to be highly effective for a variety of psychological difficulties (Grossman, Niemann, Schmidt, & Walach, 2004).

An important aspect of mindfulness meditation is the notion of "distancing" oneself from one's experience. More specifically, as the independent observer, people are directed to pay close attention to their thoughts and feelings as they occur in the present moment but simultaneously attempt to separate their thoughts and feelings from themselves. In other words, to eventually be able to realize that such thoughts and feelings are just that—thoughts and feelings—and that as such, they do not need to direct his or her actions—"the thought doesn't own you, nor does it define you—it's just a thought" (Nezu, Nezu, & Jain, 2005, p. 172). Whereas it does take practice to be able to quickly distance oneself from a negative emotional response, for some people, mindfulness mediation can be a powerful means of decelerating such reactions in order to better understand why the situation is a problem and what to eventually do about it. A Patient Handout is included in Appendix III that provides instructions on how to "get distance from one's internal judge."

Deep Muscle Relaxation

Muscle relaxation (also known as progressive muscle relaxation) helps to relieve muscle tension and provides a feeling of warmth and well-being to the body. The exercises help individuals to focus on various muscle groups (e.g., right hand) and to tense and then release such tension in that muscle area in order to feel relaxed. One progresses through all the various muscle groups in the body to the point where the entire body feels relaxed. Extensive research shows this to be a very effective means for overall stress management (Ferguson, 2003) as well as improving emotional and physical well-being among individuals who recently experienced a myocardial infarction (i.e., heart attack; Loewe et al., 2002). Becoming proficient in this strategy does take significant practice. However, again, it can be a powerful tool not only for general stress management, but as a slow-down technique as well. We include a Patient Handout in Appendix III to provide for a progressive muscle relaxation script.

Exercise/Mindful Walking

Another slow-down strategy involves a wide variety of exercise activities. These can include walking, jogging, bicycling, hiking, and so forth and recommended according to the patient's abilities and physical stamina and strength. Whereas exercise is a robust stress management tool overall, in this context, brief exercise activities can serve as an effective slow-down approach.

One specific way to combine exercise and another type of slow-down strategy is to go on a "mindful walk." In doing so, individuals can benefit from exercise, decelerate their negative emotional arousal and consciously capture the full experience of their day-to-day activities as being important and valuable. In practicing this activity, one can become more proficient at distancing oneself from one's negative arousal as a means of preventing such arousal from escalating. A Patient Handout is included in Appendix III that provides instructions on carrying out this strategy.

Talking to Someone

Talking to a family member, friend, or colleague can be one method of slowing down. We would highly recommend, however, that one does not attempt to engage the other person in a dialogue geared toward helping justify or supporting one's emotional arousal. Rather, this should be previously discussed with a given person and mutually agreed upon that a conversation subsequent to a strong emotional reaction serves a slow-down purpose. For example, based on a previous plan, the support person can remind the client to engage in various stress management techniques (e.g., deep breathing, mindful meditation, etc.), provide guidance and help in applying these strategies, or engage in a conversation that allows the person to be distracted from the situation that triggered the initial reaction in order to prevent the "train from going out of the station." For some individuals, catharsis (i.e., talking about how one feels in a strong emotionally demonstrative manner) can be helpful (e.g., allows one to externalize his or her feelings; engenders fatigue); for others, it can serve the opposite function, that is, exacerbate one's arousal. As such, it is important for the therapist to assess the likelihood of positive versus negative consequences of systematically applying this strategy with a given client or client/support person pair.

Prayer

Prayer can be a very powerful slow-down strategy for those individuals who consider themselves religious or spiritual in nature. Recommending this strategy requires being sensitive to a client's values and belief systems.

Gum Chewing

This can be seen as another "strange" recommendation. However, recent research has suggested that chewing gum can actually attenuate negative mood, enhance alertness, reduce salivary cortisol, and improve performance (Scholey et al., 2009; Xu, Liu, Xia, Peng, & Zhou, 2010). Whereas the mechanisms underlying this effect remains unknown, it is possible that chewing gum serves to increase cerebral blood flow.

Others

In addition to providing the above menu of strategies as potentially effective and relevant ways of "slowing down," it is also important for the PST clinician to inquire about other techniques that may have worked for a particular client in the past. These can be added to the overall list.

REVISITING "MEGAN": DISCUSSING *SSTA*

In subsequent sessions, Megan was introduced to the "STOP and Slow Down" approach as the "S-S" part of the *SSTA* toolkit. It was thought that this was a particularly important skill for her to learn, as she quickly escalated when experiencing any negative feelings. When combined with her tendency toward worry and cognitive overload, she quickly became overwhelmed and hopeless. This triggered even more catastrophic worries that she would "lose her mind" and become completely dependent on others. The following is a dialogue between Megan (M) and her therapist (T):

T: When you describe your feelings as shutting down and detaching, many of the situations you described involve other people.

M: Yeah . . . but it's like I'm not in the present. It's so hard to describe, but it's like there is this world going on around me . . . people around me, but I'm not part of it. I start to get scared that I won't be able to change that and that I may be going crazy.

T: Okay. Let's begin by looking at a situation in which this occurs.

M: It's going on right now. I hear what you're saying and I agree that I need to learn new things, and I want to . . . but it also seems a little surreal. It's like I'm not fully here. I know it's not real and it's just a feeling, but it makes me feel detached and out of control.

T: These are feelings called "depersonalization," and I know that they lead to your feeling disconnected from people you care about. Most of us experience them at one time or another in our lives, and people with certain kinds of anxiety or past drug use may be especially prone. How long do the feelings that you have right now typically last?

M: They come and go, but sometimes for hours.

T: And you indicated that you have experienced this in recent years, when you are abstinent?

M: Yeah.

T: On a scale of 1 to 10, 10 being the most detached you can be, how detached are you experiencing yourself from me right now?

M: Hmm . . . about a 5.

T: One of the things that I think may be going on here is that you have a long history of avoiding negative feelings and confrontation, and when fear or other emotions are triggered in any kind of stressful situation (like the fear and sadness you were just experiencing in talking about the problem with your roommate), you go into a type of "shut-down" mode.

Using the analogy that your feelings were like a television news show about yourself, as soon as you hear the volume being turned up about something very important you find a little scary, your mind turns off the television rather than it viewing something that it doesn't want to see.

This happens automatically after years of learning, perhaps growing up in a house where trouble was brewing that you didn't want to know about. In any event, this "shut-down" does keep the news away so you don't have to view it. On the other hand, you miss listening to these valuable feelings and you miss important information about your goals, your values, and your dreams. A system "shut-down" means that you detach yourself altogether.

M: That's pretty messed up.

T: Did you notice your tendency to go to self-critical thoughts there, as you felt a little worried? No? That's learning gone a bit awry. The good news is that you can begin to reverse this by learning to identify when your negative feelings are first starting to emerge.

M: Like when I feel scared or sad and have the uncontrollable urge to cry, and turn it off, then things start to get detached.

T: Right.

M: Okay. What should I do? Try to ignore my feelings?

T: No . . . not at all. Remember that you need to be aware of your feelings because they provide you with very important information about what is important to you. The feelings of depersonalization are a recognizable cue or signal that there may be feelings that you are unaware of, but that your brain has learned to shut down before you even feel them. When you notice this feeling, my recommendation is to view it as an opportunity to practice a slow-down technique. Soon you may be able to have the volume of your feelings at a level you can listen to. The

"Stop and Slow Down" technique we will practice together in the next few minutes is also meant to be practiced when you experience feelings directly, like the uncontrollable urge to cry, as well as when you are feeling detached from other people, a sign that you may have already "turned off" the input from your feelings. The aim here is not to stop your crying, fears, sadness, or detached feelings; just to turn down the level of volume and concern so that you can pay attention to what they may be telling you.

M: I just thought about my family always laughing at me because I cried when my favorite cousins moved away—really sobbed—they told me I was too sensitive and had to "toughen up."

Megan was then introduced to all the various strategies for stopping and slowing down. Of all the strategies, she found yawning to be the best for her because of the research that indicated that it would allow her to remain focused but calm her body and mind. Below is the dialogue from a subsequent session after she had the opportunity to practice.

M: I tried using yawning, deep breathing, and talking to myself silently in my head, and I liked the combination of yawning and talking to myself. A couple of times this week, when someone just asked me, "Megan, how are you doing?" I felt that strong urge to cry. I said "Okay" at the moment, but then left and went to a place where I could be by myself (like the bathroom) and yawned 5 times, like we practiced. I tried to listen to these feelings—they were mainly sadness—although I said "okay" even when I didn't feel "okay." I was stuffing down the aggravation that my roommate was giving me and I wanted a drink so badly, but I wanted to not drink even more, and then I got really scared and wondered if I damaged my brain from drinking so much over the years. I was scared that if I drink, I'll keep going, have a blackout, then wake up with the same problems! I think my urge to cry was coming from me realizing how hard it will be to tell other people like my roommate things that may make them upset or that I need some help and support rather than aggravation. I actually heard myself thinking some of the things from that role-play exercise that we did . . . you know, if I'm emotional in front of someone, they will be disappointed in me—even when my roommate is acting like a jerk, I still don't want her disappointed in me.

T: Can you see the value of slowing down so you can "hear" what your feelings are saying to you? In this case, your early learning experiences have taught you to focus on making sure you don't disappoint anyone . . . even if they have continually disappointed *you*.

M: I never realized this before, but I think that it really does scare me that I might end up alone—without anybody.

T: I think you are onto some very important information here about what's important to you, like developing relationships where both people can be honest and trust each other to help, rather than avoid a perception of disappointment at all cost.

Note that by using the "slow-down" techniques, Megan was able to stop avoiding certain emotions and came to be better able to understand what was really important to her. As such, she is now in a better position to articulate *meaningful* goals and objectives.

SUMMARY

This chapter focused on the second Problem-Solving Toolkit—the *SSTA* method of overcoming emotional dysregulation and maladaptive problem solving under stress. The acronym, *SSTA*, represents the phrase "*STOP, Slow Down, Think, and Act.*" The importance of this toolkit is to help individuals prevent strong emotional arousal from escalating, such that effective problem solving becomes extremely difficult to engage in. Because emotional stimuli can trigger reactions almost instantaneously, clients are taught to initially become better aware of their overall reactions to stress, including affective, cognitive, physical, and behavioral responses. Such knowledge can also help people to become more aware of what their feelings are, especially within the context of what situations, events, people (etc.) appear to engender such reactions, as well as what these emotional reactions "tell" people about themselves and their goals. This toolkit also helps individuals to become more aware of such triggers in order to provide a more complete picture of one's unique stress–distress sets of associations as well as helping to choose the various ways by which to better manage and regulate strong emotional reactions. In order to provide a greater context within which to understand emotional regulation, we described five classes or categories of such approaches: situation selection, situation modification, attention deployment, cognitive change, and response modulation. In describing each of these types of processes, we also highlighted how contemporary PST actually incorporates each of these five sets of emotion regulation strategies.

Although this toolkit focused primarily on helping individuals to "STOP and Slow Down," which are only the first two aspects of this acronym, we suggested that the acronym and associated phrase ("STOP, Slow Down, Think, and Act") provides for a useful mnemonic for individuals to use in order to approach the overall process of solving real-life stressful problems. In helping individuals to "slow down," we described a wide variety of possible techniques, some of which are logical choices, whereas others may appear novel or even "strange." Those that are novel were included due to the associated neuroscience research supporting their potential efficacy as a stress-management and "slow-down" strategy. We described the following techniques: counting, deep breathing, guided imagery, "fake smiling," "fake yawning," mindful meditation, muscle relaxation, exercise, mindful walking, talking to a support person, gum chewing, prayer, and other approaches that we have repeatedly found to be helpful to clients. We ended this chapter by revisiting "Megan" and providing a series of clinical dialogues illustrating the use of the *SSTA* approach and the yawning technique.

Key Training Points for Toolkit #2

1. Remember to discuss and review any homework/practice assignments previously given.
2. Provide rationale for Toolkit #2—that is, it helps people to prevent negative emotional reactions from escalating into more intense and long-lasting reactions that can be overwhelming and adversely influence one's problem-solving activities. Describe the acronym *SSTA* as representing the entire process of how to solve real-life problems under stress and that this toolkit will primarily focus on the first two letters, that is, S, for "STOP," and S for "Slow Down." Highlight the notion that, as described previously, emotional reactions may occur instantaneously; as such, one needs to be better able to know one's unique reactions to stress as well as one's unique triggers that engender such reactions.
3. Give out relevant patient handouts when appropriate.
4. Teach individuals how to "become more emotionally mindful" and to record their reactions to stressful problems.
5. Engage in discussion(s) regarding the importance of using such reactions to become more insightful about one's own emotional life, especially in terms of the types of triggers that "set off" strong negative emotional reactions. Help individuals to notice patterns.
6. Teach clients how to identify unique triggers or "hot" buttons.
7. Describe, discuss, and demonstrate the various "slow-down" strategies. It is important to actually demonstrate some of them (e.g., yawning) in

front of the client to ensure accurate learning as well as diffuse possible feelings of embarrassment or discomfort in practicing them in front of the therapist.

8. Identify several "slow-down" techniques that a given individual might be able to use.

9. Teach and practice in session any of the more complex strategies (e.g., mindful meditation, muscle relaxation) that may be appropriate for a given client.

10. Practice the "*Stop-Slow Down*" sequence in session in order to provide feedback to the client and to allow for more in-depth discussions about related issues. One approach involves having clients first visualize a given problem (at first, only those that elicit mild to moderate arousal) and then say "*STOP*" aloud upon their signal that they are beginning to experience negative arousal. Upon hearing the word "*STOP*," individuals are then directed to engage in various "*Slow-Down*" techniques previously practiced. Multiple additional practice opportunities can eventually lead to clients being able to say the word "*STOP*" silently in their own minds as a means of beginning the "*STOP & Slow Down*" sequence.

11. Conduct relevant assessments of progress (e.g., toward problem resolution, decreasing distress, etc.).

Toolkit #2 Patient Handouts (contained in Appendices II and III)

- Reactions to Stress worksheet (included in text as Figure 8.1)
- The *SSTA* Method
- What Your Emotions Tell You (included in text as Table 8.1)
- Unique Triggers Worksheet (included in text as Table 8.2)
- Deep Breathing
- Guided Imagery (previously referred to in Chapter 7)
- Mindful Meditation
- Progressive Muscle Relaxation
- Mindful Walking

Suggested Homework/Practice Assignments

- Record/note reactions to stress using the worksheet
- Record/note unique triggers

- Practice in a "safe" environment (i.e., when *not* under stress) several "slow-down" techniques previously identified as potentially effective for a given client
- Apply the "STOP-Slow Down" strategy in real-life situations
- Continue to complete PSSM forms if appropriate
- Review handouts

NINE

Toolkit #3—Healthy Thinking and Positive Imagery: Overcoming Negative Thinking and Low Motivation

---

The greatest weapon against stress is our ability to choose one thought over another.

—William James

If you are distressed by anything external, the pain is not due to the thing itself, But to your estimate of it; And this you have the power to revoke at any moment.

—Marcus Aurelius

Visualize this thing that you want; see it, feel it, believe in it. Make your mental blueprint, and begin to build.

—Robert Collier

To accomplish great things, we must first dream, Then visualize, then plan, believe, act!

—Alfred A. Montapert

This chapter contains the third toolkit, *Healthy Thinking and Positive Imagery*, and addresses two significant barriers to effective problem solving: that of negative thinking and feelings of hopelessness. The degree to which the therapist emphasizes these tools for a given client is determined largely by clinical information emanating from both previous and continuous assessments (see Chapter 4). This is also true regarding *when* to focus on these activities. For example, if results from formal (e.g., Social Problem-Solving Inventory-Revised [SPSI-R] results) and/or informal (e.g., clinical interview) evaluations suggest that a given client has a particularly negative problem orientation, it is likely that the need to focus on Toolkit #3 early in treatment is high.

OVERCOMING NEGATIVE THINKING

Rationale for Focusing on Negative Thinking

A central tenet of cognitive theories of emotional disorders underscores the psychological significance of people's beliefs about themselves, their personal world, and the future (e.g., Beck, 1995). Specifically, it is one's interpretation that engenders the quality and form of his or her emotional reactions rather than the objective facts of that person's life. If such an interpretation is negative (e.g., fearful, angry, hostile, sad, worried, or hopeless), then one's resulting emotional reaction is also likely to be negative. Conversely, if one's interpretation is more positive and realistic, then the emotional reaction is more likely to be positive and realistic. Of particular significance is that one's interpretation cannot only have an impact on one's emotions, but on one's physical health as well. As an example, the effects of a realistic and optimistic way of thinking have been found to be associated with a faster rate of physical and psychological recovery of men who underwent coronary artery bypass surgery (Scheier et al. 2003).

Changing Negative Thinking Patterns

The two activities in this toolkit to help people overcome negative thinking habits include

1. The "ABC" Model of Healthy Thinking
2. Reverse Advocacy Role-Plays

The "ABC" Model of Healthy Thinking

This strategy focuses on the thoughts that people say to themselves, their expectations of situations, and their understanding of how the world operates. The strategies contained in this toolkit draw heavily upon other cognitive behavioral therapies that focus on helping clients to "cognitively restructure" their negative thinking, for example, by disputing irrational beliefs (e.g., Ellis, 2003), behaviorally testing the validity of negative cognitions (e.g., Dobson & Hamilton, 2003), and modifying maladaptive core dysfunctional beliefs or schemas (e.g., Newman, 2003).

The *ABC Model of Healthy Thinking* can be presented with an explanation that how one thinks about a situation can have a *direct* impact on one's emotional state and, thus, can negatively impact on one's ability to effectively engage in planful problem solving. Based on a core tenet of a functional analysis of behavior, this framework uses the following components in order to delineate a person's internal reactions to a stressful problem:

A = Activating event
B = What you *believe* or say to yourself about *A*
C = Emotional *c*onsequences

Using an example of a current stressful problem, clients are requested to identify thoughts, beliefs, and/or attitudes (i.e., "B") related to the problem ("A"). Examples of negative "self-talk" or cognitions that are likely to lead to negative emotional reactions ("C") include (a) highly evaluative words (e.g., "should," "must"), (b) "catastrophizing" words when not pertaining to life and death circumstances (e.g., "It's awful that I was so angry, I'm terrible to be so selfish"), (c) overgeneralizing terms (e.g., "*Nobody* can possibly understand me and what I'm going through"), and (d) hostile phrases (e.g., "What a jerk!").

Using this tool, individuals are directed to examine their own internal thoughts, whereby both the therapist and client can engage in distinguishing between self-talk that is constructive and realistic (e.g., "I wish," "I would have preferred") versus maladaptive and inaccurate (e.g., "I was stupid not to," "I should have").

In essence, individuals are directed to write down a current problem in which they are experiencing emotional distress using the format of an *ABC Thought Record* (see Figure 9.1, also included as a Patient Handbook in Appendix II). This structure helps to initially identify one's negative thinking in order to change or reformulate them. Various versions of this ABC format (also referred to as daily thought records) have been developed by cognitive therapists as a first step to help people learn how to make more accurate interpretations of events and minimize the assumptions or automatic negative thought habits that have been learned over time. Note that the *Reactions to Stress Worksheet* introduced in Chapter 8 can also be used to help individuals better identify their negative thinking patterns.

ABC THOUGHT RECORD

Situation or Event (A)	Thoughts (B)	Emotional Reactions (C)	Intensity Rating (1-10)

FIGURE 9.1   ABC thought record.

The following are instructions that can be provided to clients in teaching them to apply this strategy (Note that a Patient Handout, titled "Overcoming Negative Thinking," that briefly describes this procedure, is included in Appendix II).

Step 1. Record an Emotionally Distressing Situation: Think about a stressful problem that happened to you recently in which you felt sad, angry, or tense. We will label this problem as "A." Write down a description of the problem in the ABC Thought Record Worksheet. Next, write down the thoughts that came into your mind during this event—we will label such thoughts as "B." Finally, write down the emotional reactions, "C," that you experienced in reaction to this situation.

Look over the thoughts you recorded on the ABC Thought Record. Confronting your troubling thoughts may be uncomfortable, but try staying with this exercise and review what you wrote down as the thoughts (B) associated with a specific problem A and the experience of negative emotions (C). Allow yourself to say them silently in your head and just observe them, notice them, become aware of them. These are thoughts that your "mind has learned to say."

Changing negative thinking habits involves much more than just thinking positively. It means practicing the way you look at and interpret a situation from a new and more accurate perspective. By using the steps below, you will learn to consider each situation you experience from many different perspectives, including positive, negative, and neutral viewpoints, in order to reach more accurate and balanced conclusions.

Step 2. Rate the Intensity of Your Emotional Reaction: As you become aware of your emotions (C), rate them using a scale of 1 to 10. With regard to the example you wrote down, what was the intensity of the emotions you experienced in the situation? Rate your emotional intensity with "1" indicating the most mild and "10" indicating the most distressing and intense.

Step 3. Guided Self-Questioning: This step is also referred to as guided self-discovery and is adapted from a form of psychotherapy known as Cognitive Therapy. In this step, objectively consider the thoughts that you wrote down for their accuracy. Look for both supporting and disconfirming evidence. For example, in completing this step, a patient who complained of problems in his marriage, Steve, reviewed his thoughts of "I hate it when my wife acts so stupid." In reading these thoughts over carefully, he knew that his wife was not stupid or dull-witted.

In fact, she was an intelligent and competent professional. Based on discussions with the therapist, Steve began to realize how inaccurate he was and, as a consequence, also began to further understand what was really going on. More specifically, Steve realized that he got very frustrated when he had difficulty getting his wife to see his point of view. When they disagreed, he felt vulnerable and scared. The thoughts of "how stupid she is" served to make him feel better about himself. However, instead of leading to better communications, as he acted more aggressively toward her to compensate for these fears and feelings of vulnerability, his wife got more fearful of his angry outbursts and found it even more difficult to listen to Steve, thus often leading to more relationship problems.

Returning to the thoughts (B) that you identified for yourself, now provide any factual evidence that you think can support the accuracy of such thoughts.

Getting evidence to support your thoughts associated with strong negative emotions is not that easy. That's because many negative thoughts are based upon assumptions, not facts, and tend to be irrational, illogical, and inaccurate. (*Note: If the client is having particular difficulties separating "facts" from "assumptions," engaging him or her in the* "Facts versus Assumptions" *exercise in the* Problem Definition *section of Toolkit #4,* Planful Problem Solving, *can be very helpful*).

Next, write down the evidence that you can find that goes against your thoughts. Finding evidence that does not support your thoughts requires your willingness to see another viewpoint. One way to do this is to ask family and friends whom you trust for help by repeating the thought or assumption to others who can provide disconfirming evidence, as they are more likely to be able to see a different side of the situation if they are not involved themselves.

Step 4. Develop More Balanced Thoughts About This Situation: Balanced thoughts are those types of thoughts that are neither very negative or that strongly argue against the negative thoughts, but rather that describe facts about the situation more neutrally. For example, after objectively looking for both supporting and disconfirming evidence regarding his own thinking, Steve's new balanced thoughts were "If I try, I can manage my reactions . . . I start to get frustrated when she has difficulty seeing my viewpoint . . . but I will try to communicate calmly to help change this situation for the better.

Your previous thinking habits may have stopped you from thinking these more balanced thoughts in the past. However, new balanced thoughts can be developed through the process of trying to find evidence against your negative thinking.

Step 5. Repeat These Balanced Thoughts to Yourself: These will be more accurate, realistic, and optimistic descriptions of the situation. Remember that it takes many years to learn negative thinking habits. Therefore, it is likely to take practice and time to develop new patterns of thinking.

Step 6. Stop to Notice How You are Feeling After Practicing Your New Thoughts in Similar Situations: Once again, rate your negative feelings after changing your thoughts about the situation. See if the rating changed.

Step 7. Practice Using Your New Balanced Thoughts: Whenever you experience negative emotions or an increase in your distress level, continue to use the ABC format to record your thoughts, to objectively evaluate your thoughts for accuracy by looking for supportive and disconfirming evidence, and to develop new, accurate, and balanced thoughts to practice under stressful situations. Such feelings of distress may be mild (for example, you find yourself mildly anxious while driving in traffic), moderate (for example, you notice that you are irritated and angry toward coworkers after a meeting), or very intense (for example, you find yourself extremely sad and hopeless following an argument with a family member).

The Case of Amy

Amy, a previous client, was experiencing significant distress that was "caused" in part by her negative problem orientation. Similar to many other college graduates, due to excessive loans and problems getting a job, she had moved back home with her parents. This ultimately led to many problems that involved adjusting to a loss of independence, increased parental restriction and supervision, and financial dependency upon her family. One problem that she selected to discuss when talking about negative thoughts and feelings involved a decrease in social activities and increased time with her parents. The dialogue below represents the discussion between Amy (A) and her therapist (T) regarding the use of the *ABC Model of Healthy Thinking.*

A: The "A" part happened last week when my parents invited a bunch of their friends over for a Sunday BBQ and party. I had really been looking forward to quietly spending the afternoon in my room, getting my new computer set up and online, and surfing the web. These friends are okay, but I have nothing in common with them and they can be very boring. I didn't want to waste another Sunday being bored, so I was feeling trapped and then depressed when I thought about not having my own place.

T: That's a good example, Amy. Let's look more closely at your thoughts that occurred when you learned about the party. That way, you can begin to take apart this event, using the ABC method. The "A" was that friends of your parents had been invited over for a BBQ party, but you preferred to do something else. Now let's list what you were actually thinking or saying to yourself when your parents told you about their plans.

A: I feel so bad right now even saying it . . . I was a selfish creep.

T: You feel bad saying that you were feeling so badly that you cannot even report what you were thinking and feeling at the time?

A: I can talk about them . . . I just feel so bad about it.

T: Please explain this to me.

A: I was first real[ly] mad and feeling sorry for myself. I was thinking, "I don't want to spend another boring Sunday, how come I don't get to do one thing I want to do anymore, like work with my computer? Since I graduated college, rather than feeling like an adult, I'm just like a little kid again. Then I started to feel real[ly] bad and guilty—I thought, "You creep, how can you be so totally selfish when your parents took you in, cared about you, and were nice to you?" I started to think I really shouldn't be so picky and I should be more willing to do what they want to do. I should want to spend more time with their friends. Then I started to feel really bad and wondered if I can't get a job because God was punishing me for being such a selfish person.

T: Okay, let's list out these thoughts: "I would rather not spend my Sunday with my parents' friends," "I'm just like a little kid again because I have to live with my parents again," "I am a no-good creep and totally selfish for having these thoughts," "I should be nicer to my parents," "I should want to spend time with friends of my parents," and "I'm being punished by God because I deserve it."

At this point, Amy and her therapist looked at each statement, searching for examples of evaluative language (e.g., "should," "selfish"), catastrophizing statements ("totally selfish," "no-good creep"), and over-generalizations ("punished by God because I deserve it"). Amy was then taught to dispute this negative self-talk and challenge these self-statements with more constructive and truthful self-statements. In addition, the therapist told Amy that she would try to point out examples of this type of negative self-talk during their sessions together, such that she would have multiple opportunities to practice challenging these thoughts. The method of "disputing negative thinking" consisted of arguing against irrational beliefs or negative self-talk by taking an opposing or challenging viewpoint. For example, self-statements that include words such as *should* or *ought* need to be countered with questions such as "*Why should I . . .?*"

Amy gave the following argument against her initial belief that she *should* want to spend time with her parent's friends:

A: After thinking about it, there really is no reason why I should want to be with my parents' friends. We don't have that much in common and they may not particularly want to be with me either. What I'm really experiencing here is being stuck between wanting to do something that will be a nice way to say thank you to my parents and wanting to do something for myself. I'm kind of angry that I'm in this dilemma, because if I had my own apartment, I wouldn't even have to make these decisions.

Challenging oneself in the use of catastrophic words while analyzing the real damage potential is an effective way to challenge these types of negative thoughts. Amy's example illustrates the point as she challenges her own thought that "I'm a selfish creep."

A: My parents enjoy their friends and assume that I do too. If I tell them the truth, they will probably be a bit disappointed but won't necessarily see me as selfish, especially if I tell them that I appreciate all that they do, and if I don't try to make them give up on everything they want.

Challenging one's overgeneralizations involves objectively observing the actual validity of what is being (even silently) stated. This includes an honest assessment of what generalizations may be "fueling" particularly distressful feelings. Amy, again, provides an example:

A: I am angry that I am so dependent upon my parents and worried if I will be able to ever be on my own two feet again. At the same time, I know my parents have gone out of their way for me and I feel guilty when I get mad. Unemployment, especially in this economy, is not a punishment by God— I know that. I'm exaggerating because sometimes it feels like I'm being punished, when I'm really feeling stuck and overwhelmed. I wish that I could have my independence back.

For Amy, the therapist found it useful to give her a handout with brief cues and instructions regarding how to identify negative self-statements and "convert" such internal dialogue into more positive and realistic self-statements. An example is provided in Figure 9.2 (Minding Your Mind: Identifying Negative Self-Talk and Converting It to Positive Self-Talk). As can be seen, this handout provides brief guidelines for recognizing and challenging negative thinking. Contained in another Patient Handout (see Appendix III) is a list of *positive* self-statements that we also give to clients that can be used to substitute for the negative ones. These are

SIGNS THAT YOU ARE USING NEGATIVE SELF-TALK

- Using "judgmental" words such as "must" and "should"
- Using *catastrophizing* words for circumstances NOT related to life and death matters
- Overgeneralizing

STRATEGIES FOR "DISPUTING" NEGATIVE SELF-TALK

- Argue against negative self-talk with logic
- Argue against "should" or "ought" with "why should I?"
- Question catastrophic words and assess real damage potential of situation
- Challenge overgeneralizations
- Use challenging POSITIVE self-statements

FIGURE 9.2 Minding your mind: identifying negative self-talk and converting it to positive self-talk.

TABLE 9.1 Positive Self-Statements

- I can solve this problem!
- I'm okay—feeling sad is normal under these circumstances.
- I can't direct the wind, but I can adjust the sails.
- I don't have to please everyone.
- I can replace my fears with faith.
- It's okay to please myself.
- There will be an end to this difficulty.
- If I try, I can do it!
- I can get help from _____ if I need it.
- It's easier once I get started.
- I just need to relax.
- I can cope with this!
- I can reduce my fears.
- I just need to stay on track.
- I can't let the worries creep in.
- Prayer helps me.
- I'm proud of myself!
- I can hang in there!

also contained in Table 9.1. Individuals are encouraged to use this list as a means of combating negative self-talk. Note that by arguing against irrational beliefs and overgeneralized self-statements, one can begin to realize that solution options are actually possible. For example, Amy's worries about regaining her independence became a major focus of treatment. Developing a plan for incremental steps toward regaining independence was more productive for Amy, in contrast to silently criticizing herself for her current dependence upon her parents.

Reverse Advocacy Role-Play

A second tool to help individuals overcome their negative thinking involves an in-session role-play procedure and is aimed at helping patients change their maladaptive beliefs and distorted perceptions of external stimuli. In this exercise, any or all maladaptive and irrational attitudes toward problems-in-living are to be temporarily adopted by the problem-solving therapy (PST) counselor using a role-play format. Examples of such irrational or maladaptive attitudes are contained in Table 9.2. The client is then directed to play a friend, counselor, or therapist, in order to "argue" against such statements by providing reasons why the statement is incorrect, maladaptive, or dysfunctional. In this manner, he or she will begin to

TABLE 9.2   Common General "Irrational" Beliefs Regarding Problems and Problem Solving

1. Most people do NOT have similar kinds of problems—no one else has difficulty coping with stress like me (unless they are psychologically weak).
2. ALL of my problems are ENTIRELY caused by me.
3. It is best to avoid facing problems or making decisions. Most problems disappear on their own.
4. The FIRST solution that comes to mind is the best. I should ALWAYS operate on instincts.
5. There is a RIGHT and PERFECT solution to most problems—I just have to find it before I try to do something new.
6. Only someone who is experiencing the EXACT same problem as me can be helpful—NO one else can understand.
7. People can't change—you can't teach old dogs new tricks! The way I am is the way I'll ALWAYS be!
8. Average people CANNOT solve most of life's problems on their own.

actually verbalize those aspects of a positive problem orientation. The process of identifying a more appropriate set of beliefs toward stressful problems and providing justification for the validity of these attitudes helps the individual to begin to personally adopt such an orientation. This strategy also lends itself well to a group setting, whereby different members of the group can take turns playing both "sides of the statement" (i.e., maladaptive versus adaptive). Below is an example of such a role-play with Ed, a heart failure patient whom we worked with who appeared to have significant difficulty believing that it is "okay" to have problems dealing with a chronic illness.

T: Ed, I would like to try a role-play exercise with you where I take the part of a friend of yours at work. But, I want you to argue with what I say as a means of helping me to change my beliefs. Your job is to not go along with what I say, but rather to disagree with me. I'll explain more fully after the exercise, but for now, try your best to make a valid and realistic case against any irrational, illogical, or incorrect statements that you hear, okay?

E: Okay, I'll give it a try.

T: I know that I seem really down lately. With all the times I cry now and think about the possibility of death, I feel like such a nutcase. Other people have heart disease and seem to be a lot more courageous than me. If I have difficulty coping, it must mean that I can't cope at all and that I'm psychologically weak.

E: That's not true. A lot of people have difficulty coping with all the terrible things that we have to go through. I cry all the time. Sometimes it's real hell on earth. (Note here that Ed has begun to personalize the situation and may not be able to effectively argue. Therefore, the therapist needs to bring him back to the task.)

T: Remember now Ed, your job is to focus on what I am saying and argue against my point. You're doing well, but try to look for a way to argue with me. Okay, let's return to the role-play. You probably don't cry as much as I do. Everyone is stronger than me. That's what makes me such a lousy patient.

E: Okay, let's see where I'm at . . . Okay, you have no right to be so hard on yourself—look what you're going through—you didn't ask to get sick, and now you have so much more to deal with. It's hard for *anyone* to get sick—it may make you feel crazy, but you're not.

T: If I feel crazy, I must *be* crazy.

E: That's just an expression—it means you're upset.

T: So I guess I should just try to figure out a way to help myself not to be so upset?

E: Sure. You're not nuts—you're just upset.

T: So, basically you're saying that just because I'm upset that doesn't mean that I'm crazy, but that thinking that way can actually make me feel worse!

E: Yeah—that sounds right.

T: (Returning to become the "real" therapist) So, Ed, maybe when you catch yourself thinking this way, you need to "Stop, Slow Down, and Think more reasonably!"

E: Okay, but I think it's going to take practice!

Whereas it appeared that Ed was able to quickly come up with reasonable arguments against the therapist's "irrational beliefs," often it takes several attempts to try to elicit more rational arguments from a client who had been living with such beliefs for a long time. If this is the case, the PST counselor can take a more extreme version of the irrational or maladaptive belief (e.g., "*No one* experiences the kind of stress I feel, absolutely *no one*") in order to hopefully allow the patient to respond with a more reasoned response (e.g., "Are you saying that there has never been anybody in the history of the world, even now, that has even come close to experiencing a similar level of stress?"). It is at this point that the therapist notices the client is consistently providing rational explanations as arguments against the therapist's reversed role-play comments, and that he or she (i.e., the therapist) begins to develop a "conclusion" whereby it is in the person's best interest to think more logically (and accurately).

Revisiting Megan: Reverse Advocacy Role-Play

We revisit Megan at this point with regard to the use of the reverse advocacy role-play exercise. Working with Megan, it was apparent that her negative thinking patterns served as a major obstacle to her being able to increase her positive problem orientation and decrease her negative orientation. This negative thinking was generally triggered by emotions concerning her parents, especially her role as "the favorite one who is supposed to provide care to everyone in her family." For example, when her mother was distant or sarcastic, she provided her father with companionship. Her older sister, who experienced bouts of depression, usually sought Megan for support. Further, their mother counted on Megan as the one in the family who would always be ready to go out to the local pub for a drink; Megan's friends regularly congregated at her house to party and play cards. The reverse advocacy role-play technique was helpful in providing Megan with a more objective view of her negative thinking, which often was an obstacle to her coping with stressful problems. Below, the technique is employed in response to her negative thought of "I'm the favorite one that everyone counts on, so I should always help out."

T: I've noticed how many times your heart seems to be hurting the most when you say things such as "I can't imagine talking to my roommate about the problems we have," or "I haven't said anything to my mom about stopping drinking." Even with your best friend, Charley, you are having difficulty discussing your abstinence.

M: I know. Charley and his boyfriend Mike are coming into town this weekend and staying with me, and they suggested that we could go to a movie instead of a bar, and I started to say, we can still go to the bar . . . I don't want to change anything you do on my account.

T: And?

M: (Starts crying) And Charley says, "But we care about you"—so I started crying, and when he asked if I was okay, I cried more. I always cry when people ask me if I'm okay.

T: Because you don't want the focus on you. You're supposed to care for them (Megan nods). Megan, I would like to try an exercise with you. I'm going to pretend to be a good friend of yours—someone that you care about and want the best for. I am going to tell you about something that has me upset, and your job in this exercise is to argue against the points I am making. Even if you feel any initial tendency to agree, your job in this brief exercise is to argue against what I'm saying, as if we were in a debate and you want to prove that your point is the correct one.

M: I'll try, but I'm probably not a good debater.

T: Thanks for trying. Okay. Let's say I'm a nurse and I'm telling you that I'm having some medical problems and have to take off work, but believe that I can't tell the doctors and nurses at my hospital about it. Ready? (Megan nods.)

T: I'm so messed up right now. I have a medical problem that I need surgery for, but I can't imagine telling the hospital that I have to take off for four weeks.

M: Don't you have vacation days?

T: That's not the point. I'm the one people count on to run my unit and if I admit that I'm sick and ask them for something they will be disappointed in me and won't like me.

M: I see what you're trying to do (smiles).

T: Try to stay with this role-play exercise, Megan. Okay, back to my character—I can't disappoint anyone by having them know I'm not what they think I am. Worse yet, some of them might have to cover for me at work.

M: How would being sick disappoint them? They will probably be concerned and want to help.

T: No they won't. They don't care about me—just what I can do for them. I must do what they expect to make their life easier or they won't admire me or love me anymore . . . I'll be fired. I'll be alone.

M: Wow, is that what I'm saying to myself? (Realizes that she is supposed to argue.) Oh . . . sorry. Nobody is going to stop loving you or fire you. That's not true.

T: Yes it is. I have to be the one to please everyone and take care of everyone else. I have to be the favorite person in their life or all of them will leave me in the dust.

M: But you're human . . . they know that. Sure they expect you to do your job, but if you're sick, I'm sure that some of them will want to be there for you.

T: You don't understand. I am different. I must be the best and favorite worker in the entire hospital.

M: That's ridiculous! That's so easy to argue because no one can possibly be that.

T: I disagree. I'm special, and being the best and favorite nurse in the world is what makes me special and make people want to be with me.

M: That's like saying you're better than everyone else.

T: Maybe I have to be.

M: But if you ignore your surgery, I'm guessing it's pretty serious, you could die.

T: But I may have to take that chance, rather than disappoint anyone.

M: That's crazy—it's not worth dying or hurting yourself to make the whole world comfortable.

T: Could you repeat that?

M: I guess I get what you're trying to say. I really do need to change the way that I've been thinking.

Note that the role-play continued until Megan began to adopt a more positive problem orientation.

POSITIVE IMAGERY: OVERCOMING FEELINGS OF HOPELESSNESS AND VISUALIZING SUCCESS

Other potential barriers to coping effectively with stressful problems are feelings of hopelessness and poor motivation characteristic of a negative problem orientation. A phrase that we often hear when a client feels overwhelmed and hopeless is—"I just can't see the light at the end of the tunnel." In other words, some individuals feel that they "just can't see themselves successfully resolving a problem or achieving a particular goal."

With regard to the power of visualization to overcome hopelessness, a story that we often share with patients as an example of a profound use of this technique involves Victor Frankl, psychiatrist, author, and holocaust survivor. In his book, *Man's Search for Meaning* (1984), Dr. Frankl describes a person's ability to visualize the future as "salvation in the most difficult moments of our existence." He recalled the poignant and powerful memories of his experience of pain and humiliation in a Nazi concentration camp during World War II and the endless problems that continually consumed him. However, he also described experiencing a type of personal epiphany when, during some of his darkest moments, he was able to force his mind and thoughts to another time and place. For example, on a forced march during the winter, suffering from malnutrition, a severe cough, and lack of warm clothing, he dropped to his knees overcome with exhaustion. As was typical when a prisoner stopped marching, a Nazi guard began to beat him, yelling that if he did not get up, he would be left to die. At this point, Frankl simply said to himself—"This is it for me" and thought he was going to perish.

However, he managed to actually get up by visualizing himself in the future, standing at a podium in a warm and well-designed lecture room, with a full and attentive audience, giving a lecture on "the psychology of the death camps." He later stated in his book ". . . by this method I succeeded somehow on rising above the situation, above the sufferings of the moment, and I observed them as if they were already past . . . emotion which is suffering, ceases to be suffering as soon as we form a clear picture of it" (p. 95). Those familiar with Frankl's biography know that after he survived the atrocities of this experience, he did go on to become an internationally known psychiatrist and author who actually lived out his visualization to the extent that no one would have believed possible.

Obviously, we are not advocating that simply visualizing a solution to difficult and complex problems alone will solve them. However, we are confident that people who can successfully visualize an improved future or a "problem solved" are more likely to be motivated to persevere in their problem-solving efforts. Therefore, in this toolkit, we offer two specific visualization tools to help individuals overcome feelings of hopelessness and continue to move toward goal attainment. They include

1. Positive Visualization to Overcome Hopelessness
2. Positive Visualization for Goal Attainment

Positive Visualization to Overcome Hopelessness

This PST activity is useful when it is apparent that a client feels particularly hopeless and has significant difficulty moving forward within treatment. In other words, he or she does not feel that success in coping with problems is likely. This visualization exercise asks individuals to use their imagination or "mind's eye" to "travel to the future" *after* they successfully solved a difficult problem. They are instructed *not* to think about how one got there—just that he or she did reach a problem-solving goal. Because feelings of hopelessness are usually accompanied by depressive affect and feelings of fatigue and sluggishness, the emphasis, similar to other visualization exercises, is to attempt to *experience* as much as possible a variety of positive physical sensations, including sight, sound, touch, taste, and smell in order to really *feel* differently in the moment, as compared to simply thinking about it.

At times, when people feel overwhelmed, they pay more attention to all the negative feelings associated with the problem, rather than the potential positive consequences associated with the problem being solved. This exercise is to help individuals to *experience* something positive in order to feel somewhat more motivated to try to do something different. This is similar to the situation where a runner, upon seeing the finish line or ribbon, actually becomes more motivated to run faster in order to reach his or her goal (i.e., to complete the race).

Such an exercise can easily be used in the very beginning of treatment if the therapist perceives the client to feel particularly hopeless. It can also be applied throughout treatment whenever clients indicate difficulty in applying the various other problem-solving tools as a means of coping with stressful situations. Note that this activity is directed by the therapist, who should be competent in creating strong imaginal pictures for clients.

Below is a script describing a visualization induction.

Close your eyes and take a deep breath—filling all the spaces in your abdomen, just under your rib cage and hold it for a count of three . . . (wait for three seconds) . . . now release it and let all the air flow out. Do this one more time and notice that when you hold your breath, your abdomen is full and deflated as you let it out. Now, just allow your breathing to be normal, calm, and regular, no special rhythm, just whatever comes natural, and just focus on your breath. Notice where you experience the breath, maybe your nostrils or abdomen . . . keep your focus on your breath for a moment (wait three seconds).

Now use your imagination to visualize yourself at a future point in time—it could be a few months from now or a year from now when the problem that you are facing is largely past—largely resolved, such that it is no longer a major problem for you. It doesn't matter how you got there. Just that you are on the other side of the obstacles between you and your goals. Use all your senses to fully put yourself there in this visualization where your problem is largely improved. Picture your surroundings . . . where are you? Do you see yourself as inside or outside? Picture what you see close by and picture what you see at more of a distance. Think to yourself, if I was describing this to someone, how would I describe what this looks like? See if you can imagine the smells or the sounds of this scene in the future . . . using all of your senses. How does it feel in your body? Imagine what you would be touching or what your body would feel like. What would you be doing? If you are with other people, how do they appear? How are they relating to you? If you are alone, what are you thinking? Now fully experience this future point in time, thinking, "How would my life be different in this scene from how it is now before my visualization?" Try to imagine all of the positive thoughts and feelings associated with this moment.

Now take a deep breath, open your eyes. Write down the visualization you just experienced in as much detail as possible. Write down how you felt believing that the problem was solved—that you actually finished the race!

Positive Visualization for Goal Attainment

This visualization exercise is more of a self-directed tool for the client to learn and practice on his or her own, with the therapist's guidance, in contrast to the above exercise that is therapist-directed and conducted within a session. It involves using all three problem-solving multitasking strategies to help create positive images of the future as a means of becoming increasingly motivated to work toward one's goals. Individuals are guided to focus on a 5-year goal that is subsequently broken down into yearly, monthly, and weekly goals. A Patient Handout ("Positive Visualization for Goal Attainment") that provides for specific and detailed instructions in carrying out this exercise is included in Appendix III.

Clinical Example: The Case of "Jessica" (Integrating the Tools)

The following involves a clinical example of how a PST therapist attempted to integrate many of the tools described thus far in working with clients. The patient is Jessica (J), a 28-year-old medical student with a family history of depression and early life stress (i.e., mother's had a life-threatening illness and required hospitalization when Jessica was younger). She had previously been in PST treatment and had experienced significant improvement at that time. However, she was experiencing a new stressful situation and requested a "booster" session. When under stress, Jessica tended to experience a relapse involving ruminative thought patterns and depression.

Below is a clinical dialogue between Jessica and her therapist when she returned to classes after a winter break during which she had volunteered for humanitarian work in Guatemala.

J: Last weekend was good. Even though I was returning to classes and felt a lot of pressure after the break, I ended up being able to have a good weekend. I was social with friends and actually did enjoy myself, really trying to be in the moment, not get bogged down in worry about school. But then today, I went to look at my new apartment and started having doubts about making that place cozy and comfortable. I feel really sad about school starting, like a deep, sad, dread, as if my break in India and this wonderful time of discovery and happiness is coming to an end—the door is closing, and it is gone. I'm so anxious, full of anticipation and fear about the studying and pressure. I thought I would come in and try to talk to you and try to use the PST techniques to accept my feelings better by just letting them come and go, and to share my attempt at "externalization" until I understood what I wanted.

T: I'm glad you did. I believe that if you are able to externalize—just putting your feelings on paper, talking to me, to yourself, to your friends. This is a great start!

J: I was in school this past year and it was, in many ways, a harrowing year. By this fall, I was so stressed out that I didn't have any time for much enjoyment or time with family and friends. Then, the break came and the relief of it swept over me. My friend Carolyn told me I was like a different person . . . that while in India, I was a happier and more carefree person, someone who wasn't consumed with worry and exhaustion. I managed anxieties for traveling there, although they got somewhat bad right before leaving, but nothing like they have been in the past for me, thanks to PST. Moreover, I then hit a whole other level in Guatemala. I was purely full of joy with what I was doing.

T: Can you list some of the things you actually did while you were there?

J: Okay. I liked waking up early and having a long day. I liked going to sleep early and feeling so well-rested. I liked not having headaches. I liked doing physical labor involved in building a school. I liked speaking in Spanish. I liked meeting people that I may not have been so crazy about but nonetheless not focusing on that or their faults. I enjoyed myself. I liked that I could feel irritated, but do something to change my environment.

T: Has it struck you that these are aspects of yourself that you can put into practice here? Although a whole day involved in physical labor of building a school may not be feasible, getting some type of physical exercise is.

J: I don't know. I was so different there than here . . . like when I didn't want to hike to some ruins with Caroline and Steve (fellow volunteers), I went off and did my own thing. Although that made me anxious, I knew myself well enough to know that I didn't want to be with them. I woke up in the morning with a sense of excitement about the day and what it would bring. I remember traveling with the other volunteers I met from New York and instead of feeling anxious about being with people I didn't know, I actually felt excited. I felt excited about what we were going to find or explore. Things that usually make me anxious, like getting lightheaded due to no water or food, I was able to control by drinking lots of water and having food with me if I needed a snack. I had limited internet (Facebook) contact and so I wasn't comparing myself with others. In all of my reflections, I kept thinking that I'm proud of myself. This is where I want to be and one of my fellow med students could get married, or win a scholarship, or have a baby, but I am here in India and I made this happen and I am seeing things and having experiences that are all mine.

T: Perhaps this is an insight that you can use toward your goal of completing your med school training. For example, a visualization to remain hopeful, for example, "I'm proud that I'm doing this, facing this challenge. This city is not where I ultimately want to be but where I now need to be. This person or that person may be competitive, get higher scores on an exam, have a boyfriend, or get married, but only *I* made Guatemala happen, which was an important and powerful choice for me and I am my own agent, seeing things and having experiences that are all mine. I can focus on accomplishing my goals at med school or

I can narrow my focus on all the negatives . . . I have a choice . . . not easy, but a choice."

J: I can try. Over there, I felt a lightness of being, a freedom so to speak. No one there knew of my lifelong struggle with anxiety and depression and so it was almost helpful in allowing me to portray and believe in myself as that. I also felt attractive. I even had a little romance— it wasn't anything that was so satisfying and something that I am currently focusing on, but I felt attractive and more self-assured there. I even felt like the group I was with really appreciated me and vocalized that to me. I didn't necessarily reveal that much about myself, which still is a problem I tend to have, but I also didn't fixate on those things. I was in the moment a lot more than I am here, where I am constantly worrying about time or how this thing or that thing is going to make me feel, or predicting how I am going to handle a particular situation. It was more day-by-day and I felt a comfort level with my surroundings that I seldom feel here.

T: So the choice is more difficult for you here, for sure. You make a case for two "Jessica's" that coexist . . . which Jessica will you feed and nurture? Let's see which Jessica is closer to the real "you"— you mentioned that you wrote down some of what you have recently experienced?

J: (Taking out a piece of paper). Here is what I wrote down—I began to feel very sad the day before leaving Guatemala. I was in a beach town on the coast and, in that time, the lifestyle was so appealing. No med school, no stress, but beautiful beaches, being outdoors with nature and the sun, guys surfing and catching good waves being the highlight of the day, going out at night and knowing you'd see familiar faces. I wanted this life on one hand, but then in another way, I thought I would get bored. But I wanted to be able to stay there at least until I *did* get bored, to see what things bored me, and to see what I really did like. I came home and the first day I felt like I was moving very slowly, trying desperately to hold onto Guatemala and the calm I felt there. But slowly, as the days passed, I became sadder. My face is starting to look drawn and I don't feel like I want to look in the mirror. I don't "sparkle" like I did when I was away.

I looked full of life, even when I would wake up to go to the bathroom in the middle of the night. [Then] I started to worry again. I worry here. I worry and I obsess. I worry that med school isn't right. I worry about disappointing people if I don't want to keep doing it. I worry that I am not excited at this point in time about being a doctor. I worry about my life. I feel anxious about the passage of time and trying to understand how I feel, what will make me feel better, what will make me feel worse. Sometimes I think that I have a breaking point and what if I just can't do it anymore? What if I do break?

And when I have these feelings, even though I can talk to friends about it, I start to feel so alone. I feel trapped in my head with these thoughts that are making me literally feel like a different person. There is "worried me," there is "happier me" here in the states, and there is "contented" me in Guatemala, and a feeling of wonder that I could feel so good . . . and to come slamming back to my reality here is a reality that I feel like, at this point in time, I do *not* like. So what do I do about that? How do I make it more appealing? There are people I could see, but some of them I'm not even that excited about seeing. I want a reality where I am content more often than I am not. Being back on "Facebook" all the time in the past couple of days has undoubtedly made things worse. I am premenstrual, and not sleeping well also is not helping. Having the beginning of classes once again and a big move coming up are all things that are making me feel this pit. This pit in my being that I keep checking for and, sure enough, it's still there. For minutes or for times when I may be distracted, it leaves me . . . but then it comes rushing back as soon as I get off the phone or enter my apartment and am quiet. I know that I am not alone and yet these feelings are so isolating . . . and I know that I become different and my needs are different. I wonder if anyone could love me like this . . . knowing that I have these ups and downs my whole life. When can I get better and stay better? I have worked hard enough, challenged myself enough that I'm ready to move past these feelings. I know how powerful the anxiety is and its power over me has been terrifying at times . . . in one week's time, I can feel so utterly different. I want to look nice and then I don't care what I look like. I want to be social and then I don't want to be social. I want to eat and then I don't have an appetite. I'm excited about life and the adventures and feeling fortunate, and then it all feels hard and I feel sad without something to look forward to. This is where I find relief only in sleeping and in knowing that it is temporary, and my sleep isn't even that good. I get more upset. I tell myself that these feelings won't always be around. I should know that coming home from a trip coupled with a new start is a recipe for me to feel this way . . . and that it will pass . . . it always has passed . . . and it's learning how to master the feelings or let them be here when they are here that I have to do.

T: (In response to Jessica's written words): The last part of this paragraph is very uplifting because of the realization that you came to that "these feelings won't always be around. I should know that coming home from a trip coupled with a new start is a recipe for me to feel this way . . . and that it will pass . . . it always has passed . . . and it is learning how to let the feelings or let them be here when they are here that I have to do." One important clarification, however . . . this is an example of how one word and all its associative properties can make a huge difference in our reactions to our own reactivity. I am circling the word "master" here in your diary because none of us, *ever, master feelings*—actually they direct and often "master" us, don't they? The important thing is to listen to them, rather than simply react to them and allow them to escalate and intensify. If we work hard, we can manage, not master, our negative feelings and use them constructively to help see our life dreams and values that are important to us. In your feelings, for example, I tend to see values and life dreams that you have—love for other people, to do meaningful work, to heal and self-nurture, a need to affiliate and be with others, a commitment to be discriminating and not affiliate with people who are phony, have very different values, or who don't want to take the time to "get" you, to foster your spirituality and sexuality, to let go of the past. I would write these down, post them in your new home or in a card in your purse, and make a commitment to move a tiny bit closer toward these, *not* on necessarily feeling better, although, over time, I believe that living more consistently with one's values and life dreams ultimately results in our feeling better. The negative feelings of course will be there, up and down, as you do this. They are like the sun and the rain in the Guatemalan rain forest—they are what they are. Here are some additional ways to use the tools that you have: Visualize—picture the "Guatemalan Jessica" in your mind's eye—really try to visualize what she would do with these feelings and visualize a future point in time, for example, the end of the next term, and how it will feel if you can ultimately be successful in managing these highs and lows.

J: I think she would say, "Take it as it comes . . . some of what you are learning is interesting, and it's all good."

T: Excellent! I agree. Additionally, try using simplification—write down the three most challenging aspects for your getting back to your life here and med school. For example, you said earlier that there is an incessant stress on your mind and body of studying and the feeling that you are missing out on life.

Stress is different from missing out—" I'm missing out" is a thought that's triggered when you are burdened by the stress. Change the thought to be more accurate with what is truly going on: "This stress sucks—there's lots of pressure in med school." You are living life . . . not missing out . . . sometimes life sucks . . . anywhere. Now break down the stressful tasks in terms of what you will accomplish first—that is what "Guatemalan Jessica" would say. With regard to your current social situation, you indicated that it reinforces the idea that you don't feel as though you belong and you continue to be disappointed in the people at school, the first part, and this experience makes you somehow feel inadequate, the second part. The first part makes sense—more data that you're not most "at home" with your current cohort of students. It's the second part that reflects habitual thinking. Your perception of your current cohort of students, for the most part, not being a good match for you, seems accurate. With regard to the second part, the interpretation, that is, viewing yourself as inadequate, could actually be just as easily interpreted as you feeling superior, as many of your fellow students are less mature, younger than you, and without your life experience. Of course, we both know that neither interpretation is true—that they are somehow better than you or you are somehow better than them. It just reflects what environment and people are the best matches for you.

J: But I feel as though I may not be as competent or as smart as others in med school.

T: Of course this is another *thought*, not a *feeling*, and it flows from the previous thought. Here's the chain of thinking as you describe it: "This cohort in med school is a poor social match . . . I'm not happy about being back and facing all this work . . . therefore I must be inferior, therefore I *am* inferior." A more accurate description would be—"This sucks . . . I wish I was back in Guatemala . . . sure learned about myself there and what I am capable of . . . much to explore regarding what I want to do next when the burden of this year lightens up. For now, as the Buddhists say, "Haul water, chop wood."

J: In other words, keep to the temporary goal of getting through the term, that's it . . . keep my problem solving focused on that goal and managing my inevitable negative emotions when under pressure.

T: Sounds good to me.

Note that by combining externalization and visualization, together with her increasing insights that her negative and inaccurate thinking greatly contributed to her anxiety and depression, Jessica was eventually able once again to move toward adopting a more positive (and realistic) problem orientation. If her ruminative thinking continues to interfere with her ability to engage in planful problem solving, we recommend that the therapist guide Jessica to practice more intensely the "STOP" (when such negative and ruminative thoughts arose) and "Slow Down" (in order to reconsider the accuracy of such thoughts) process in order to allow herself to minimize the likelihood that such thoughts and emotions fuel ever increasing ruminative thinking. This can take the form of having Jessica say aloud what she is thinking (i.e., ruminative thoughts), have the therapist say aloud "STOP, Slow Down" and direct her to engage in various slow-down strategies in order to then allow her to think more reasonably and planfully. For individuals characterized by significant depressive ruminations, we suggest that this type of practice be especially highlighted.

SUMMARY

The focus of this chapter was twofold—how to overcome negative thinking as well as learning how to overcome feelings of hopelessness. We suggest that the relevance and need to address these concerns is predicated on the therapist's clinical assessment and decision making (i.e., "Is the client's negative thinking pervasive and interfering with his or her ability to engage in effective problem solving?" "Does this patient appear to feel hopeless?"). Based on cognitive therapy principles, the rationale for focusing on negative thinking patterns involved the notion that how one thinks about or interprets a given event or stimulus can directly influence his or her emotional reaction. The "ABC Model of Healthy Thinking" was introduced as a means by which to better identify one's negative thinking in order to eventually dispute such inaccuracies with more positive self-statements. Given if the client has additional difficulties overcoming such negative thinking, we described the use of the "Reversed Advocacy Role-Play" exercise, whereby the roles of the therapist and client are reversed in order to eventually have the client adopt a more reasoned and adaptive way of thinking.

The second set of tools focused on helping individuals feel more hopeful and more likely to adopt a positive problem orientation. The two tools described both used visualization as the major change agent, one that was more therapist-directed, and the second, more self-directed. The first, "Positive Visualization to Overcome Hopelessness," attempts to foster motivation to continue treatment by guiding individuals to visualize seeing "the light at the end of the tunnel;" in other words, to experience having solved the problem, in contrast to attempting to visualize "how to get there." The rationale behind this approach involves enhancing a person's ability to actually experience the feelings of achievement in order to enhance his or her motivation, similar to how one might feel more motivated to run faster upon seeing the finish line. The second tool, "Positive Visualization for Goal Attainment," involved a series of steps to help individuals use visualization to "simplify" large goals into smaller, more manageable objectives in order to ultimately better engage in planful problem solving as well as engage in actual activities geared toward achieving such goals.

Several clinical cases were presented to illustrate how to apply and integrate some of these tools.

Key Training Points for Toolkit #3

1. Remember to discuss and review any homework/practice assignments previously given.

2. Provide rationale for Toolkit #3—that is, to help individuals overcome the types of negative thinking and feelings of hopelessness that serve as obstacles to effective problem solving. Negative thinking can lead to negative emotions that inhibit effective problem-solving attempts. Feelings of hopelessness serve to decrease one's motivation to continue to pursue goal attainment and problem resolution.

3. Give out relevant patient handouts when appropriate.

4. Teach individuals the "ABC Model of Healthy Thinking" and encourage them to use the worksheet to help identify negative thinking patterns.

5. Help individuals practice disputing negative thinking using the various handouts.

6. Help individuals adopt a more positive problem orientation using the "Reverse Advocacy Role-Play" exercise if necessary.

7. If relevant for a given individual, conduct "Positive Visualization to Overcome Hopelessness" exercise. It is possible that this activity should be conducted very early in treatment if the patient feels particularly hopeless. Engage in this tool as often as needed for a given client.

8. Teach individuals to use the Positive Visualization to Move Closer to Goal Attainment tool.

9. Encourage individuals to practice all tools when appropriate outside of sessions.

10. Demonstrate how all the tools learned thus far (e.g., "Problem-Solving Multitasking," SSTA approach) can be integrated and applied together to foster effective problem solving.

11. Conduct relevant assessments of progress (e.g., toward problem resolution, decreasing distress, etc.).

Toolkit #3 Patient Handouts (Contained in Appendices II and III)

- ABC Thought Record (included in text as Figure 9.1)
- Overcoming Negative Thinking
- Minding Your Mind: Disputing Negative Thinking (included in text as Figure 9.2)
- Positive Self-Statements (included in text as Table 9.1)
- Common General Irrational Beliefs (included in text as Table 9.2)
- Positive Visualization for Goal Attainment

Suggested Homework/Practice Assignments

- Practice using the "ABC Thought Record" in order to dispute negative thinking
- Practice visualization exercises
- Practice integrating SSTA tools with tools from Toolkit #3
- Continue to complete Problem-Solving Self-Monitoring (PSSM) forms if appropriate
- Review handouts

TEN

Toolkit #4—Planful Problem Solving: Fostering Effective Problem Solving

By failing to prepare, you are preparing to fail.

—*Benjamin Franklin*

A good plan is like a road map; It shows the final destination and usually the best way to get there.

—*H. Stanley Judd*

The fourth and final toolkit focuses on teaching individuals the following four sets of planful problem-solving skills:

1. *Problem definition* (i.e., clarifying the nature of a problem, delineating a realistic problem-solving goal, and identifying those obstacles that prevent one from reaching such goals)
2. *Generation of alternatives* (i.e., thinking of a range of possible solution strategies geared to overcome the identified obstacles)
3. *Decision making* (i.e., predicting the likely consequences of these various alternatives, conducting a cost-benefit analysis based on these identified outcomes, and developing an action plan that is geared toward achieving the problem-solving goal)
4. *Solution implementation and verification* (i.e., carrying out the action plan, monitoring and evaluating the consequences of the plan, and determining whether one's problem-solving efforts have been successful or need to continue)

RATIONALE FOR TOOLKIT #4

The basic rationale for teaching these tools is largely based on the notion that such skills are characteristic of individuals who are effective problem solvers, in addition to the positive outcomes associated with effective problem solving (see Chapter 1, *Planful Problem-Solving Style*). Training in planful problem solving can be useful for individuals who (a) have difficulty coping with stressful problems due to never having learned effective problem-solving strategies, (b) have difficulty applying effective problem-solving skills to *all* areas of their lives, and/or (c) have experienced significant stress (e.g., trauma) that has inhibited their ability to fully use their effective problem-solving skills as a means of coping. Note also that individuals may have particular strengths in some areas (e.g., ability to generate alternative solution ideas) but weaknesses in others (e.g., making decisions). Similar to previous recommendations, the degree to which training in a given planful problem-solving tool is emphasized is largely determined by information gleaned from continuous formal (e.g., results from the 52-item version of the Social Problem-Solving Inventory-Revised [SPSI-R]) and informal (e.g., clinical interviews, materials from completed Problem-Solving Self-Monitoring [PSSM] forms) assessments.

Such assessments early in treatment can help the therapist decide which of two approaches to take in teaching these tools:

a. "Brief" Planful Problem-Solving Training
b. "Intensive" Planful Problem-Solving Training

BRIEF PLANFUL PROBLEM-SOLVING TRAINING

For individuals who appear to have only minor planful problem-solving deficits, or if problem-solving therapy (PST) is being provided to a particular population as more of a prevention approach, we recommend that this briefer version of training in *Planful Problem Solving* involve the following:

- Brief overview of the four planful problem-solving skills (Note that a Patient Handout, "Planful Problem Solving: An Overview," is contained in Appendix III)
- Training in the use of the "Problem-Solving Worksheet" (contained in Appendix II)

▓ Continued practice in applying the skills using the *worksheet* across multiple stressful problems that clients are currently experiencing. This involves continuous discussions and feedback regarding clients' ability and competence in applying the skills to extant problems. If this process leads to the identification of a deficit regarding a particular planful problem-solving skill (e.g., difficulties in making decisions), then more intensive training in that skill, as described in the next section, should occur.

Problem-Solving Worksheet

As a means of guiding one's approach to solving a stressful problem (i.e., applying the planful problem-solving steps), individuals are requested to attempt to resolve a given problem using the 2-page Problem-Solving Worksheet. Table 10.1 contains the list of information requested of individuals in filling out this form. Note that although there is limited space for certain categories of requested information (e.g., three obstacles to one's goal, five alternative solution ideas), clients are encouraged to provide as much information as they can using the back of the *worksheet* or additional sheets of paper, their journal, computer, tablet, and so forth.

When initially describing how to use this form, it is a good idea for the client to initially identify a problem that is lower within the hierarchy of extant stressful problems in order to minimize emotional arousal that may be distracting to the learning process. Next, the client is requested to respond to each question. We recommend that an initial "go through" of the *worksheet* be mostly geared toward increasing the client's familiarity with the form itself as well as with the various steps. This is also an opportunity for the therapist to assess the client's ability to engage in these steps and to

---

TABLE 10.1   Information Requested to Complete the Problem-Solving Worksheet

- Briefly describe the problem.
- State your problem-solving goal (BE REALISTIC).
- Describe the major obstacles to achieving your goal at this time. (space provided for 3 responses)
- Think of alternative ways to achieve your goal. Be creative. List at least 3 solution ideas. (space provided for 5 responses)
- What are the major "pros" or positive consequences of these differing alternatives?
- What are some of the "cons" or negative consequences?
- Decide which alternatives are the best by choosing the ones with the best *positive* consequences and fewest *negative* consequences. Write down your action plan.
- Carry out the plan & observe the consequences: Are you satisfied with how your plan worked?

do so competently. Completion of at least the steps that culminate in developing an action plan is recommended for the first practice exercise. During this time, the therapist can provide feedback to the client both about how to use it properly as well as the effectiveness, accuracy, and appropriateness of the actual responses.

At this point, assuming that a given client continues to demonstrate only mild problem-solving deficits, feedback to the client about the process can center around the answers to the *worksheet*. However, if the client displays significant problems with applying a particular problem-solving step (e.g., defining the problem), then the therapist can use the various information and exercises described later in this chapter as a means of increasing his or her competency level. If an action plan is actually developed during the first session devoted to planful problem solving, the therapist should determine if it is "strong" enough to eventuate in the resolution of the problem at hand. If so, the client should be encouraged to attempt to carry out the plan in order to determine if it is, in fact, an *effective* solution. If, however, the therapist determines that this initial solution plan is *not* likely to produce satisfactory results, additional discussions and attempts at using the *worksheet* need to occur.

Clinical Examples

In this next section, we provide three cases as illustrations of how individuals can use the Problem-Solving Worksheet to help resolve stressful problems based on discussions with, and training by, their therapists.

The Case of "Jim" *(Problem: Adhering to a Healthy Lifestyle Regimen)*

Jim had been diagnosed with type 2 diabetes and was having significant difficulty adhering to a low carbohydrate/low sugar diet and exercise regimen. PST was geared to help him adhere more consistently.

Describing the Problem

I knew it was important to start exercising on a regular basis and to reduce my blood sugar level by reducing the number of carbs and sugars in my diet. At first, I did well. Right after my diagnosis, I educated myself about diets, started taking meds that my doctor prescribed, and signed up for a membership in a local gym. My blood glucose dropped to close to normal range! Over time, however, after my initial weight loss and some success in lowering my blood glucose, I found myself less likely to go the gym because of time constraints and grabbing fast food meals when under pressure at work. My glucose readings were starting to be more unpredictable and I was feeling like a failure for not "fixing" the problem correctly. I tried really hard to adjust my attitude to be more realistic. This idea made sense to me and it is what I would say to a good friend who was going through a similar situation. I just had to learn to take my own advice.

Goals

- To keep my motivation up
- To maintain a low carbohydrate, low sugar diet
- To exercise for at least 30 minutes each day

Obstacles

- I often rush from the house in the morning and have trouble thinking about what to have for breakfast, so I often miss breakfast
- My work schedule makes it difficult to get to the gym
- I look forward to my favorite television shows
- I enjoy the time I spend in the early evening reading to my 3-year-old daughter and I am too tired to work out afterward

Alternative Solution Ideas

This is the part of problem solving that I am good at—coming up with ideas about how to solve a problem. I knew that if I tried to reach all my goals at once, I might be setting myself up for failure. That's probably a good example of how my tendency to try and fix everything worked *against* me. So, I further separated my goals into both a dietary goal and a workout goal. I decided to work on the dietary goal first. Breakfast was often missed because I did not have the time to make decisions and prepare breakfast before leaving the house before my 30-minute drive to work. I came up with the following list of ideas:

- Make breakfast the night before
- Buy prepackaged breakfasts
- Eat a breakfast snack bar on the way to work
- Ask for help from a nutritionist to prepare my meals
- Ask for advice and suggestions from a diabetes support helpline on the Internet
- Ask my wife for help to select a number of different low-carb, low-sugar breakfast alternatives when she shops and brings home samples for me to test out

Decision Making and Developing a Solution Plan

I weighed each alternative with a series of plusses and minuses . . . Many of them had very few positive consequences—for example, most breakfast bars are high in sugar and I don't like the taste of the other ones. Several alternatives were expensive (prepackaged foods) or costly in terms of my time and money (setting up consultation from a professional nutritionist). Some had further health risks (forget the diet, eat whatever I want, and ask my doctor for larger doses of meds). There were two that had the highest ratings—sample food with my wife's help and prepare my breakfast to be eaten on the way to work at the beginning of the week. These two alternatives seemed to go well together and, when combined, offered me the most positive consequences and the least negative ones. Foods I discovered liking were a low-carb cereal, blueberries, and nuts.

Trying Out the Action Plan

My wife and I made up packets of the cereal on Sunday in baggies, mixed with nuts and blueberries. I took a packet each day when I left for work, along with a bottle of water.

Rating the Outcome

I discovered that I was less hungry for lunch and less likely to gobble down fast food. I actually liked my own special cereal mix and found myself looking forward to my commute and breakfast "on the road." Most of all, this was a great head start for me to realize that there are ways that I can improve my glucose management and tackle the trouble spots as they come up. I used the same principles to work on the exercise problem. The end product? A before-dinner "Gymboree" with my daughter that gave us great exercise and a time to bond each day!

The Case of "Mary" (Problem: Difficult Relationships With Family Members)

Mary was a 48-year-old woman who described herself as having huge difficulties setting limits and boundaries regarding her elderly parents and brother, Jack.

Describing the Problem, Goals, and Obstacles

My problem was pretty clear—how to put limits on the demands that my parents and brother were making on me without feeling so guilty and worried when I have to say "no." I wanted to tell my parents that I loved them and want to be of help, but there are times when I can't be present because of my work and plans that I make with my husband. The big obstacle was that when they "pushed my guilt buttons," I started to feel a sense of panic about doing something wrong. I realized that these feelings were very exaggerated because my parents were robust seniors, had resources, and were there for each other. Another big obstacle was that I had been taught not to trust anyone other than my family, and my first husband, who was physically abusive, seemed to provide "proof" that this was true. However, the status of my current marriage was very different. My husband, Frank, was very caring and respectful of what I wanted, more than anyone I had known. On the other hand, my parents and brother behaved in ways that were very immature—getting angry and having tantrums when they didn't get their way. I was trying to change them and at the same time keep them happy 100% of the time—an impossible expectation.

Alternative Solution Ideas

- Use the thinking techniques provided by my therapist to help me think more positively and rationally about my right to a marriage and a personal life that is separate from my parents
- Tell my parents that I love them and will do what I can
- Try to convince my parents to change
- Move across the country (or out of the country) to get away from my parents
- Not talk to Frank about the problems with my parents
- Ask Frank's help in changing the way I react to my parents
- Join a support group about how to deal with aging parents
- Break down the problems with my parents into the smaller, day-to-day decisions

Decision Making and Developing a Solution Plan

In looking at the various alternatives, the last alternative I wrote down really hit home. I realized that since I was feeling like this problem was so big and overwhelming, it would be important to first break down the problem of setting limits with my parents into smaller ones, dealing with one situation at a time (simplification). I rated this alternative as an important first step that I could then combine with some of the others. I chose a family event (a wedding shower) that my mother wanted me to take her to in the coming month. Frank and I had planned to be away at that time in the Outer Banks of North Carolina with friends. My mother wanted me to travel north in order to take her to the wedding shower, but I wanted to keep the plans I made with my husband and friends. After reviewing the other alternatives, I realized that my parents were not likely to change their way of thinking. I would have to work hard at accepting this and maybe change my own exaggerated guilt and worry in reaction to their unfair demands. Knowing this helped me to circle back and redefine my problem a bit to be focused on how to help *me* reduce *my* exaggerated guilt reaction and to use this situation as practice for the future. I generated some additional alternatives that included asking Frank to stay calm and help me to work out what to say (I noticed that when he became angry at my parents, it made me feel worse). In addition, I worked with my therapist to be able to use self-statements that I could tell myself whenever I started to feel guilty. These statements were based on facts and helped me work against the years of guilt and unfair self-criticism I had learned to pile on myself over the years.

Trying Out the Solution Choice With an Action Plan

I told my parents that I loved them, but there are times that I couldn't always do what they wanted. I was careful not to try and convince them that it was wrong to make such demands, because that usually led to an argument, and I had to accept that they would not always be 100% pleased with my decisions. I asked Frank to practice with me, and this was helpful because he knew the things that my parents would say to "push my buttons." I practiced saying various self-statements silently to myself that I prepared with my therapist in order to hit the "off switch" when my parents started in on me. I had a helpful alternative prepared in which I offered to help my mother think about who else could take her to the shower. After several minutes of complaining, she agreed to call a cousin to take her.

Rating the Outcome

I was very uncomfortable initially, but when I started to see how manipulative my parents had been, I realized that I was actually contributing to the problem by not thinking about me and always self-sacrificing. I also came to trust Frank's support and help more, and my marriage has never been better. My parents still complain and believe that my brother and I should always be ready to drop everything at their whim, but I'm working on accepting that they're not going to change. As a result, I experience much less guilt and panic, my brother and I are closer, and they are not able to push my buttons as much anymore.

The Case of Catherine *(Problem: Depression and Loneliness)*
Catherine was a 64-year-old woman who was divorced from her husband 10 years prior and came to therapy because of strong feelings of depression and loneliness.

Describing the Problem, Goals, and Obstacles

First, I started a fresh journal and thought about the situations in which I most experienced a sense of loneliness. As discussed with my therapist, I asked myself the questions—"who, what, when, where, why, and how" in order to help me better define my problem. I discovered that I felt most painfully alone and sad on weekends. The most accurate explanation I could figure out when

I looked objectively at the situation was that my children had all grown and moved out of the immediate area. Weekends were usually taken up in the past with family activities—now I had so much free time on the weekends without any real plans.

I often ended up calling my grown children who were generally kind and supportive, but I knew that they had their own work and families that needed their time. After such talks, I would start to have thoughts that my usefulness as a person was over. Next, I thought about my goals. Although I would love to have back some of the years in which I was raising my family, I realized that it wasn't possible, and the truth was, I currently had few friends and very little sense of purpose in my life. That was hard for me to admit. Therefore, I knew that I should develop a realistic goal of meeting new people with whom I could plan a few weekend activities in the next few months.

Next, I thought about what was standing in my way or blocking the path to my goal. I realized that before I even gave any idea a chance, I started to think of all the things that could go wrong. What if I didn't like the new people I met? Worse yet, what if they didn't like me? Because I was a homemaker most of my life and had few formal skills, what if I couldn't find any purposeful activities on the weekend?

In defining my problem, I realized that I had a strong tendency to be a "worrier" about everything. I listed a secondary goal of trying out some new alternatives in spite of my worries (especially if my worries were bigger than they had to be!). For example, throughout my life, many people have said they enjoyed my company and I have enjoyed the company of others. There was an equal chance of being liked or liking others, as much as there was a chance that we would not like each other. This next part was tough for me to face—as I thought about feeling bad over not having a strong purpose in life, I asked myself why I only felt this way now. Then it hit me . . . I had a strong sense of purpose when I was raising children. It might not make sense to try to discover some *general* life purpose but to think of *current* goals as my life purpose. This part of trying to better understand my problem was important because it helped me to see my current goals as very important to my life *right now*!

Alternative Solutions Ideas

- Sign up for a cooking or foreign language class at the senior center
- Join a gym
- Volunteer to help at the church
- Volunteer to help at the animal shelter
- Join a community choir
- Join a support group for retirees
- Put an ad in the newspaper
- Join a discussion group on the Internet
- Work for a political cause such as AARP

Decision Making and Developing a Solution Plan

Two major concerns she had when evaluating the alternatives included the costs involved (i.e., she had very little money to spend) and the overall convenience. Because she lived in the city, she didn't want to have to travel very far away. After rating all of the alternatives, she chose volunteering for a church activity as one that had the most predictable positive consequences and the least amount of negative consequences. She stated, "The activity I volunteered for was to cook for the church's soup kitchen every Tuesday afternoon. This church worked with other churches in the area to provide meals to the homeless and gave me the opportunity to meet new people from this affiliated church."

Trying Out the Solution Choice With an Action Plan

One of the reasons why I chose this solution had to do with it being very cost effective and also pretty easy to carry out. I had to sign up for the Tuesday afternoon time slot and show up with my sleeves rolled up and ready to cook. I had some skill as a cook, so this activity had the added bonus of feeling good about myself.

Rating the Outcome

After working for three Tuesdays, I met a woman from the other church who loved good food and wine as much as I did. We decided to take ourselves out for a nice dinner and movie on the weekend. We had such a nice time, that we are now discussing the possibility of starting a "movie and dinner" club for older single women in our two churches. Some surprises that occurred when I look back in hindsight was how much energy I put into feeling sorry for myself being lonely, sad, and worried about not having a purpose in life, that it actually kept me from trying to meet new people and discovering my day-to-day, moment-to-moment purpose. I can now say that my current purpose in life is to help less-fortunate people, make good meals, and be a good friend to some of the women I have met recently. Not all will work perfectly, but some will result in a better quality of life for me. Isn't that what it's all about?

INTENSIVE PLANFUL PROBLEM-SOLVING TRAINING

In the event that PST is being provided to a population presenting with problems that are described in the literature as being associated with ineffective problem-solving ability (e.g., depression, suicide, generalized anxiety, chronic medical illness, substance abuse), the remainder of this chapter provides for a more intensive training in each of the four planful problem-solving skills. These tools and exercises are also appropriate for individuals found to have significant deficits in one or more of the skill areas. Once again, the degree to which any or all of the tools should be emphasized in PST for a given individual is based on prior and continuous assessments.

"If I Know What I Want, Why Should I Do All These Steps?"

This might be a question asked by clients with regard to the numerous worksheets and forms they may be requested to complete as part of the training in any of the following intensive training modules. It is important to note that it is the therapist's judgment which worksheets or activities, if any, are crucial to use. They are included in this manual as instructional aids for potential use depending in a given individual's strengths and limitations. We believe that such intense training is necessary for individuals with significant deficits in a given problem-solving area. As such, when asked such a question, we have responded—"In a game of golf, if two people have the same skills, who is more likely to eventually get a hole-in-one, the person who looks for the flag near the hole, estimates the directions of the wind, and carefully selects the correct golf club, *or* the person who swings hard but *aimlessly* at the hole?"

Problem Definition

> *It isn't that they can't see the solution.*
> *It's that they can't see the problem.*
>
> —*G. K. Chesterton*

There is an old saying by John Dewey—"A problem well-defined, is a problem half-solved." A similar adage is "measure twice, cut once." Both sayings suggest the notion that if we take the time to fully understand the nature of the problem we are experiencing, solving it will take less time and effort. More importantly, paraphrasing Chesterton above, "seeing the problem" helps to "see the solution." We believe that this activity is the most difficult of the planful problem-solving tasks, as it requires one to be able to adequately identify not only "why" it is a problem, but to do so from multiple perspectives (i.e., oneself, others involved).

In describing this process to clients, we often use the analogy of defining a problem as being similar to laying out a course or route for travel. Even if several people have the same destination, they may not all have the same resources, such as time or money, to be able to take the same exact trip. If one has never traveled to a particular destination, it becomes especially difficult due to its unfamiliarity. Simply looking at a map without knowing a specific destination would be overwhelming. As such, defining a problem is similar to first identifying a road map where one wishes to go. Another way of saying this is to first identify one's goals. In this way, one can later determine "how to get there" (i.e., the solution plan).

According to our model, correctly defining a problem involves the following 5 steps:

1. Seeking the available facts
2. Describing the facts in clear language
3. Separating facts from "assumptions"
4. Setting realistic goals
5. Identifying the obstacles to overcome in reaching such goals

Seeking the Available Facts

Sometimes people try to solve a problem before they know all the facts, especially if they tend to be impulsive or careless. As an example, it is likely that before people agree to buy a certain car, they usually wish to obtain a sizable amount of information about the car in order to make a good decision—how much gas mileage it gets, its safety record, what other consumers think about it, and so forth. In this context, we suggest that people do the same with regard to their stressful problems. With any situation that is causing some distress, it is important to seek out any facts or information that are not readily available. If we do not actually know what the problem is, we might wind up working on the wrong one.

For example, one patient we worked with, Sam, was getting more and more angry because he felt that since he had been divorced, he experienced his family and friends as being overly worried and treating him very "delicately." This often led Sam to believe that they were avoiding him. He told us that they seemed very careful not to talk about his ex-wife and were starting to avoid telling him about good times they had for fear they would upset him. Sam thought that his friend Bill, particularly, was beginning to think of him as a "fragile person." This made Sam angry, which often led to arguments that left them both feeling sad and frustrated. However, after encouraging Sam to find out more about why his friend acted this way, he learned that Bill was starting to feel like there was nothing he could do to help Sam get past his divorce and his avoidance had more to do with his own feelings of failure as a friend. Thinking of all the times that Sam helped him made Bill feel like he was failing as a friend because he could not be of more help. Ironically, all Sam wanted from Bill was to behave toward him the way he always had and not try to make things better. As such, it seemed that one thing both Sam and Bill needed to do was to "seek the facts."

We recommend to clients to think of themselves as a detective, scientist, or newspaper reporter, whose job it is to get the facts. They should ask specific questions, such as who, what, when, where, why, and how. Moreover, as would be required for a detective, such questions would have to be answered in a manner that is objective and thorough in order to allow for an uninformed person to understand what actually happened. We also remind clients to remember the "externalization" principle—that is, to write information down in their notebooks, journals, computers, smartphones, and so forth. In reading their answers, they can ask further questions, such as "Do I have *enough* facts?" "Do I need to get some more?" It is suggested that they put on the "detective's hat" and go out and seek more facts if necessary. Table 10.2 contains a list of specific questions to help guide this process in order to ultimately define the problem accurately (Note that this is also contained in Appendix II as a Patient Handout—"Getting the Facts").

Sometimes it is difficult to try to sort out what is relevant or useful information when attempting to answer these types of questions. If so, we recommend that people use visualization as a means of clarification, that is, to help identify relevant information in order to answer the above types of questions. Below is a sample visualization induction to help foster this activity.

> Close your eyes and reconstruct in your imagination a recent experience that was an instance of a recurring problem or part of a current, ongoing problem. First, imagine that you are in the situation, not viewing it as an observer, and experience it in your mind's eye as it actually happened. As you are experiencing the situation, ask yourself—"What am I thinking and feeling?" Next, repeat the experience, but this time as an observer, as if watching a movie or videotape of the situation. Play it in slow motion and ask yourself—"What is happening? What is the other person(s) saying, doing, and feeling? What am I saying, doing, and feeling?"

After this exercise, clients are directed to write their answers down, for example, using the "Getting the Facts" form.

TABLE 10.2   Questions to Help You Get the Facts

- *Who* is involved?
- *What* happened (or did not happen) that bothers you?
- *Where* did it happen?
- *When* did it happen?
- *Why* did it happen? (i.e., known causes or reasons for the problem)
- *How* did you respond to the situation? (i.e., actions, thoughts, and feelings)

Describing the Facts in Clear Language

Especially when people feel stressed, they tend to use language that may be emotionally laden, and thus, potentially unclear. Getting back to "Sam," for example, he originally stated that he felt that Bill was treating him "like he was some kind of psycho" and that he was making him feel so frustrated that "his head was going to explode!" Being presented with these problems, imagine Sam's reaction if the therapist told him that, based on such descriptions, she would "get him a room on the 'psycho ward' and 'remove the fuse from his head so it wouldn't explode!'" Of course, Sam's initial description provides a colorful way of explaining his feelings, but for anyone to provide reasonable care to him, it would be very important for Sam to be able to describe his feelings and problems using *clear* language. This is very much in keeping with the third problem-solving "multitasking" principle—*simplification*.

Another example involves Juanita, who sought therapy because of feelings of anxiety. She initially stated—"Riding in elevators is a nightmare. It's like I'm going to die or something!" A more accurate and factual description might be—"My anxiety is at its most intense when I ride in elevators. As the doors open and I step inside, my heart beats fast, my skin feels clammy, I think about my family's history of heart disease, and have thoughts about dying. As soon as I step off, I have immediate thoughts of relief and feel my heart rate returning to normal."

When people do not use clear and unambiguous language, they can exaggerate or have other people misunderstand what is being stated. For example, Sam, when angry, tended to "overstate" the frequency of his friend's avoidant behavior. When he first described the situation, he indicated that his friend "never shared anything with him anymore." In fact, after being encouraged to focus on the "facts" and use clear language, he admitted that it happens only about half of the time that he originally claimed.

Separating Facts From Assumptions

Sometimes people make assumptions, especially when they are emotional, without paying attention to this automatic thought process. Assumptions have a way of becoming a fact before anyone tries to determine if it is really true. Continuing with the theme of "thinking like a news reporter or a scientist," we recommend that people attempt to seek *facts* and not rely on *assumptions*. A fact is something that most people would collectively agree to be true; an assumption involves a person's *beliefs, opinions, or interpretations* they "*think* to be true" without initially determining its validity.

When people act on assumptions, they are likely to be unsuccessful in their problem-solving attempts. Therefore, we strongly recommend that clients are vigilant in trying to determine what are facts and what are assumptions before concluding that they have a clear and accurate understanding of the nature of their problem. For example, getting back to Sam, he assumed that his friend, when he avoided telling him about positive things in his life, thought he was no longer any fun to be with and thought Sam was a burden. Note that this was not only false (i.e., an assumption), but Sam tended to blow this idea up even more and began to feel that Bill no longer valued him as a friend. Based on these supposed facts, Sam felt justified in his anger and his arguments. Further, his immediate reactions to such assumptions, and not actual facts, led to his continued anger, frustration, arguments, and sadness. So, in this case, Sam interpreted his friend Bill's change in behavior as evidence that he no longer wanted Sam for a friend, when the facts later revealed that Bill was fearful that he wasn't being as helpful as Sam needed him to be.

We have found that a very useful exercise to help people to "separate facts from assumptions" is to show them pictures cut out from a magazine or newspaper. Clients are directed to "look at the picture for a few moments, put it down, and then begin writing everything they can think of to describe the picture." After writing down what they saw or thought was "going on" in the picture, the instructions are to look through the list and to differentiate between those aspects of the picture that are facts versus those that are assumptions. By seeing the picture one more time, the client can then become more cognizant of what is a fact as compared to something that is really more of an interpretation, which may require one to seek more information in order to verify its validity. We include the picture in Figure 10.1 as an example of an ambiguous situation that can easily elicit people making assumptions about what is going on in the picture.

FIGURE 10.1 Sample picture describing the "facts versus assumptions" exercise.

Common "Thinking Mistakes" That Can Lead to Assumptions

The following is a list of common ways that people often "distort" information when making automatic assumptions. If a client consistently displays any of these "cognitive errors," it would be advisable to use the tools contained in Toolkit #3 (Chapter 9—*Healthy Thinking*) in order to help him or her overcome the adverse influence of such errors.

Arbitrary Inference: This "thinking mistake" occurs when a person draws a conclusion without sufficient facts to support it or rule out alternative interpretations. For example, Jennifer turns down a request for a date from Frank, and Frank *automatically* concludes that she thinks he is unattractive and boring.

Selective Abstraction: This involves a situation where an individual focuses on certain selected information and draws a conclusion based solely on this information while ignoring other important information that contradicts this conclusion. For example, Henry participates as a member of a team in an athletic contest and concludes that it was his mistake that cost the team a victory the previous week, while ignoring the fact that several other team members made more serious errors.

Overgeneralization: When people make assumptions about the general characteristics of people or situations within a given class on the basis of a single event, they engage in "overgeneralization." For example, when Alice made a single mistake, her boss, Roberto, concluded that she is "incompetent."

Magnification or Minimization: Magnification occurs when an individual exaggerates the value, intensity, or significance of an event. Minimization refers to the opposite distortion, that of inappropriately devaluing or reducing the significance of an event. An example of magnification is exaggerating the possible threat or risks associated with meeting new people at a party ("Nobody is going to like me—I'll be so embarrassed!"). An example of minimization would be inappropriately minimizing the danger of leaving one's car unlocked in an unfamiliar neighborhood at night ("Nothing can happen, I'll be right back").

Misattribution: This refers to the tendency to be extreme when incorrectly attributing or identifying the cause of the problem to be oneself (e.g., "It's always my fault") or others (e.g., "It's not me—it's usually my wife's fault").

Setting Realistic Goals

In setting goals, it is important to remember to identify ones that are actually *attainable*. This means that they have to be reasonable and reachable. Although we recommend not to discourage clients from "following their dreams," unless goals are reachable, it is unlikely they will be able to solve most stressful problems. Expecting oneself to reach unrealistic goals essentially "sets one up for failure." Research has repeatedly shown that one major reason why people get depressed is that they set too high goals for themselves and are never able to reach them. If a goal seems initially too large to try to accomplish, clients are guided to follow the simplification technique, that is, to break the problem down into smaller ones, while still keeping their "final destination" in mind. For example, setting the goal of attaining "financial independence by next year" is likely to be out of most people's reach. However, by stating that they wish to "decrease their overall expenses in order to save an additional 5% of their salary by the end of one year" appears more manageable and certainly in the right direction.

Problem-Focused Versus Emotion-Focused Goals

It is also important for individuals to understand the difference between "problem-focused goals" and "emotion-focused goals." *Problem-focused goals* are objectives that involve changing the nature of a situation so that it is no longer a problem. Such goals are more appropriate for situations where the situation *can*, in fact, be changed. Examples include saving more money, improving communication, or losing weight. On the other hand, *emotion-focused goals* are objectives where a situation *cannot* be changed or where one's emotional reaction, if unchanged, would create more problems in the long run. For example, fear that one may never be able to get a job that is satisfying, while understandable, is likely to cause more harm if unchecked. "Holding onto" resentment, anger, or jealousy are other examples.

Therefore, when setting goals, individuals need to determine which types of goals are appropriate for the problem they are trying to resolve. Going back to Sam, one of the things he *cannot* change is the fact that he was divorced and that some aspects of his social life had changed, such as going out as a foursome with Bill and his wife. Because he cannot be married to his ex-wife again (as per her own goals), that part of the situation is unchangeable (although he may meet someone in the future). However, decreasing his frustration, embarrassment, and view of himself as a failure as negative emotional reactions he had about being alone are appropriate and important *emotion-focused goals* for him to consider. The goal of *accepting* that his marriage was really over represents another important emotion-focused objective. In addition, his current difficulties with his friend might be possible to change. So, having his friend more relaxed around him and less avoidant to share stories about his own wife and family can be appropriate *problem-focused goals*. This example illustrates the notion that most stressful problems in life usually involve many different types of goals, both emotion-focused *and* problem-focused.

Accepting that certain problems cannot be changed may be especially difficult for some to achieve. From a PST perspective, if a particular client is having difficulty accepting some of "life's negatives" (e.g., loss of a family member, break-up of a relationship, getting older, being diagnosed with a chronic illness), that very goal (i.e., "How can I accept _____") should be identified as a "problem to be solved," and handled using the entire problem-solving process (i.e., applying any of the tools comprising the four toolkits that are relevant). For example, for some, the difficulties in acceptance may be more cognitive (e.g., "I'm not supposed to fail"), emotional (e.g., "I can't deal with my anxiety"), or motivational ("I can never get over losing my spouse—I can never move on") in nature. As such, the therapist can guide individuals to use the appropriate problem-solving tools to foster acceptance that a given problem situation cannot be changed.

Identifying the Obstacles to Overcome

Once one has articulated a goal or set of goals, the next step in *Problem Definition* involves identifying obstacles that exist in preventing one from reaching such goals at the present time. Using the analogy of the "problem solver as traveler," goals represent the destination and identifying obstacles to reaching one's destination (e.g., far distances, time pressure, lack of available resources, conflicts between people regarding where to go to and how to get there) help greatly to better generate alternative solution ideas (i.e., the means and routes by which to reach the destination).

Identifying these obstacles basically asks the question—*what makes this situation a problem?* This is a key question to answer in order to help one correctly define the problem. Problems, by definition, involve obstacles to overcome or conflicts to resolve. We may not have sufficient resources or knowledge to reach a goal or there may be too many goals to choose from. As with most of life's more difficult problems, there are usually multiple factors that exist that contribute to the creation of a problem. Identifying such factors also helps us to identify more realistic goals. Sometimes if a problem feels very overwhelming, it is likely that we need to break it down into a set of smaller problems and tackle the various obstacles one at a time (i.e., simplification).

For Sam, one of his obstacles was to overcome his "quick anger trigger" whenever he felt frustrated. He was also experiencing conflicting goals—on one hand, he did want to have Bill's support as well as his friendship. On the other hand, he wanted to feel that he was not becoming a burden and that Bill *wanted* to spend time with him. However, he also wanted to remain honest and be able to tell his friend when he was feeling upset about his divorce.

TABLE 10.3   Possible Obstacles to One's Goals (What Makes This Situation a Problem?)

- *Barriers*—something or someone blocking your path to a goal.
- *Conflicting goals*—conflicts between yourself and others or regarding two opposing goals you have.
- *Conflicting opinions about who "caused" the problem*—arguments with others regarding whose "fault" it is that the problem exists.
- *Reduced resources*—lack of necessary skills or resources that makes reaching your goal very difficult.
- *The unknown or unfamiliar*—a situation you haven't encountered before makes it difficult to know what to do.
- *Complexity*—the situation seems very complicated and overwhelming.
- *Emotional difficulties*—your emotional reaction itself is difficult to overcome

To correctly define a problem, we should answer the following questions:

▓ What present conditions are unacceptable ("what is")
▓ What changes or additions are demanded or desired ("what should be")
▓ What obstacle(s) exist that limit my ability to go from "A" to "B" (i.e., what makes it a problem?)

Table 10.3 provides a list of various factors that often make a situation a problem for a given individual. By using this structure, clients may be more able to identify factors that make a given situation particularly complex and problematic. Developing such a list becomes especially important in order to eventually create an action plan that truly addresses the most important factors involved that make the situation a problem in the first place.

Continuing to view oneself as a "problem-solving traveler," the question to specifically ask is—"What is preventing me getting from *A* ("where I am now") to *B* ("where I want to go")? As such, we direct clients to use the list on Table 10.3 to complete the "Problem Map Worksheet" (Figure 10.2; also contained in Appendix II as a Patient Handout). Specifically, to write down what are any obstacles, conflicting goals, complexities, lack of resources, emotional difficulties, or unknown/unfamiliar aspects that make this situation a problem. Using the travel analogy—"What kind of roadblocks, long tunnels, expensive tolls, winding roads, or dangerous hills do you need to take into account when planning a trip to get to one's destination?" We also remind individuals to use clear language and to separate facts from assumptions when completing this task.

Problem Definition Worksheet

As an instructional and practice aid, we provide another worksheet, *Defining the Problem* (see Table 10.4 for the specific questions; note that the worksheet

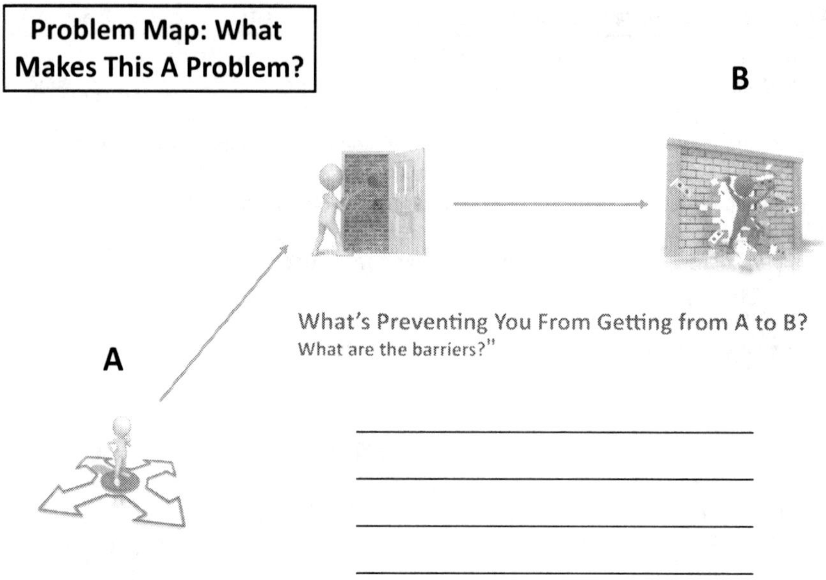

FIGURE 10.2   Problem map worksheet.

itself is contained in Appendix II as a Patient Handout), to help individuals better define the problem they are currently experiencing or wish to focus on.

Special Considerations When Defining the Problem
The following are important additional issues to consider when training clients in this skill area.

1. *Confusing a solution with a goal.* A common mistake that people often make when attempting to define a problem is to think of a "solution as a goal." As an example, consider Jane, a patient we worked with who was under lots of stress on her job. Her boss gave her assignments that were rarely given to others. As a result, she felt that he was taking advantage of her and consequently felt overwhelmed with resentment. When Jane first tried to define the problem, she stated—*How do I let my boss know that I don't appreciate such bad treatment.*" Although she deserved credit for trying to tackle this difficult and stressful problem, criticizing his way of running the office with her boss may be *one* possible alternative solution, but is not a clear description of the problem. When Jane was able to stay focused on *defining* the problem, she took the time to state the facts, separate them out from assumptions, and clarify her goals and obstacles. In her attempt to correctly define

TABLE 10.4 **Questions Comprising the Defining the Problem Worksheet**

1. *What are the facts?* Write down the facts concerning your problem. Remember to separate facts from assumptions. For example, if you experience many arguments with your spouse or significant other, state this clearly as a fact, such as "my partner and I are experiencing increased arguments about . . ." rather than stating an assumption, such as "my partner does not care about me."
2. *Why is this a problem for you?* If you are unable to improve this situation or the way you are feeling, what are the consequences? Why is this an important problem for you to improve? How will improving this problem improve your life (even in a small way)?
3. *What are your goals?* Be sure to make them realistic and attainable! Start with small goals that are steps to your larger goals. For example, if you want to improve your communication with your partner, a first goal might be to decrease arguments by 50% or increase the quality time alone to communicate by 1 hour per week.
4. *What are the major obstacles to your goal?* What is actually getting in the way of your ability to work toward your goals? With regard to the example in #1, possible examples of obstacles might include the following: you may not know how to communicate calmly or assertively without some guidance; your partner may be unavailable to you; you may lack confidence or hope.

the problem, Jane now focused on "the bigger picture problem," rather than how to solve it. She restated her goal to be: "*I want to do my job and not constantly have my boss demand more from me; I want my coworkers not to resent me when I can't help them do their work. I want to keep my job secure but also use my spare time to do some things that bring me joy.*" Using this more objective and comprehensive description, there are likely to be many more alternative ways to reach this set of goals beyond the one where Jane tells her boss that she does not like the way he operates the office.

Another example of confusing a goal with a solution involves a veteran we recently worked with who had recently come back from Afghanistan. During his two deployments, Mario had missed spending time with his preteen son. However, during this same time, Mario's wife and their son's mother functioned essentially as a single mom, therefore, serving as the only parent. Mario originally stated his goal as "wanting to spend more time with his son, Mario Jr." However, upon delving more deeply into the specifics of the situation via discussion and completion of the various worksheets related to problem definition, it appeared that Mario and his wife had frequent disagreements about parenting, especially because Mario Jr. tended to listen more to his mom than his dad. This left Mario feeling "impotent" as a father. Given this scenario, Mario's goal was reformulated as "*wanting to improve both parenting compatibility with my wife and the quality of my relationship with my son.*" As such, he was then able to have a much better understanding of the overall problem, identify the relevant obstacles to these goals, and to generate multiple alternatives to reach such goals beyond simply spending more time with his son.

2. *Whose problem is it anyway?* Most of the time when we describe a problem that we are facing, we tend to think of it solely from our own perspective. Asking this question addresses the notion of whether other people involved in the situation would also consider it to be a problem, as well as whether they would take any responsibility for either "having created it" or for "fixing it" (regardless if justified or not). In essence, it becomes important for the therapist to ask such questions of clients in order to broaden their perspective of how other people might react to the situation, especially with regard to identifying additional obstacles. Getting more facts may be an important initial response to this type of question.

3. *What is the real problem?* In Chapter 5, one of the "PST Do's and Don'ts" we included was the admonition to not focus only on "superficial" problems. We often give the handout shown in Figure 10.3, indicating that a given problem may only be the "tip of the iceberg." For example, frequent arguments with a spouse or partner about childrearing may be indicative of a "deeper" set of problems with the basic relationship. Being bored at a job may be more symptomatic of a deeper disillusionment with how one's life is progressing. As such, it is always important for therapists to keep "their eyes and ears open" to such possibilities. It is frequently the case that going through the entire planful problem-solving process involves circling back to previous steps to reformulate one's problem definition based on more detailed analysis and considerations.

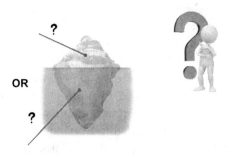

FIGURE 10.3 What's the "real" problem?

One recent example of this issue involved Marty, an Operation Iraqi Freedom veteran, who came to one of our groups indicating that his major problem was "how to become a better suitcase packer," noting that he was "terrible at packing his clothes properly when taking a trip." Upon initial further questioning, he continued to be adamant about how important it was for him to learn this skill and that he was hopeful that PST could help him do so. Focusing on a detailed analysis of his "packing problem," plus having him become more comfortable with the group intervention per se, however, allowed him to later reformulate his problem definition to, *"How can I become less anxious when leaving on a trip away from my family?"* Going through the detailed process of problem definition training, it became apparent that he was very anxious about leaving his family to travel for work because it reminded him of being deployed and being away from them for long periods of time. Having his suitcase packed perfectly somehow came to represent a safe trip, one where he would be able to come back in a timely manner. Whereas this would appear to be a rather extreme example of this issue, we strongly recommend that the PST therapist be diligent in helping clients to identify and work on the real problem.

4. *When the problem is confusing.* At times, individuals may get stuck when trying to accurately define the problem, delineate goals, and/or identify salient obstacles. We have found the set of questions below to be useful in beginning a dialogue that can increase a client's understanding and insight into this process.

- What are your feelings connected with this problem?
- Is there anything in your past that makes this situation or set of feelings especially challenging for you?
- Is this situation or problem related to a particular life dream of yours?
- How is this situation related to your life values?
- How would your life be different if this problem changed for the better? For the worse?

Generation of Alternatives

Nothing is more dangerous than an idea, when it's the only one you have.

—*Emile Cartier*

The second planful problem-solving skill involves generating alternative ideas to help overcome those obstacles to goal attainment previously identified.

If we continue to think of problem solving as a journey, reaching one's goals can be thought of as getting from A to B; in other words, reaching one's goals at destination B. As in any journey, even if one is clear about where he or she wants to go, there might be several paths or roads to take to reach B. Often, there are different consequences related to taking different paths— one might be longer but cost less money, another might be more expensive but is quicker, and yet another might be more scenic yet takes more time. As such, we recommend that individuals consider "multiple routes to get to their destination."

Not only are there differing consequences associated with differing alternatives, but believing that there is only one route to take can inhibit one's motivation to actually take the trip (i.e., to solve the problem). To make this point with clients, we would ask them to—*"Think of having only one route to take. Think how you would feel if there was only one cereal to choose from the next time you went to the grocery store, or if there was only one movie listed in the entire town where you live to see this coming weekend?"* When a person is only able to see a very limited number of alternatives to choose from in life, he or she is likely to experience high levels of hopelessness and helplessness. At its most extreme, such "tunnel vision" can lead to suicidal thoughts and behavior. As noted in the quote from French philosopher Cartier at the beginning of this section, having only one idea can be a "dangerous" situation. Conversely, when people feel that they have multiple choices, they tend to feel more in control, safe, and full of hope.

Therefore, with real-life stressful problems, we argue that it is generally a good idea for people to think of a *variety* of ways to solve the problem, not only in order to eventually arrive at the best solution, but also to feel more hopeful. The task at hand here is to creatively think of a sizable list of possible ideas. To accomplish this, we recommend applying certain *brainstorming* principles. Brainstorming helps to minimize dichotomous or "black and white" thinking. In addition, it helps to decreases one's tendency to react impulsively—if people are guided to think of a range of ideas, they are forced to be more reflective and planful. Brainstorming also increases one's flexibility and creativity, which actually improves the quality and quantity of the solutions that are generated.

Using brainstorming principles also helps to discourage judging ideas while thinking about novel solutions. This becomes particularly important when people have strong emotional reactions to problem situations. Emotions can often dominate or influence thinking, such that individuals might rigidly think only of options that maintain their negative thoughts and feelings. When emotions do seem to become overwhelming, brainstorming can help them to get "back on track." Moreover, using brainstorming techniques helps to redirect a person's time and energy to focus on the task of solving a problem. One can concentrate on *productive thinking* rather than on the negative emotions that surround the problem.

Productive thinking involves confronting problems directly by creatively developing a list of possible ways to resolve them. This is in contrast to *nonproductive thinking*, which refers to thoughts *unrelated* to solving a problem, but focused on the consequent emotional distress instead.

In making this point with clients, we offer the following rationale:

> Consider the following differences in the reactions between Rita and Naomi, who both missed the last train home from work. Both had dinner engagements scheduled for later in the evening. Rita focuses her attention on her negative thoughts of irresponsibility, carelessness, and unreliability as well as negative emotions of sadness and anger at herself. She also concentrates on her disappointment that the train was gone, which meant that she would arrive home late, causing her to miss her dinner date. She continues to lament on these negative thoughts, which eventually spirals into more negative thoughts and emotions. Four hours later, Rita is still sitting at the station "counting her woes." This is the result of nonproductive thinking.
>
> On the other hand, Naomi chooses to "Stop, Slow Down, Think, and Act" rationally about her problem ("I have missed the train") as well as her goal ("How can I get home as quickly as possible without ruining my evening, given that I have missed the last train?"). Following this path of productive thinking, Naomi attempts to generate a variety of alternative ways to reach her goal. Her partial list includes calling to delay her dinner date, taking a bus, taking a taxi, asking someone for a ride home, calling home and having someone pick her up, and taking a train to a different station and going straight to the restaurant to meet her dinner date rather going home first. Four hours later, Naomi is enjoying the evening with a pleasant companion who picked her up from a different train station.

There are three major brainstorming principles to use to foster one's creativity:

- Quantity leads to quality
- Defer judgment
- Variety enhances creativity

Quantity Principle

This principle suggests that it is important to generate a large pool of solution options. The concept of generating numerous responses to problems, and to elaborate upon these responses, is supported by research findings that show that people can improve the selection of high-quality ideas by increasing the number of alternative solutions. In addition, in keeping with the externalization rule of problem-solving multitasking, drafting a written list of ideas, rather than composing a list of ideas in one's head, can help people to improve both the quantity and quality of thinking. Recording ideas on paper (in a computer, smartphone, etc.) keeps the problem solver focused on the task at hand and reduces repetition of ideas or "getting stuck on the same idea." Furthermore, the externalized results of the brainstorming exercise can be maintained for future reference and can serve as a concrete reinforcement of one's problem-solving attempts. Note that we provide a "Generating Alternative Solutions Worksheet" as a Patient Handout in Appendix II as an instructional aid.

Providing analogies as examples can also aid individuals in their attempts to use brainstorming principles. For example, we have often asked our patients the following question—"Which store is more likely to have your size and selection, a large store or a smaller store?" Obviously, we all would prefer to go to the larger store to increase our selection choices. Parenthetically, we have come across skeptical patients, who because they may be resistant to learning new techniques, have challenged this analogy. Consider Don, a 46-year-old man, who upon hearing the "store" analogy, retorted—"Well, that's not really true because when I went to buy my son's baseball pants, I checked out a few stores and the department store was more expensive than the little shop near our house! I saved twelve bucks!" In response, we pointed out to him, "That's great! Yet, had you never checked out *several* stores, you would have never known what a great deal you got."

Deferment Principle

To further facilitate brainstorming, we recommend that individuals *defer judgment*. This principle suggests that it is important to record all ideas that come to mind as a means of increasing the quantity of solutions without judging them. Prematurely rejecting ideas can limit productive and creative thinking that could lead to ultimately identifying the more effective ones. Therefore, we suggest that it is important to refrain from evaluating solutions at this point in the problem-solving process. There is only one criterion to use at this time—that the idea is *relevant* to the problem at hand. Otherwise, we indicate to clients that there is no right or wrong alternative at this juncture—"If you catch yourself (even silently) judging any ideas you have, *STOP* and remind yourself that this will cut down on creativity."

At times, clients may be reluctant to allow themselves to express ideas that they believe are silly, unrealistic, stupid, or could reflect badly upon themselves. We respond to such concerns by emphasizing that deferring judgment actually increases one's effectiveness. For example, even if an idea seems silly or initially impossible, it may spark another related idea that is *not* silly or impossible. Some of the practice exercises that we use when working with people to improve these skills involve having people deliberately offering alternatives that might be regarded as outlandish or impractical if evaluated critically simply to spark creativity.

Some people may have difficulty adhering to the deferment-of-judgment principle. For example, some individuals we have worked with develop the "yeah, but . . ." syndrome in response to their own alternatives or alternatives offered by another. We have heard the following—"Yeah, *but*, that won't work because . . ." "Yeah, *but*, I would never do that because . . ." "That sounds okay, *but*, what if . . ." "I thought of that, *but*, I didn't write it down because . . ." In response to this type of reaction, we ask individuals to consider the following analogy:

> Think of the list you are putting together as a dinner menu that you need to prepare for your restaurant. On most dinner menus, there are a variety of options to please the tastes of children, adults, senior citizens; people who are very hungry; people who only want a snack; people who want late-night breakfast menus, desserts, or steak dinners. There may be some items on the menu that certain people might not enjoy, or others that they might not have thought of eating at a particular time of day. But, by the very fact that your restaurant offers a variety of choices, you will be more likely to satisfy the vast majority of your patrons. Likewise, deferring judgment about the menu of alternative solutions you create to solve your problems will increase the likelihood that you will have a variety of choices or satisfactory ideas that will meet your goals. You may not like all of the alternatives; however, there is no harm in listing them on the menu. When you engage in decision making at a later point, you can select which solutions are best suited for you."

The Variety Principle

According to the *variety* principle, the greater the range or variety of solution alternatives generated, the more good quality ideas will be made available. When generating solution alternatives, some individuals can develop a way of thinking that produces ideas that reflect only *one* strategy or general approach to the problem. This narrow set of ideas can occur even when one applies the quantity and deferment-of-judgment principles. To change such a perspective, we recommend that individuals peruse their list of solution alternatives after using the quantity and deferment-of-judgment principles and identify the *different* strategies that they have. In essence, one is trying to identify differing classifications—that is, to group solution alternatives according to some common theme.

If any of the strategies have very few specific solutions, people are guided to think of more specific solution alternatives for that particular strategy.

Next, they are asked to think of new strategies that are not yet represented by any of the available solutions and generate additional specific solution ideas or tactics for those strategies.

Learning to differentiate between strategies and tactics can serve to enhance one's brainstorming options. *Strategies* are *general* courses of action that people can take to try and improve a problem situation. For example, Sophie, a former client, described herself as "angry, sad, and hurt" following several incidents in which her daughter and son-in-law had left her out of holiday plans and special events that involved her grandchildren. She brainstormed multiple ideas in which she might communicate with her grown daughter and son-in-law regarding ways she hoped their relationship might be improved. Her goal was to communicate how important the relationship was to her and what she believed needed to take place for it to change. She listed a few general *strategies* first. These included the following:

- Ignore their acts of insensitivity
- Express her anger and feelings of hurt
- Invite them to stay with her for a few days to talk
- Ask them to be kinder to her and include her in family celebrations
- Threaten to remove them from her will unless they changed
- Tell them that it is important to her to see her grandchildren
- Communicate clearly and specifically how she hopes to be treated in the future

We define *tactics* as specific steps involved in putting a strategy into action. When thinking about different tactics, we encourage people to generate as many options as possible, while continuing to defer judgment. Getting back to Sophie, she also generated tactics in her list of alternatives. For example, with regard to communicating clearly and specifically how she hoped to be treated in the future, she generated the following *tactics*:

- Speak to her daughter and son-in-law in person the next time she sees them
- Make specific arrangements to discuss the matter
- Send an e-mail
- Write a letter
- Have another family member communicate her feelings
- Have someone neutral mediate the discussion
- Call them on the telephone

By providing differing ways to think of alternatives, the strategy-tactics principle often provides new viewpoints from which to identify alternative solutions. Overall problem-solving efforts are likely to be less effective or productive if limited by the use of only one strategy. Therefore, we recommend that people think of a variety of both strategies and tactics rather than focusing on one or two narrow tactics or limiting oneself only to general approaches.

For example, getting back to Sophie once again, based on feedback from her therapist, she became aware that all of her strategies were centered on the theme of ways to get her daughter and son-in-law to change. When she realized this, she decided to try to think of other available general strategies. With her therapist's help, she realized that getting herself and her husband to change and accept their daughter's behavior as out of their control represented a whole series of other options that she had not previously recognized. There were many new tactics she was able to list under the category of "ways that I can change to improve the relationship." These included the following:

- Arrange her own family celebrations and events
- Communicate directly with her grandchildren
- Change her view of their behavior as less negative
- Ask her husband's help in setting special visits
- Reduce her expectations

By applying the variety principle, in thinking of both strategies *and* tactics, Sophie ultimately was able to choose from a larger pool of ideas about how to handle this problem.

Using Emotion Regulation Categories

In Chapter 8, we described five differing classes of emotion regulation strategies as delineated by Gross and Thompson (2007). These included the following:

- Situation selection
- Situation modification
- Attention deployment
- Cognitive change
- Response modulation

In attempting to generate a variety of different types of solution alternatives, we further recommend using these categories to spark additional ideas for solutions. As such, the therapist might engage the client in a general discussion of what these classes of strategies are (see Chapter 8) and guide him or her to think of at least one option per category. Doing so can easily lead to additional ideas.

Keeping the Creative Juices Flowing

Sometimes people get "stuck" in being able to generate multiple ideas for solutions. We offer the following ways to help "get unstuck" and become more creative:

- *Combine ideas*—take two or more ideas, put them together to make a third idea.
- *Slightly modify an idea*—take one idea and slightly change it (e.g., make it larger, smaller, change its color, add more people, etc.).
- *Think of how others might solve the problem*—think of various people, such as role models (e.g., sports figures, politicians, TV personalities, community or religious leaders) or favored relatives or friends, and think of what they might do to solve the problem.
- *Visualize*—imagine various obstacles to the problem-solving goal and then imagine oneself (or others) jumping over these hurdles—what did they have to do?

Practice Generating Alternatives

Learning any new skill often requires that people first practice the easier steps or tasks. For example, we often suggest to clients: "*You probably did not go on a major highway the first day you learned to drive; you probably did not enter a tennis tournament the second time you took a tennis lesson.*" If generating multiple ideas proves a bit difficult for certain individuals with regard to the real-life problems that they are currently experiencing, one way to improve their basic creativity skills is to practice with "fun" examples or problems that only may be hypothetical.

For example, we often use the following example when working with groups—to generate as many ideas about what one can do with a "single brick." We suggest that therapists use this exercise standardly with clients. It tends to be a fun exercise but also generally promotes the insight that a large pool of ideas actually exists. More importantly, clients learn how to use the various tools with regard to a nonemotionally provoking example. For this exercise, clients are directed to write down as many ideas as possible, different things one can do with a single brick within a 5-minute time limit. If they experience creative blocks, guide them to apply the various brainstorming and creativity tools contained in this toolkit.

A second "fun" idea might be to think of as many things one can do with a wire hanger. A more real-life problem, perhaps one that a client is currently experiencing, might be to think of as many ideas regarding how one can meet new people having moved to another neighborhood and feeling somewhat isolated. Note that in addition to providing practice, if one engages in these types of mental exercises (e.g., categorizing alternatives), their ability for subsequent creative problem solving becomes enhanced (e.g., Chrysikou, 2006).

Handling Interfering Emotional Reactions

On occasion, one's emotional reactions to discussing a stressful problem can inhibit a person's creativity in generating alternatives. If this occurs, the therapist should circle back to some of the strategies contained in the *SSTA Toolkit* to help such an individual overcome this type of obstacle. In addition, research in the sphere of cognitive problem solving has indicated that distancing oneself from the problem can actually serve to enhance creative problem solving. For example, extrapolating from this research, we suggest that by imagining that the problem is actually situated far away in distance (e.g., miles away) or in time (e.g., one year from now), one's ability to solve problems can be greatly enhanced. Additional research also suggests that if one is stuck regarding a difficult or complex problem, one effective option is to "take a break" or engage in a different activity, as nonconscious processing has been found to engender effective answers to difficult problems when such problems require an extensive search of stored knowledge.

Decision Making

> *Where there is no decision, there is no life.*
>
> —*John Dewey*

> *There are in nature neither rewards nor punishments,*
> *There are only consequences.*
>
> —*Robert Ingersoll*

The third planful problem-solving skill involves decision making. This set of tools helps individuals to

1. Better predict the consequences of their actions
2. Conduct a cost-benefit analysis regarding the previously generated alternatives
3. Develop an action plan that constitutes an overall solution

Time to Judge

In an attempt to increase the number of high-quality solutions, our recommendations when generating alternative solutions involved applying the brainstorming principle of deferring judgment. Now that alternatives have been generated, it is time for the problem solver to make judgments. This involves evaluating the likely success of the various options and deciding which ones to carry out. This initially involves predicting the positive and negative consequences of each alternative idea. People, especially when they are distressed, may initially wish only to consider how effective a solution might be in terms of "taking away the problem ASAP." By being more objective and systematic in order to evaluate each idea, one stands a better chance of minimizing negative consequences and maximizing positive consequences. However, whether a consequence is positive or negative depends heavily on the situation and can differ greatly depending on *who* is having the problem. The same consequence may be evaluated positively by some but negatively by others. That is why we strongly recommend, especially for individuals who have particular difficulty with this task, to use a systematic approach when evaluating alternatives and making decisions. As the quote by 19th century American lawyer, Robert Ingersoll, suggested at the beginning of this section—*consequences are neither inherently positive or negative, but exist nonetheless.*

The "Fallout" of Bad Decisions

Often, people think of solutions as *any* action taken to solve a problem. What sometimes we forget is that there are many ineffective solutions that may solve a *part* of the problem but simultaneously also create additional problems, distress, and various other negative consequences. For example, drinking, gambling, avoidance, aggressive statements and behavior, or thinking in ways to try and convince oneself of something that is not accurate are all ways that people try to "solve" problems every day. These solutions often provide some short-term relief or distraction but can have many lasting negative consequences. Such actions often create additional problems and the individual eventually is left feeling frustrated, hopeless, and ineffective. As such, it is important for individuals to try to predict both the benefits as well as the *costs* of a course of action, as well as its impact on one's overall well-being and that of others.

As defined in Chapter 1, effective solutions are defined as not only helping to achieve one's goals but *also* one that reduces negative side effects or fallout. Sometimes, effective decisions may be a bit more difficult to implement in the short-term but can ultimately have many positive short-term and long-term consequences.

To illustrate this point, consider Bernice, a person who had a history of relationships in which she sacrificed herself for the needs and desires of others. Although she was the only person who had a full-time job in her family, Bernice frequently accommodated her plans based on the "whims" of her aging parents who lived nearby. When she wanted to move away from them to take a better paying job, for example, she received little support. Her parents complained— "Who would take us to doctors' appointments or family get-togethers?"

Bernice had a long pattern of blaming herself and believing that she had to always please others, even though her partner, Lisa, tried hard to convince her to become more independent. She was also very grateful that her parents were always supportive of her same-sex relationship with Lisa. Therefore, in trying to cope with this problem, one of Bernice's initial solution alternatives was *"to convince my partner, Lisa, that the move and the new job isn't so important— I'd rather stay put so I don't have to deal with guilt from my family— after all, they are supportive of us!"* However, Lisa often felt frustrated watching others take advantage of Bernice's generous nature and became frequently angry that Bernice's family was not supportive of the move, especially since it meant a significant boost for her career. Unfortunately, Bernice often fought with Lisa and secretly wished that Lisa would just do what her parents wanted so the problem could be avoided. However, the more that Bernice considered this alternative, the more she realized that there were many long-term consequences for choosing this option. For one, she was missing out on an important and well-earned job. In addition, there were consequences for her relationship with Lisa. Finally, she realized that her family members were unlikely to change, and no matter how much she thought "well, there always will be another job offer," it was likely that she would continually face the same problem. As Bernice became more creative in generating alternatives, she discovered that there were other ways she could objectively be a resource to her parents, but without having to sacrifice her career and her own happiness.

Making Effective Decisions

Making decisions about what to do to solve a difficult problem can be hard. As Irish novelist, George Moore, once said—*"The difficulty in life is the choice."* However, even though making decisions can be tough, it can lead to more control over one's life and enhanced well-being.

Our model involves the following four steps to making effective decisions:

- Screen out obviously ineffective solutions
- Predict a range of possible consequences
- Evaluate the predicted solution outcomes
- Identify effective solutions and develop a solution plan

Rough Screening of Solution Alternatives

The decision-making task can be made easier if one conducts an initial rough screening of the list of possible alternatives in order to eliminate any that are clearly inferior. Remember that the only criteria that should have been used during the process of generating alternatives is one of *relevancy*. Therefore, it is possible that several ineffective ideas were generated "in the spirit of brainstorming." Rather than spending time rating each alternative, it is advisable to conduct such an initial screening. At this point, alternatives can be considered "clearly ineffective" if they have (a) obvious unacceptable risks associated with their implementation, and/or (b) low feasibility. *Unacceptable risks* refer to likely serious negative consequences that significantly reduce the effectiveness of the solution. *Low feasibility* refers to the low likelihood that the solution could actually be implemented by the problem solver due to the lack of ability, lack of resources, or other major obstacles.

Predicting Consequences

In evaluating the remaining solution options, individuals are further taught to think of two major categories when predicting consequences: (a) likelihood estimates and (b) value estimates. *Likelihood* estimates involve two assessments:

1. The likelihood that a given solution alternative will actually achieve the stated problem-solving goal(s); that is, *will this solution work?*
2. The likelihood that the problem solver will be able to actually implement the solution in an *optimal* manner; that is, *can I carry it out?*

Value estimates involve predicting the total expected positive consequences (i.e., benefits, gains) *and* negative consequences (i.e., costs, losses) of a particular solution alternative, including long-term as well as immediate consequences, and social as well as personal consequences.

Personal consequences that should be considered include the following:

a. Effects on emotional well-being
b. Time and effort expended
c. Effects on physical well-being
d. Effects on psychological well-being (e.g., depression, anxiety, self-esteem)
e. Effects on economic well-being (e.g., job security)
f. Self-enhancement (e.g., achievements, knowledge)
g. Effects on other personal goals, values, and commitments

Some of the more important *social consequences* that should be considered include

a. Effects on the personal and/or social well-being of significant others
b. Effects on the rights of others
c. Effects on significant interpersonal relationships
d. Effects on personal and/or social performance evaluations (e.g., reputation, status, prestige)

It is clear from the above checklists that solutions for real-life problems may have many different consequences. Considering the limited capacity of the conscious mind to handle large amounts of information, it is important to write down the major significant expected consequences (e.g., "I am likely to feel very guilty, my parents will be very hurt, in the long run I could lose my job"). This will help to facilitate the task of evaluating one's solution alternatives.

Evaluating Solution Outcomes

In evaluating the various solution options, we direct individuals to further ask themselves the following four questions:

1. Will this solution solve the problem?
2. Can I really carry it out?
3. What are the overall effects on me, both short-term and long-term?
4. What are the overall effects on others, both short-term and long-term?

For each alternative idea remaining after the initial screening, individuals should use a simple rating scale in response to these four questions (e.g., -1 = negative; 0 = neutral; $+1$ = positive). More "complex" rating systems can be developed for "high-risk" problem solving, where the consequences of a relatively ineffective solution might be serious (e.g., a scale of 1 to 5, where 1 = slightly satisfactory and 5 = very satisfactory). Further, if appropriate, individuals could place more weight or emphasis on a particular outcome criterion by establishing a minimum rating for a given criterion. For example, if it was thought that emotional well-being was particularly important for a given problem, one might decide to eliminate any solution alternative that is not rated as a "+" for this criterion. Individuals can also add new outcome criteria or eliminate criteria, depending on their appraisal of the significance of different outcomes for different problematic situations. For example, in some situations, financial cost might be a particularly significant criterion to consider when judging solution alternatives (e.g., "what to do when your washing machine breaks down"). Instead of considering this criterion as part of the overall personal effects criterion, it can be given special emphasis by considering it separately. The point here is to establish a systematic method of conducting the cost-benefit analysis. However, unless the problem is extremely complex, we advocate using a rather simple scale (i.e., -1 to $+1$) in order to make the decision-making process more "user-friendly."

Keeping in mind the externalization rule, the various solution alternatives and ratings should be written down. To simplify the task of comparing alternatives, they can be summarized in a chart, such as the one provided in Appendix II as a Patient Handout entitled "Decision Making Worksheet."

Difficulties in Anticipating and Evaluating Solution Alternatives

It is not always easy to predict and evaluate specific consequences of solutions before they are experienced, especially subjective consequences such as feelings and emotions. Two visualization procedures that might be helpful in this regard include behavior rehearsal and imaginal rehearsal. *Behavior rehearsal* or role-play (with the PST counselor or other group member if conducting group PST) is particularly useful with regard to solving interpersonal problems (e.g., dealing with the offensive behavior of another person). *Imaginal rehearsal* involves experimenting with different coping options using visualization. Both of these rehearsal procedures may help a person identify and evaluate the various social and emotional consequences of different solution possibilities.

Identifying Effective Solutions and Developing a Solution Plan

On the basis of the systematic evaluation of the available solution alternatives, individuals are directed next to ask the following three questions:

1. Is the problem solvable? (i.e., "Is there a satisfactory solution?")
2. Do I need more information before I can select a solution or combination of ideas to carry out?
3. What solution or solution combination should I choose to implement?

Is the Problem Solvable?

Answering this question requires that one begins to add up the ratings for each alternative (e.g., how many "plusses," how many "minuses," and how many "zeros"). If one is able to actually identify effective solutions based on these ratings, then the answer to the above question should be "yes." In other words, effective alternatives are those with the least number of negative consequences (i.e., less minuses) and the most number of positive consequences (i.e., more plusses). However, when making this evaluation, individuals are reminded that *no solution is perfect*. If one's alternative solutions with the highest ratings continue to have some negative consequences that are likely to occur, people are directed to look over the other listed alternatives and determine if any alternatives exist that did not have the same negative effects. Some people have found that through this process, they are able to think about how to slightly change or adjust the highest rated alternative to further reduce the negative consequences associated with it. However, it is important to remember that it may not be possible to reduce *all* negative consequences.

Do I Need More Information Before I Can Select a Solution or Solution Combination for Implementation?

If the result of the above scrutiny suggests that one's alternatives appear to be rated as basically negative (i.e., associated with a lot of minuses), then it is likely that one should reconsider whether the problem was correctly defined or if a sufficient pool of alternatives were generated. If so, individuals are then directed to circle back and engage in either or both steps once again.

However, another possibility exists if there are very few potentially effective solution ideas—individuals may begin to realize that after contemplating the various options and their consequences that, in fact, this problem is *not* solvable. If so, they then need to reconsider the goals and reformulate them to ones that are more *emotion-focused* (for example, changing one's emotional reaction to the problem; accepting that the situation cannot be changed the way one would like), as compared to continuing to try to "solve an unsolvable problem."

What Solution or Solution Combination Should I Choose to Implement?

Individuals are next directed to choose those alternatives that have the best ratings in order to develop an *action plan*. We use the phrase "action plan" to emphasize the notion that the solution plan needs to be carried out and put in motion, even if it involves "nonaction" (e.g., attempting to accept that a given problem cannot be changed). In keeping with our definition of an *effective solution*, an action plan should be consistent with the general goal of resolving the problem satisfactorily, while maximizing positive consequences and minimizing negative effects.

The action plan should be consistent with the general goal of attempting to resolve the problem satisfactorily, while maximizing positive consequences and minimizing negative effects. The solution plan may be *simple* or *complex*. For a simple plan, based on the evaluation ratings, one can choose a single solution or course of action. When there is one solution that is expected to produce a highly satisfactory outcome, such a simple plan may suffice. There are two types of complex plans—a *solution combination* and a *contingency plan*. For a solution combination, one might choose a combination of solution alternatives to be implemented concurrently. This is done when it appears that the combination is likely to have greater utility than any solution alone, or when several obstacles are targeted for change either sequentially or simultaneously. As noted previously, many problems in life are complex and involve multiple obstacles to overcome prior to effective problem resolution. Therefore, identifying several specific solution tactics to comprise an overall solution plan at times is highly advisable. Contingency plans involve choosing a combination of solutions to be implemented contingently—that is, implement solution A first, if that does not work, implement solution B, if that does not work, carry out solution C, and so forth.

Another type of contingency plan occurs when one first implements a particular course of action (A) and, then, depending on the outcome of A, the problem solver carries out either B or C. Such a contingency plan is chosen when there is enough uncertainty about any one solution or solution combination that it seems advisable to have a contingency plan to save time in case the initial solution choice(s) is unsuccessful. Once the solution plan has been prepared, the final step before solution implementation is to fill in the details as to exactly how, when, and where the solution plan will be implemented.

Practice Example

As an example to allow clients to practice these decision-making tools, we, at times, use the following problem:

Problem:

> *You and your family are driving to a movie, but running late. You see that you are low on gas. You might be able to make it to the theatre without stopping, and yet, looking at the time, if you do stop, you will probably be late. On the other hand, you may not have enough gas to get to the theatre and back home. What do you do?*

Problem-Solving Goal:

> *To have a nice evening with your family, possibly watching a movie together.*

Possible Alternatives

- *Do not stop and keep driving to the movie*
- *Stop for gas*
- *Forget about the movie for tonight*
- *Stop and call Triple A*
- *Go to a restaurant closer to where you are now*
- *Go to a shopping mall instead*
- *Call a friend to bring gas to you*
- *Park the car and call for a taxi*

Are there additional options you can think of?

Predicting Consequences

In predicting the consequences, let's consider the first option, "Do not stop and keep driving to the movie." For now, try practicing how to identify, predict, and evaluate the hypothetical effects that might occur if you were experiencing this problem. Write down the various consequences in your journal, notebook, or computer and then evaluate each one. As an example, note what one person we worked with, Fred, wrote down in terms of possible consequences:

- *Effects on me—feel very anxious while driving; exhausted from walking if we run out of gas; feel bad for getting family stuck; feel angry with myself for not stopping earlier (an important value I have for myself is being better prepared); we may not get to the movie if car runs out of gas; we may have to walk for gas; I don't know where the nearest station is; I might feel relieved if we make it to the movie in time; gas station may not be open after movie.*
- *Effects on others—family would be scared and upset if we don't make it; family would be happy if we make it to movie in time; I set a bad example for my kids being unprepared.*

This example obviously has no perfect answer, but it was designed to give clients practice in predicting consequences and rating alternatives and to become aware that most alternatives lead to *some* positive and *some* negative consequences. In part, the actual ratings given by different people may reflect differing values, priorities, or interests. Once again, that is why we underscore the notion that the same problem for differing people is likely to lead to differing solutions. For additional practice, we strongly recommend that clients apply these decision-making tools to their own personal problems.

Solution Implementation and Verification

There are costs and risks to any program of action,
But they are far less than the long-range risks
and costs of comfortable inaction.

—John F. Kennedy

The fourth and last planful problem-solving activity involves both carrying out the action plan (solution implementation) and assessing its outcome (solution verification). Although it is likely that the problem solver might feel satisfied once the action plan is carried out, according to our approach, doing so is not the end of the process. A more careless/impulsive approach is to cease being systematic and planful once a decision is made and the action plan is carried out. In order to be an effective problem solver, we strongly recommend that there is one more component to this last step—to monitor and evaluate the actual success of the solution plan *after it is carried out*. This is important in order to

1. Determine whether one needs to continue to work on the problem, or if the problem is actually successfully resolved
2. Understand what areas, if any, of one's problem-solving skills require some additional "fine tuning"

The Problem-Solving Outcome Will Not Always Be Perfect
We emphasize this *Healthy Thinking* concept with clients because some individuals continue to hold unrealistically high expectations for themselves. We have heard people say, "*But I really tried hard and it still didn't turn out the way I wanted it to.*" Being an effective problem solver is to keep one's expectations realistic. In addition, it is important to focus on the positive consequences rather than only on the negative effects. As such, if this becomes an issue for a given individual, we recommend that the therapist circle back to salient activities contained in Toolkit #3 (*Health Thinking*).

Carrying Out the Action Plan
This step in the problem-solving process involves the following activities:

1. Motivate oneself to carry out the action plan
2. Prepare to carry out the action plan
3. Implement the action plan
4. Observe and monitor the effects of the solution
5. Reinforce oneself for engaging in the planful problem-solving process
6. Troubleshoot areas of difficulty

Motivating Oneself to Carry Out the Action Plan
Although many individuals are eager to carry out their action plans, especially having gone through all the previous steps of defining the problem, generating alternatives, and making decisions regarding the content of one's action plan, others may remain trepidacious, or even fearful about taking action. This can occur either because of what it means about changes in

oneself (e.g., changing the way one has been thinking for such a long time) or changing the nature of the problem situation itself (e.g., trying to change others' behavior or certain situations). For those individuals, we recommend that they engage in a motivational exercise to foster their willingness to complete the process.

Specifically, individuals are directed to use the "Motivational Worksheet" (contained as a Patient Handout in Appendix II), which essentially asks them to list those potential benefits and costs associated with *not* solving the problem in the left-hand column, and listing, in the right-hand column, possible benefits and costs that might occur if a given goal is achieved. In doing so, they are guided to compare these overall consequences and apply the cost-benefit analysis learned previously to reappraise the problem with regard to their well-being. We remind individuals to consider possible *immediate* benefits and costs, possible *long-term* benefits and costs, as well as benefits and costs to *themselves* and to *significant others*. This worksheet can be posted on one's refrigerator at home or any other appropriate place to continually remind themselves of why they chose to focus on this problem and worked so hard to discover a solution. The late President Kennedy's words at the beginning of this section are offered as a motivational quote that underscores the idea that although there are risks associated with any plan of action, there are more serious consequences associated with inaction.

On occasion, it is possible that this subsequent analysis leads to the conclusion that the benefits of not doing anything at the present time outweigh the costs as compared to actually carrying out the proposed action plan. If so, it is probable that this is valid due to one of the following reasons: (a) the situation has changed for the better on its own, (b) the individual may have reappraised the problem as less of a priority than originally stated, or (c) the proposed action plan itself appears to be weak. If the latter, rather than carrying out this plan, it is suggested that the client circle back through the previous planful problem-solving steps in order to produce a stronger plan.

Preparing to Carry Out the Action Plan

The next step is to consider any predicted or perceived obstacles that might have been uncovered during the previous exercise. Obstacles that might impact the problem solver's ability to carry out the solution plan in its optimal form should be assessed. For example, consider Alicia, a client who chose to enroll in a yoga class for relaxation and stress reduction purposes. In considering the steps by which she would enroll and participate in the class, she subsequently learned that the class time conflicts with her husband's evening work shift. Therefore, a new problem emerges, that of difficulties with transportation, one that first needs to be resolved given that she is unable to drive herself and her husband is unavailable.

To help overcome newly identified obstacles to *optimal* solution implementation, questions the therapist may ask include, "*Are there ways to modify the solution plan which would overcome the obstacle* (e.g., implement it at a different time of the day, with different supports)?" "*Is there a direct approach by which the obstacle can be handled?*" Depending on the magnitude of the obstacle and the severity of the impact it may have on the problem-solving attempt, patients may need to revisit previous problem-solving activities. The focus of the problem-solving efforts at this point in the process may be to alter the existing plan, develop a new solution plan, or choose to temporarily postpone the implementation of a specific action plan in order to develop a resolution to the identified obstacle.

If certain skill deficits (i.e., problem-focused coping skills or emotion-focused coping skills) are identified related to the designated solution plan, the strategies of solving the problem need to be reevaluated. Essentially, in keeping with the problem-solving model, the therapist is faced with deciding among the following options: (a) to incorporate the appropriate skills training into the therapy (or have it obtained outside of the PST intervention), (b) instruct the individual to return to certain previous planful problem-solving activities in order to develop a new plan, or (c) to work with the patient to reformulate the overall definition of the problem situation to include the skill deficits as an obstacle to overcome in the overall solution plan of a particular identified problem. In essence, such a decision requires the therapist to engage in problem solving himself or herself with the overall goal of "helping this particular patient with his or her given limitations and strengths to overcome the short-term problem identified, and the long-term goal of improving certain coping skills in future problematic situations." If the skill deficits identified are likely to interfere with future problem-solving efforts, the individual is likely to benefit from addressing these difficulties at some point in therapy.

When individuals were making decisions concerning the options that appeared to be potentially most effective, they also developed an action plan regarding how it actually will be carried out (e.g., a simple or complex plan, a solution combination or contingency plan). This was particularly important because even with the most creative and useful ideas, it is important to have a step-by-step plan of how one will put the plan into action. We recommend that it is important to have the steps in the plan written down.

To illustrate, let us revisit Jane from earlier in this chapter. She was the individual who was experiencing a problem with her boss at work. Jane's problem-solving goals were to be recognized and compensated for the work she was expected to do that was beyond the requirements of her job as a secretary for a public television news station. More specifically, in addition to the secretarial duties that defined her job, she was often planning and managing special events, preparing promotional articles about the station for their public education campaign, and helping the station manager handling the volunteer staff. After generating and rating many alternatives to help reach her goals, Jane selected the alternative of arranging a special meeting with her boss to request a raise as an important first step. Her plan included

- Setting up the meeting during the time that budgets were being decided
- Making this appointment with her boss at the end of the day on a Monday (Mondays, in general, were less hectic and there was less stress present in the station)
- Making a list of the work that she completed that was in excess of her position
- Estimating the financial benefits to the station for her additional work (for example, successfully organizing the volunteers, the amount of donations received after a successful event, etc.)

In addition, to help her carry out this plan optimally, Jane asked her cousin, Kerry, who worked for a human resources department for a large local company, to role-play this upcoming meeting and provide tips and feedback on the words and behavior that might help get her points across effectively. Jane then made a list of everything she needed to do to optimally carry out her plan in order to be able to monitor the effects of each step along the way.

Carrying Out the Action Plan
In order to increase the likelihood that one is able to carry out an action plan in its most optimal fashion, here are some additional tips:

- Rehearse the plan in one's imagination before carrying it out.
- Like Jane, role-play the action plan with someone trustworthy.
- Think the plan aloud (e.g., *"First I need to state my goals and to think about the positive consequences that will occur when I solve this problem. Now I need to take a deep breath and go ahead and carry out the solution. When I begin talking to my boss, I realize that I might get anxious, so I need to practice what I might say to him right before I see him. Then I will remind myself to speak calmly and deliberately so I don't get more nervous . . ."*).
- Write down the steps in detail, similar to an instruction or user's manual.

Monitoring the Outcome

For individuals trying to lose weight, it makes sense to be weighed on a weekly basis. If one is trying to save additional money, it makes sense to balance the checkbook and keep sales receipts. If one is trying to lower high blood pressure, it makes sense to go for routine physicals. Such examples, in part, provide for a rationale that we provide to individuals to underscore the importance of monitoring both one's actual performance in carrying out the solution as well as the outcome itself. Depending on how complex the problem and/or action plan, there are several possible ways to record such information—the type of "measure" that is most appropriate for a particular problem depends on the type of behavior or action plan that one is evaluating. Examples include the following:

Response Frequency. This represents the number of responses involved. Examples include the number of cigarettes smoked, the number of times a child gets out of his or her seat or talks out of turn in class, the number of times a teenage daughter violates curfew, or the number of requests one makes for a date.

Response Duration. One can also record the amount of time it takes to perform a response. Examples include the time it takes to complete a report, time spent studying, time spent exercising each day, time spent commuting to work, and time spent sleeping.

Response Latency. This involves monitoring the time between the occurrence of a particular event and the onset of a particular response. Examples include the number of minutes late to class, the amount of time beyond curfew, the amount of time late for dinner, or the amount of time a child takes to get a chore completed following a parental request.

Response Intensity. One might be able to rate the degree of intensity of something, such as the degree of anxiety, the intensity or severity of a headache, the degree of depression, the intensity of sexual arousal, or the degree of pleasure or satisfaction associated with a particular activity. This can often be accomplished using a simple rating scale, such as 1 to 5, where *1* = little to no anxiety, and *5* = severe anxiety.

Response Product. This involves the "*by-products* or *effects*" of a behavior. Examples include the number of dates accepted, the number of boxes packed per hour, the number of sales made, the number of chapters studied, the number of arrests made, and the number of problems solved.

We recommend (what a surprise!) that clients externalize (record) such information. We are amazed by the number and variety of smartphone applications that can help one to accomplish this quite easily.

Evaluating the Outcome

The next step is to evaluate one's actual performance, when relevant, regarding the implementation of the action plan. For example, Jane observed that she experienced significant anxiety and fear thinking that asking for financial recognition would seem too pushy (i.e., she was always hesitant to assert herself). However, she discovered that listing out the actual financial benefits of her work was helpful to her to better realize and accept her own value to the station. As such, Jane actually found it easier (although still somewhat anxious) to ask for increased compensation for this extra work. In addition, she was able to become aware that until she role-played with her cousin to practice what she would say, she was not feeling very confident. However, the role-play practice and advice from her cousin helped her to develop a script with which she felt more comfortable and less anxious.

In addition, individuals are further directed to evaluate the overall effects of the solution, at least those that have occurred thus far (i.e., it is unlikely that "long-term" effects have yet occurred). In essence, they are guided to determine how well the actual outcomes match those that were previously predicted during the decision-making process.

Table 10.5 contains a series of questions that can help this evaluation process in a concrete and focused manner and comprise the "Action Plan Outcome Evaluation Worksheet" (also contained as a Patient Handout in Appendix II). Essentially, clients are directed to answer these questions using a scale of 1 (*not at all*) to 5 (*very much*). Based on the answers to these questions, they are then asked by the therapist the basic question—"*Was the match between what you predicted or expected to occur and what actually happened a strong one?*"

If the answers to this question is essentially "yes," then individuals are directed to go to the next step in this set of planful problem-solving activities—self-reinforcement.

TABLE 10.5   Questions From the "Action Plan Outcome Evaluation Worksheet"

1. How well does your solution plan meet your goals?
2. How satisfied are you with the effects on you?
3. How well do these results match your original prediction about personal consequences?
4. How satisfied are you with the impact on others involved in the problem?
5. How well do these results match your original prediction about the consequences concerning others?
6. Overall, how satisfied are you with the results of your action plan?

Giving Self-Reinforcement

If patients are successful in their problem-solving efforts, evaluating the actual resulting consequences allows them to acknowledge their accomplishment and helps them to accept responsibility for their productive and positive actions. To facilitate recognition of effective problem solving, we direct individuals to use self-reinforcement as an additional skill in the process of resolving problems. Self-reinforcement helps to underscore the importance of any and all problem-solving attempts. Planning a specific and desired form of self-reinforcement as a reward for successfully overcoming a particular problem can also motivate people to initiate problem-solving attempts in the future. Whereas the primary motivation for engaging in problem solving should be to reduce distress, overcome difficulties, and increase or decrease a particular behavior, feeling, or situation, self-reinforcement is intended to be a "bonus" for achieving goals.

Self-reinforcement can take many forms. A reinforcer may consist of a concrete reward such as purchasing a new object, engaging in a pleasurable activity, praising oneself, or relieving oneself of an obligation or chore. In our experience, clients have purchased albums, clothes, sporting equipment, or computer products as rewards. Others have made time for themselves or allotted finances to engage in activities they typically did not have the opportunity to enjoy (e.g., going to the movies, taking a day off from work, sleeping later than usual). The temporary relief of certain obligations or stressors may also serve as a reward for some individuals. A 32-year-old mother, Anna, described her self-reinforcement as hiring a babysitter while she spent one day doing pleasurable activities for herself without having to take care of her 4-year-old daughter. Individuals should be encouraged to begin brainstorming a potential list of reinforcers prior to implementing a given action plan. As problem-solving attempts are initiated for different problems, the list of reinforcers may change to reflect a reward that is more closely related to overcoming the difficulty at hand (e.g., purchasing new clothes as a cancer patient improves her body-image concerns after breast surgery).

The practice of self-reinforcement is particularly important for individuals who think of themselves as poor problem-solvers and who have poor self-efficacy beliefs with regard to their ability to cope with difficult problems. Recognizing their ability to successfully resolve a problem will increase their belief that they will be able to handle difficult problems in the future. Furthermore, if people increase their awareness of how the application of problem-solving skills aided them in resolving problems, they will also be more likely to rely on these skills when problems arise.

Troubleshooting When Problem-Solving Efforts Are Not Successful

Clients should be prepared during the training sessions to expect that everyone encounters situations in which their problems are not solved by the *first* solution plan attempted. The importance for the therapist to discuss this likelihood cannot be overstated. However, patients should also be reassured that after troubleshooting and recycling back through other problem-solving operations, most problems are likely to eventually get resolved. Therefore, having implemented a solution plan that results in less than optimal consequences is not a reason for giving up. Those whose solution plans were not found to be effective should follow the course of troubleshooting.

Troubleshooting for the individual represents reviewing each step of the problem-solving process in order to identify where the complications surfaced. Specific to solution implementation, troubleshooting refers to identifying the areas where the actual consequences do not match the predicted consequences and subsequently attempting to understand why the discrepancy occurred. In completing the "Action Plan Outcome Evaluation Worksheet," people will be able to determine where changes are necessary. For example, did the solution plan fail to achieve the desired personal effects, social effects, or goal attainment? Evaluating the difficulties that arose will lead to a quicker optimal resolution than immediately dismissing the entire problem-solving effort as a failure. By choosing not to review the problem-solving steps and overall solution plan, people risk repeating ineffective methods for coping with their problems. If clients do need to find new approaches by which to solve their problems, it is recommended that the entire set of tools (where relevant) across the four toolkits be reviewed and employed to increase the structure of renewed attempts.

SUMMARY

This chapter focused on Toolkit #4, *Planful Problem Solving*. Planful problem solving is comprised of four major activities: (a) defining the problem (i.e., clarifying the nature of a problem, delineating a realistic problem-solving goal, and identifying those obstacles that prevent one from reaching such goals), (b) generating alternative solution ideas (i.e., thinking of a range of possible solution strategies geared toward overcoming the identified obstacles), (c) making decisions as to which alternatives to include in an action plan (i.e., predicting the likely consequences of these various alternatives, conducting a cost-benefit analysis based on these identified outcomes, and developing a solution plan that is geared to achieve the problem-solving goal), and (d) carrying out the action plan and verifying its outcome (i.e., carrying out the solution plan, monitoring and evaluating the consequences of the plan, and determining whether one's problem-solving efforts have been successful or need to continue). Two versions for training in these tools were provided: (1) "Brief" Planful Problem-Solving Training and (2) "Intensive" Planful Problem-Solving Training. Which one to engage in with a given client or population depends on both findings from the literature as well as individualized assessment data.

The briefer form of training in this toolkit involved providing individuals with an overview of the four planful problem-solving steps, as well as guided practice applying the "Problem-Solving Worksheet," which provides for a specific structure to effectively cope with various extant problems. The more intensive training program allows for additional extensive training in any or all of these four tasks. Training in *Problem Definition* involved teaching individuals to engage in five specific activities: (a) seek available facts, (b) describe facts in clear language, (c) separate facts from assumptions, (d) set realistic goals, and (e) identify obstacles to overcome in order to reach such goals. As an instructional aid, we advocated thinking of the process of problem solving as analogous to mapping a travel plan to reach a particular destination. The importance of differentiating between problem-focused goals and emotion-focused goals was underscored. Additional problematic issues involved in accurately defining a problem were highlighted, including confusing a solution with a goal, not looking at the problem from other people's perspectives, focusing only on "superficial problems," and being confused if the problem is complex.

Training in the *Generation-of-Alternatives* tool focused on applying three brainstorming principles when attempting to think creatively of possible solution options. They include the quantity principle, the deferment-of-judgment principle, and the variety principle. Ways to overcome "feeling stuck" when generating ideas were also presented. Practicing this tool with "silly" examples, such as thinking of differing uses of a single brick, was strongly recommended as a standard task to engage individuals in order to foster creativity.

The *Decision Making* tool teaches individuals to engage in the following steps: (a) screen out obviously ineffective solution ideas, (b) predict a range of possible consequences of the various alternatives, (c) conduct a cost-benefit analysis of these consequences, and (d) identify effective solutions and develop an action plan. In helping individuals to be successful in their predictions of the likely effects of a given action plan, we strongly recommended that they consider personal consequences, social consequences, short-term effects, and long-term effects. Based on such predictions, individuals are then guided to evaluate each alternative according to (a) the likelihood that the action plan will, in fact, help reach their goals (i.e., overcome the identified obstacles), (b) the likelihood that they are able to carry out the action plan optimally, (c) the short- and long-term personal consequences, and (d) the short- and long-term social (i.e., effects on others) consequences.

The fourth and last planful problem-solving task involves carrying out the action plan (i.e., solution implementation) and evaluating the outcome (i.e., solution verification). Training in this set of tools included helping individuals to (a) motivate themselves to carry out the action plan, (b) undergo certain preparations to ensure the plan can be carried out optimally, (c) implement the solution, (d) monitor the actual effects of the plan, (e) self-reinforce for attempting to solve a problem, and (f) troubleshoot if the solution was not successful.

Key Training Points for Toolkit #4

1. Remember to discuss and review any homework/practice assignments previously given.
2. Decide which training approach to focus on initially (i.e., brief versus intensive training).
3. Provide rationale for Toolkit #4—i.e., these are the specific skills involved in effective problem solving and characterize those individuals who have been identified as effective problem solvers.
4. Give out relevant patient handouts when appropriate.
5. If conducting the brief training version, teach individuals to use the "Problem-Solving Worksheet," practice using the worksheet regarding multiple current problems, and provide meaningful and extensive feedback during this process. In addition, continue to determine if more extensive training in any or all of the problem-solving steps becomes necessary.
6. If providing more intensive training in any or all of the four planful problem-solving toolsets, follow manual regarding the various steps, exercises, and activities described.
7. Encourage individuals to practice all learned tools when appropriate outside of sessions.
8. Demonstrate how all the toolkits can be integrated and applied together to foster overall effective problem solving.
9. Circle back to any previous tools if warranted (e.g., motivation decreases, difficulties in overcoming negative thinking or emotional arousal occurs).
10. Conduct relevant assessments of progress (e.g., toward problem resolution, decreasing distress, etc.).

Toolkit# 4 Patient Handouts (In Appendices II and III)

▪ Planful Problem Solving: An Overview
▪ Problem-Solving Worksheet
▪ Getting the Facts (also see Table 10.2)
▪ Defining the Problem Worksheet
▪ Problem Map (included in text as Figure 10.3)
▪ Motivational Worksheet
▪ Action Plan Outcome Evaluation Worksheet

Suggested Homework/Practice Assignments

▪ Practice using "Problem-Solving Worksheet" if receiving brief training
▪ Practice applying any of the specific planful problem-solving skills that were taught using relevant worksheets or forms
▪ Practice integrating the tools across all four toolkits, especially *SSTA*
▪ Continue to complete PSSM forms if appropriate
▪ Review handouts

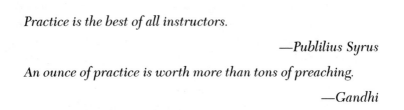

ELEVEN

Guided Practice, Future Forecasting, and Termination

Practice is the best of all instructors.

—*Publilius Syrus*

An ounce of practice is worth more than tons of preaching.

—*Gandhi*

After the major problem-solving therapy (PST) training has taken place, the remainder of treatment is devoted to practice. The importance of such practice is conveyed in the two quotes above by Syrus and Gandhi. As with any new skill, the more one practices, the better one gets. Beyond actually solving stressful problems, continuous practice in this context serves three additional purposes:

a. Applying the entire problem-solving model (i.e., *SSTA*) under the guidance of a therapist allows for helpful professional feedback.
b. Increased facility with the model through practice can decrease the amount of time and effort necessary to apply the model with each new problem.
c. It helps to facilitate maintenance and generalization of the skills.

GUIDED PRACTICE

The therapist's goals for these practice sessions are to

1. Help patients fine-tune the problem-solving skills they have acquired
2. Monitor their application of these principles

221

3. Help individuals to integrate the various tools
4. Reinforce patient progress as a means of further increasing their sense of self-efficacy

The number of practice sessions required after formal training ends is dependent on the competency level that a patient achieves as well as actual improvements in the areas related to the initial reasons for seeking treatment (e.g., decreases in depression, anxiety, anger; improvements in self-confidence and self-esteem; improved adjustment to a chronic medical illness; enhanced overall quality of life). However, regardless, we do strongly encourage that several sessions be devoted specifically to practice. A useful approach to guide practice sessions to is use the acronym *SSTA to* continue to inform to inform clients how to approach various stressful situations in order to instill and reinforce the basic process (i.e., to *STOP, Slow Down, Think, and Act*).

A typical practice session begins and ends in a similar manner as the previous skills-training sessions. Patients are asked to review how they applied various problem-solving tools to assigned or new problems since the past session, as well as to discuss areas that have been difficult for them. Extensive feedback should be provided as appropriate. If some individuals find they could not complete any of the problem-solving worksheets due to confusion or feeling stuck, it is important for the therapist to provide guidance and additional practice. At times, the therapist may need to circle back to various training exercises or activities to enhance a patient's understanding or skill acquisition regarding a particular area.

Therapists are advised to continue evaluating and monitoring patients' motivation to apply and practice the various problem-solving tools. The importance of practice cannot be overemphasized. Yet, some patients may value practice sessions less than skills training sessions because they misperceive the bulk of their necessary effort to be done. Other individuals may believe that the skills training sessions adequately addressed the problems that brought them in for therapy and, therefore, no longer believe additional sessions are necessary. For these reasons, it is imperative that the purpose of the practice sessions be underscored at the end of formal training.

INTEGRATING VARIOUS PROBLEM-SOLVING TOOLS: THE CASE OF "JOHN"

As noted above, these practice sessions, in part, can be helpful in teaching clients how to "put it all together" (i.e., to integrate various tools).

The following example illustrates how multiple tools were applied together to help reduce a patient's feelings of hopelessness. John was a 36-year-old national guardsman who recently returned from deployment in the Middle East and was wrestling with significant issues of readjustment, particularly feeling overwhelmed and confused. He was attending a PST group at the counseling center at his local university where he had recently returned to school. John was experiencing significant difficulty defining his problem. We include this example as a demonstration of how to help individuals handle the challenging task of defining complex problems by using certain SS tools in concert with planful problem solving.

T: Okay, John. I see that when you indicated you were wrestling with the worksheet for homework that your problem had to do with trying to clean up your house and that you were feeling pretty upset with your difficulty organizing things. You listed your goal as "clean house" and your obstacles as "motivation" and "playing video games."

J: Yeah . . . and there's only one alternative I can think of to reach my goal—just get off my butt, stop whining, and do it! But I end up getting out of bed late, playing video games, and living like a slug—if I could do that, don't you think I would? Not sure if I buy this problem solving.

T: I can see how frustrating this is for you and that you're feeling pretty hopeless about ever being able to accomplish what you want to get done. I also hear a lot of self-criticism.

J: You got that right Doc—I'm so mad at myself.

T: I'm wondering, though, if we can try to define your problem differently by using the visualization and simplification tools you've already learned. Let's do this to see if we can look at the problem, your feelings about it, and the goal you have set in a different light. Is that okay?

J: Can't hurt.

T: Can you tell me a little more about how you feel about this problem? Does it represent some block to any important value or life goal you have for yourself?

J: It really gets me angry. I always wanted to be sort of a hero, you know? Really do something meaningful to make life better for other people and (he starts to hold back tears at this point) . . . now I can't even clean a room . . . see this . . . these feelings? Whenever I think about doing anything, I realize that my feelings are so close to the surface . . . dealing with all the sh°t I saw . . . and I don't feel like I can do anything . . . so I just veg out and say, I'll deal with all that when I'm feeling better.

T: Thanks for trusting me, John, and letting me help with this problem. So now I see that cleaning and organizing the house is more than just about making things tidy. It's one strategy you can think of that may lead you to feel like you can do anything, nonetheless, something meaningful. But when each day goes by that you don't do it, you feel worse and angry at yourself, on top of the hopelessness. I think it may make sense to hold off on strategies for now and look at the real problem here . . . becoming more hopeful that you can make a meaningful contribution here, back at home, in your post-deployment life. Does this sound right?

J: Yeah . . . when you taught me that visualization stuff, I started to think that I really could get myself going . . . but now I'm not so sure.

T: Let's start by having you write down your "real" goal—the one that your feelings cue you into and that is aligned with your values—making a contribution. What obstacles come to mind that prevent you from reaching your goal?

J: Well, I start thinking that if I can't clean my apartment, how can I do anything else?

T: Okay, negative thinking . . . remember how this is one of the barriers to planful problem solving?

J: Oh yeah, and the others were negative feelings and hopelessness. I guess I have all the barriers operating here.

T: Excellent, yes, you have identified them correctly, and particularly when you become very angry at yourself, your arousal combines with these other barriers and you will need to use the "SS" part of *SSTA* to calm your brain and body so that you can begin to generate alternative ideas about what you can do . . . to start coming up with creative ideas that are ways to make a contribution. I'm going to give you a hint here and ask you to consider also using simplification in order to break down your ideas into smaller steps that you could take toward this goal.

J: (Starts to get aroused) . . . but if I can't even clean my apartment . . .

T: Stop . . . Slow down . . .

J: Okay . . . give me a second, I'm going to stand up and breathe a few times.

T: Great . . . I'll do it with you . . . remember . . . no active thinking while we're   breathing . . . just allow any thoughts or feelings to occur and pass. (A minute of breathing has passed.)

J: (Smiling) I guess using *SSTA* is one alternative.

T: It sure is! Now what else can you do?

J: Okay . . . I can check the Internet to learn more about different opportunities to help people.

T: Wow, when your brain is calm you can really think creatively!

J: Or volunteer at the vet center or my church.

T: Any others?

J: I could help my nephew with his baseball game.

T: Another creative idea that could start a whole series of ideas about helping family and friends as well as charities. Now, what about your apartment? Remember my hint to simplify.

J: Well, I could do just one thing each day, that way I wouldn't get as over-whelmed and I would at least be able to say I did something.

T: Great, John! Now, what about those negative thoughts that you can't do anything useful if you have difficulty cleaning your apartment?

J: So, I would be able to get something done in my apartment if I don't try to do everything. That would make me feel more helpful . . . and I suppose I could still do something like the volunteer work.

T: Right! If you develop this as an action plan that you can carry out, you could learn that you can do just a small part of the apartment cleaning, while at the same time, begin doing something helpful to others. I think we're on our way to overcoming some of these obstacles. Let's look at what tools you used to overcome your hopelessness about feeling useful. You used "Stop and Slow Down" in order to be able to listen to your feelings, with the volume turned down a bit so they were not screaming at you, and without becoming overwhelmed by them. Paying attention to your sad and angry feelings put you in touch with how much you wanted to feel useful again and contribute something to the lives of other people. It's your negative feelings put to "better use." As such, you were able to think of some creative ways to do what matters to you. Because you were able to think this through with a calm and reasonable mind, you can now develop an action plan to carry out—this will give you an opportunity to learn new information, specifically that you can commit yourself to helping others while you slowly work on organizing your apartment. You don't have to complete the apartment organization all in one step before you can get started with making a meaningful peacetime contribution to the lives of others.

J: I could also help other vets with computer skills . . . that's something that I'm good at. Thanks, Doc. This has been very helpful.

FUTURE FORECASTING

As a means of enhancing maintenance and generalization, potential problems that may occur in the future should also be discussed to help individuals plan accordingly and begin to associate the possibility of managing these difficulties by using the newly learned tools. More specifically, they can be given various problem checklists such as those previously completed (see Chapter 4), in order to identify any changes in their lives that might occur in the near future, both positive and negative, as a means of developing effective action plans to address them effectively. We suggest that even positive events be addressed, such as moving to a new house, getting married, having a baby, or getting a promotion, as all such events, however positive, basically represent stress. As such, there are likely to be differences in one's "fantasies" about the future versus the reality of change. This is not to suggest to patients that all life is filled with negativity; rather, a positive problem orientation recognizes that problems *do* exist. A quote by Theodore Rubin is apropos here—"The problem is not that there are problems. The problem is expecting otherwise and thinking that having problems is a problem."

TERMINATION

When the therapist and patient agree termination is appropriate, the therapist may wish to provide additional worksheets for duplication and future use. During these final sessions, the therapist should discuss various termination issues, especially within the context of the therapeutic relationship. The therapist should also review the goals of PST as discussed during the initial sessions. Individuals should be asked for examples of how these goals have been met. Feedback regarding the therapist's perspective of treatment progress is also important. Areas of weaknesses and strengths may be addressed and discussed, and recommendations of how to maintain gains (i.e., practice, monitor self-improvement) should be provided to clients. Reinforcement is especially important during these final sessions, as patients often experience some trepidation about "losing" their support. Furthermore, people often recall the most recent message given by therapists and words of encouragement may be internalized as positive self-statements in future stressful situations. In general, patients should be encouraged to practice the problem-solving tools in as many day-to-day situations as possible in order to facilitate a true incorporation of the philosophy and skills underlying this approach into their daily thoughts, feelings, and actions. They are especially encouraged to maintain all of the handouts and worksheets given to them during treatment. In the event that only the briefer form of training in planful problem-solving skills was provided, it may be helpful to provide all of the additional handouts and worksheets for the individual's future reference.

Problems With Termination

For some patients, termination itself may represent a "problem-to-be-solved." In addressing these issues, therapeutic tactics for termination are built upon the general strategy of helping patients to use learned problem-solving skills and apply them to any problems concomitant with ending treatment. For example, *SSTA* tools can be employed when encountering feelings such as sadness, fear, anger, guilt, or abandonment. Such emotions are often mixed and represent a *powerful* signal that can help a client better understand what is happening and that a problem exists. Individuals should be encouraged to use problem definition tools to help them become more aware of what is going on and acknowledge the loss of the therapy relationship. They should define problems in order to address any difficulties they are experiencing regarding leaving therapy. Each patient's goals for, and personal obstacles to, an optimal end of therapy can then be specified. After they are clearly defined, various strategies can be generated to meet these goals. In this manner, the last session(s) can serve as the time to self-monitor and evaluate the effectiveness of the strategies mutually chosen by the therapist and client to ease termination difficulties.

REVISITING MEGAN

Before we end this chapter, we will revisit Megan one more time. The following focuses on her difficulties attempting to define her problems. While teaching Megan to use the "Problem Definition Worksheet" to help her define a problem, it became apparent that she needed additional aid. Her therapist decided that visualization may be of help in order to increase her motivation toward managing her anxiety, as well as to help her clarify her problems more clearly.

Because of her past focus on the exaggerated negative outcome of being alone if she were to disappoint or be the source of any discomfort to others in even the smallest way, it was important for her to see the possibility of alternative interactions. Although she continued to keep a journal as a means of documenting her continued need for alcohol abstinence, she would often write down things she has observed about herself (e.g., her improved energy at work) and her experiences during the week in order to develop an initial description of her goals for therapy. Specifically, along with maintenance of sobriety, Megan listed important current goals as "Facing the problem that I have with my roommate, feeling connected to the world, and feeling purposeful with my life."

When considering the many problems that stood in the way of her achieving her life goals, Megan listed her three most troublesome problems as anxiety, sad feelings, and low motivation. Below is a brief dialogue between Megan and her therapist discussing the worksheet that she was completing with regard to these goals.

M: I think the most important thing for me right now is confronting this situation with my roommate. Sleep is one of the areas where I usually don't have a problem, but now when I go to my room to sleep, I am freaked out, especially now that I'm not drinking. I lay there just waiting for my roommate to come home with some guy and start partying in the other bedroom. Our rooms are right next to each other and I can hear everything! I don't know half the guys that she brings back and I don't know how stable she is.

T: What have you tried to do so far? What discussions have you had?

M: Not a word. I started sleeping on the couch in the front living room with the TV turned on. Even though they come in and walk past me, it's not as bad as being in my room and waiting for them to come in, come up the stairs, and start screwing.

T: What has been the major barrier for you to talk with her?

M: I guess I don't want to upset her. I'm so scared of that.

T: So . . . you're telling me that you have carried all the tension and fear for some time now because you want to avoid any confrontation that may be distressing to her? What do you believe will happen if she is upset?

M: (Crying) I don't know. I don't know . . . the anxiety is so bad and it gets in the way. It's that same old thing—I just don't want to have any bad feelings or tension . . . I think my anxiety is a major issue here. I can see that I need these skills.

Below is another dialogue where Megan describes her use of the visualization strategy of imagining herself in the future after the problem (dealing with her roommate) is solved.

M: It was hard to imagine. When we first started and you asked me to visualize the problem as successfully resolved, I kept thinking, "I can't . . . I can't." Then when you told me not to worry about how I was ever going to do it but develop the visualization like a scene at the end of a movie, I started to see myself sitting and talking with my roommate, with us both and planning on setting up a garden in the backyard on a beautiful spring day.

T: Can you use this visualization now? Close your eyes, take a few deep breaths, and put yourself back into that scene. How are you feeling in your body?

M: Really calm . . . nice . . . we actually used to do things like that together. In my mind we're both sober. Yes, calm . . . because my anxiety is not in the way and I got a good night's sleep.

T: And what are you thinking?

M: Let's see . . . this is hard . . . I'm happy because I'm looking forward to doing that kind of project with her and I'm thinking that we're actually going to do it.

T: Describe the visualization experience in detail using all your senses.

M: Sure (closes eyes) . . . I'm just sitting in my front living room with the window open and a nice breeze is coming in. I'm looking at my friend and she is happy and sober, too. I can smell the pretzels from the pretzel shop across the street. I'm thinking, maybe I'll have some friends over and have some hot pretzels and mustard and play some board games. Wow! That would be so nice.

T: Realizing that there may be hard work ahead to experience this, do you believe that it is possible?

M: Yeah . . . we actually liked to do things like that when we weren't drinking . . . we just let it all slide. It's why I want to stay sober now.

T: That's the very idea behind using visualization in this way. It's to give you an image in your mind's eye that you can work toward, a reason to keep trying when things get difficult. Remember the examples we talked about, such as Victor Frankl—the visualization did not save him from his immediate pain . . . it gave him hope . . . it brought him to his feet.

M: I get it . . . a first step on the journey, right?

T: Right.

With the therapist's help, Megan began to understand that many of her previous panic attacks and urges to cry were partially related to her inability to access her emotional triggers without becoming overwhelmed. Her use of the planful problem-solving strategies was boosted by the knowledge that in order for her to reach her goals, it is important for her to experience her emotions and learn from them, rather than to react to her feelings with embarrassment, fear, and a desire to avoid them.

When Megan first began to define the problems with her roommate, she focused on the fear that her roommate would be angry with her for trying to impose her abstinence on her. Below is an initial dialogue between Megan and her therapist as she faced the complexities of problem definition.

M: So the goal I wrote down is to get my roommate, Chelsea, to stop drinking, too, because I used visualization again to help me picture where I wanted to go with my problem. In my visualization, I saw her as sober, but she doesn't see herself as an "alcoholic" like I do. She says that sobriety is fine for me if I want it, but she doesn't need to do that.

T: And it's really tough if you focus on trying to change her mind. That might be what we call an unrealistic goal. Let's discuss for a moment the visualization you just described with regard to you.

M: You mean the part where I was happy because I was planning a project to work on with Chelsea and thinking we could actually do this?

T: Is it necessary for Chelsea to fully embrace Alcoholics Anonymous in order for that to happen?

M: No, but I would need to do this with someone who is reliable and wants to do it with me. Someone I can count on to not go off on some drama when we have this project to work on to fix up the yard.

T: Okay . . .

M: And I don't know if Chelsea will be able to do that.

T: Have you asked her if this is something she believes that she can do?

M: Oh, gosh, here come the tears again (starts crying).

T: What an opportunity to use the "Stop and Slow Down" tool you practiced earlier.

M: Okay . . . Okay . . . breathe. . . (Makes a yoga position with her hands over her head and breathes deeply.)

T: What are your feelings telling you?

M: I'm scared she won't follow through and I'm afraid to tell her because she may think I don't trust her . . . that's why I want her to commit to total sobriety.

T: Great Megan . . . good insight. Of course, though, that's just one solution. After we define the problem, list your goals and barriers; we'll also think of many others.

Megan continued to define her problem, which included separating facts from assumptions. For example, she was assuming that Chelsea could not engage with her in the yard project if she didn't totally give up drinking, but needed to see if that was a fact. In addition, she knew that Chelsea's drinking and past behavior may have contributed to an expectation that she could be counted on, and realized that if she wanted Chelsea's partnership in this project, she would need to take this lack of trust and her fears about discussing it with Chelsea into account.

Megan ended up listing her goal as developing a collaborative project to make her yard more attractive and to grow a small vegetable garden. She indicated that Chelsea would be the person she would like to enlist for the project. The major barrier was talking to Chelsea about her goals and letting her know that her (Chelsea's) continued drinking on many weekends made her concerned that they would not be able to complete the project. She also listed her anxiety and negative emotions as major barriers to discussing the situation with Chelsea.

This problem was becoming more well defined in that it led to many ideas that Megan brainstormed concerning how she might discuss the problem with Chelsea, such as ask other friends for support, have a back-up plan if Chelsea agreed to the project then disappointed her, involve other friends, and calm her body down when she became anxious.

Ultimately, after several weeks of brainstorming and frequent practice combining the strategies of visualization, SSTA, and the simplification strategies, Megan developed the following action plan that took into account the emotion-focused and problem-focused aspects of her problem.

Megan's Action Plan

1. Construct a letter to Chelsea with the support of my friend Charley, my sister Katie, and my therapist, that communicates how much I enjoyed the times that we worked on projects together in the past. Also tell her that I miss these times and let her know that if she chooses to drink as much as she does, it makes me sad and I miss her company.
2. Tell her that I would like to start a garden project next weekend and that I am hopeful that she will join me. Also make it clear that I would like a no-drinking rule while working on the project. If she chooses not to do it with me, I will understand but will miss her company.
3. Agree to have Charley and my sister Katie as part of the gardening team, so if Chelsea decides not to in, we will still get it done.

Megan implemented her plan, and, to her surprise, Chelsea indicated that she welcomed the chance to not get "smashed" each weekend and do something more productive. This increased Megan's use of PST strategies and motivated her to continue to apply her new skills to other problem areas as well.

A Summary of Megan

Megan had a long history of emotional suppression and interpersonal fears of disappointing others. During her adolescence, she discovered the anesthetic and calming effects of alcohol and this remained her primary means of coping until the time she referred herself for treatment. In one of her journal entries, she commented that it seemed to her that her ability to mature and learn how to cope with life had been stunted for the past 10 years. This was a metaphor that was often useful as she continued to practice using the tools that she learned in PST treatment. One particular challenge that Megan and her therapist confronted concerned the habitu-ated styles of avoidance and dependency that would be triggered during times of increased stress, particularly when an interpersonal confronta-tion or conflict was present. For example, as Megan began to improve her skills at work and demonstrated both an increased energy and sense of competency at work, she began to encounter a competitive situation with several of her fellow workers. When this initially occurred, she was pulled to return to well-worn and largely nonconscious patterns of interpersonal avoidance and hopeless crying episodes with an occasional return of a detachment episode.

Below is one entry in her journal:

> I have to talk with one of the people I supervise at work and give her an ultima-tum about her absenteeism. But I have now been working myself up into this state of anxiety and anticipation of talking to her that I keep hearing myself say that she will be upset and I can't stand this part of my job. I want to leave. I want to run away from the office. I don't even want to see her face. What happens if I cry or have a panic attack right here in the middle of the office? I'm so glad I have my PST cue cards and worksheets to look at. Here is what I have tried so far: writing out instructions for myself to breathe, to relax, and rehearse what I will tell her.
>
> I will go to the bathroom and yawn 5 times before the meeting with my supervisee. I have worked so hard and I am continuing to do that now. But even though I logically understand that it is not my responsibility to keep everyone comfortable, I still get this huge surge of dread about seeing someone disap-pointed or angry. I just really want to save everyone, even if it hurts me. It's times like this that I am so glad I have a way to calm down and a plan that has a good chance of working. One good thing that I have learned from PST ther-apy is that If I get through this okay, I'm not going to beat myself up because it's hard for me or think of myself as crazy—I'm doing something really nice for myself.

SUMMARY

After formal training in the four problem-solving toolkits is concluded, mul-tiple sessions should be devoted to guided practice, where clients address various problems they are currently experiencing across various life areas (e.g., family, health, career/job, finances, social relationships, leisure time, etc.) using the overall SSTA approach. Such sessions can provide basic prac-tice in the various tools, as well as the opportunity to identify possible new problem areas or any remaining problem-solving skill deficits or limitations. Clients are also directed to engage in future forecasting by predicting any changes in one's life circumstances, positive or negative, that might occur in the near future as a means of adequately addressing them via problem solving. Any problems with termination (e.g., a client feeling a loss of support) should be addressed by the therapist and client as a problem to be solved. Individuals should be encouraged to keep all handouts and worksheets for future reference and encouraged to apply them more formally if appropriate and necessary.

Key Training Points

1. Remember to discuss and review any homework/practice assignments previously given.
2. Direct clients to apply problem-solving tools to extant problems across various areas of life.
3. Provide additional training and practice in a given problem-solving tool if required.
4. Encourage individuals to practice all learned tools when appropriate outside of sessions.
5. Continue to demonstrate and discuss how all the toolkits can be integrated and applied together to foster overall effective problem solving.
6. Conduct relevant assessments of progress (e.g., toward problem resolution, decreasing distress, etc.).
7. Guide individuals to engage in future forecasting to identify potential sources of stress in the near future.
8. Review the overall model prior to last session.
9. Review what the client has learned from PST and provide meaningful feedback.
10. Reinforce any progress and continued attempts to use the problem-solving tools.
11. Focus on potential termination problems and address them using the problem-solving approach.

Suggested Homework/Practice Assignments

- Practice applying any of the problem-solving tools with extant problems
- Practice integrating the tools across all four toolkits
- Continue to complete either Problem-Solving Self-Monitoring (PSSM) forms or Problem-Solving Worksheets

CONCLUSION

We would like to end this book with a quote by Helen Keller, the woman who struggled with becoming deaf and blind due to a childhood illness, and who eventually became a strong role model for millions of people related to her charity work as an adult. We believe her statement sums up our basic philosophy of Problem-Solving Therapy:

> *All the world is full of suffering;*
> *It is also full of overcoming it.*

References

Alexopoulos, G. S., Raue, P., & Areán, P. (2003). Problem-solving therapy versus supportive therapy in geriatric major depression with executive dysfunction. *American Journal of Geriatric Psychiatry, 11,* 46–52.

Allen, S. M., Shah, A. C., Nezu, A. M., Nezu, C. M., Ciambrone, D., Hogan, J., & Mor, V. (2002). A problem-solving approach to stress reduction among younger women with breast carcinoma: A randomized controlled trial. *Cancer, 94,* 3089–3100.

Anderson, R. M., Funnell, M. M., Butler, P. M., Arnold, M. S., Fitzgerald, J. T., & Feste, C. C. (1995). Patient empowerment: Results of a randomized controlled trial. *Diabetes Care, 18,* 943–949.

Areán, P. A., Hegel, M., Vannoy, S., Fan, M., & Unuzter, J. (2008). Effectiveness of problem-solving therapy for older, primary care patients with depression: Results from the IMPACT project. *The Gerontologist, 48,* 311–323.

Areán, P. A., Perri, M. G., Nezu, A. M., Schein, R. L., Christopher, F., & Joseph, T. X. (1993). Comparative effectiveness of social problem-solving therapy and reminiscence therapy as treatments for depression in older adults. *Journal of Consulting and Clinical Psychology, 61,* 1003–1010.

Areán, P. A., Raue, P., Mackin, R. S., Kanellopoulos, D., McCulloch, C., & Alexopoulos, G. S. (2010). Problem-solving therapy and supportive therapy in older adults with major depression and executive dysfunction. *American Journal of Psychiatry, 167,* 1391–1398.

Audrain, J., Rimer, B., Cella, D., Stefanek, M., Garber, J., Pennanen, M., . . . Lerman, C. (1999). The impact of a brief coping skills intervention on adherence to breast self-examination among first-degree relatives of newly diagnosed breast cancer patients. *Psychooncology, 8,* 220–229.

Baker, S. R. (2003). A prospective longitudinal investigation of social problem-solving appraisals on adjustment to university, stress, health, and academic motivation and performance. *Personality and Individual Differences, 35,* 569–591.

Barrett, J. E., Williams, J. W., Oxman, T. E., Frank, E., Katon, W., Sullivan, M., . . . Sengupta, A. S. (2001). Treatment of dysthymia and minor depression in primary care: A randomized trial in patients aged 18 to 59 years. *Journal of Family Practice, 50,* 405–412.

Barrett, J. E., Williams, J. W., Oxman, T. E., Katon, W., Frank, E., Hegel, M. T., . . . Schulberg, H. C. (1999). The treatment effectiveness project. A comparison of the effectiveness of paroxetine, problem-solving therapy, and placebo in the treatment of minor depression and dysthymia in primary care patients: Background and research plan. *General Hospital Psychiatry, 21,* 260–273.

Bechara, A., Damasio, H., Damasio, A. R., & Lee, G. P. (1999). Different contributions of the human amygdala and ventromedial prefrontal cortex to decision-making. *The Journal of Neuroscience, 19,* 5473–5481.

Beck, J. S. (1995). *Cognitive therapy: Basics and beyond.* New York: Guilford.

Bell, A. C., & D'Zurilla, T. J. (2009a). The influence of social problem-solving ability on the relationship between daily stress and adjustment. *Cognitive Therapy and Research, 33,* 439–448.

Bell, A. C., & D'Zurilla, T. J. (2009b). Problem-solving therapy for depression: A meta-analysis. *Clinical Psychology Review, 29,* 348–353.

Benson, B. A., Rice, C. J., & Miranti, S. V. (1986). Effects of anger management training with mentally retarded adults in group treatment. *Journal of Consulting and Clinical Psychology, 54,* 728–729.

Berry, J. W., Elliott, T. R., Grant, J. S., Edwards, G., & Fine, P. R. (2012). Does problem-solving training for family caregivers benefit their care recipients with severe disabilities? A latent growth model of the Project CLUES randomized clinical trial. *Rehabilitation Psychology, 57,* 98–112.

Biggam, F. H., & Power, K. G. (2002). A controlled, problem-solving, group-based intervention with vulnerable incarcerated young offenders. *International Journal of Offender Therapy and Comparative Criminology, 46,* 678–698.

Black, D. R. (1987). A minimal intervention program and a problem-solving program for weight control. *Cognitive Therapy and Research, 11,* 107–120.

Black, D. R., & Threlfall, W. E. (1986). A stepped approach to weight control: A minimal intervention and a bibliotherapy problem-solving program. *Behavior Therapy, 17,* 144–157.

Brack, G., LaClave, L., & Wyatt, A. S. (1992). The relationship of problem solving and reframing to stress and depression in female college students. *Journal of College Student Development, 33,* 124–131.

Bradshaw, W. H. (1993). Coping-skills training versus a problem-solving approach with Schizophrenic patients. *Hospital and Community Psychiatry, 44,* 1102–1104.

Bucher, J. A., Loscalzo, M., Zabora, J., Houts, P. S., Hooker, C., & BrintzenhofeSzoc, K. (2001). Problem-solving cancer care education for patients and caregivers. *Cancer Practice, 9,* 66–70.

Cameron, J. L., Shin, J. L., Williams, D., & Stewart, D. E. (2004). A brief problem-solving intervention for family caregivers to individuals with advanced cancer. *Journal of Psychosomatic Research, 57,* 137–143.

Cape, J., Whittington, C., Buszewicz, M., Wallace, P., & Underwood, L. (2010). Brief psychological therapies for anxiety and depression in primary care: Meta-analysis and meta-regression. *BMC Medicine, 8,* 38.

Caspi, A., Sugden, K., Moffitt, T. E., Taylor, A., Craig, I. W., Harrington, H., . . . Poulton, R. (2003). Influence of life stress on depression: Moderation by a polymorphism in the 5-HTT gene. *Science, 301,* 386–389.

Castles, E. E., & Glass, C. R. (1986). Training in social and interpersonal problem-solving skills for mildly and moderately mentally retarded adults. *American Journal of Mental Deficiency, 91,* 35–42.

Catalan, J., Gath, D. H., Bond, A., Day, A., & Hall, L. (1991). Evaluation of a brief psychological treatment for emotional disorders in primary care. *Psychological Medicine, 21,* 1013–1018.

Chang, E. C., D'Zurilla, T. J., & Sanna, L. J. (Eds.). (2004). *Social problem solving: Theory, research, and training.* Washington, DC: American Psychological Association.

Chang, E. C., D'Zurilla, T. J., & Sanna, L. J. (2009). Social problem solving as a mediator of the link between stress and psychological well-being in middle-adulthood. *Cognitive Therapy and Research, 33,* 33–49.

Cheng, S. K. (2001). Life stress, problem solving, perfectionism, and depressive symptoms in Chinese. *Cognitive Therapy and Research, 25,* 303–310.

Chrysikou, E. G. (2006). When shoes become hammers: Goal-derived categorization training enhances problem-solving performance. *Journal of Experimental Psychology: Learning, Memory, and Cognition, 32,* 935–942.

Ciechanowski, P., Wagner, E., Schmaling, K., Schwartz, S., Williams, B., Diehr, P., . . . LoGerfo, J. (2004). Community-integrated home-based depression treatment in older adults: A randomized controlled trial. *The Journal of the American Medical Association, 291,* 1569–1577.

Clum, G. A., & Febbraro, G. A. R. (1994). Stress, social support, and problem-solving appraisal/skills: Prediction of suicide severity within a college sample. *Journal of Psychopathology and Behavioral Assessment, 16,* 69–83.

Cuijpers, P., van Straten, A., & Warmerdam, L. (2007). Problem solving therapies for depression: A meta-analysis. *European Psychiatry, 22,* 9–15.

Dallman, M. F., Bhatnagar, S., & Viau, V. (2000). Hypothalamo-pituitary-adrenal axis. In G. Fink (Ed.), *Encyclopedia of stress* (pp. 468–477). New York, NY: Academic Press.

Damasio, A. R. (1999). *The feeling of what happens.* New York, NY: Harcourt & Brace.

Davidson, R. J., & Begley, S. (2012). *The emotional life of your brain: How its unique patterns affect the way you think, feel and live—and how you can change them.* New York, NY: Hudson Street Press.

De La Torre, M. T., Morera, O. V., & Wood, J. M. (2010). Measuring social problem solving using the Spanish Version for Hispanics of the Social Problem-Solving Inventory-Revised. *Cultural Diversity and Ethnic Minority Psychology, 16,* 501–506.

Demeris, G., Oliver, D. B., Wittenberg-Lyles, E., Washington, K., Doorenbos, A., Rue, T., & Berry, D. (2012). A noninferiority trial of a problem-solving intervention for hospice caregivers: In person versus videophone. *Journal of Palliative Medicine, 15,* 653–660.

DeVellis, B. M., Blalock, S. J., Hahn, P. M., DeVellis, R. F., & Hockbaum, G. M. (1987). Evaluation of a problem-solving intervention for patients with arthritis. *Patient Education and Counseling, 11,* 29–42.

Dhabhar, F. S. (2011). Effects of stress on immune function: Implications for immuno-protection and immunopathology. In R. J. Contrada & A. Baum (Eds.), *The handbook of stress science: Biology, psychology, and health* (pp. 47–63). New York, NY: Springer Publishing.

DiGiuseppe, R., Simon, K. S., McGowan, L., & Gardner, F. (1990). A comparative outcome study of four cognitive therapies in the treatment of social anxiety. *Journal of Rational-Emotive & Cognitive-Behavior Therapy, 8,* 129–146.

Dobson, K. S., & Hamilton, K. E. (2003). Cognitive restructuring: Behavioral tests of negative cognitions. In W. O'Donohue, J. E. Fisher, & S. C. Hayes (Eds.), *Cognitive behavior therapy: Applying empirically supported techniques in your practice* (pp. 84–88). New York, NY: Wiley.

Dolcos, F., & McCarthy, G. (2006). Brain systems mediating cognitive interference by emotional distraction. *The Journal of Neuroscience, 26,* 2071–2079.

Doorenbos, A., Given, B., Given, C., Verbitsky, N., Cimprich, B., & McCorkle, R. (2005). Reducing symptom limitations: A cognitive behavioral intervention randomized trial. *Psychooncology, 14,* 574–584.

Dowrick, C., Dunn, G., Ayuso-Mateos, J. L., Dalgard, O. S., Page, H., Lehtinen, V., . . . Wilkinson, G. (2000). Problem solving treatment and group psychoeducation for depression: Multicentre randomised controlled trial. *British Journal of Medicine, 321,* 1–6.

Dubow, E. F., & Tisak, J. (1989). The relation between stressful life events and adjustment in elementary school children: The role of social support and social problem-solving skills. *Child Development, 60,* 1412–1423.

Dugas, M. J., Ladouceur, R., Léger, E., Freeston, M. H., Langlois, F., Provencher, M. D., & Boisvert, J. (2003). Group cognitive-behavioral therapy for generalized anxiety disorder: Treatment outcome and long-term follow-up. *Journal of Consulting and Clinical Psychology, 71,* 821–825.

D'Zurilla, T. J., & Goldfried, M. R. (1971). Problem solving and behavior modification. *Journal of Abnormal Psychology, 78,* 107–126.

D'Zurilla, T. J., & Maydeu-Olivares, A. (1995). Conceptual and methodological issues in social problem-solving assessment. *Behavior Therapy, 26,* 409–432.

D'Zurilla, T. J., & Nezu, A. (1980). A study of the generation-of-alternatives process in social problem solving. *Cognitive Therapy and Research, 4,* 67–72.

D'Zurilla, T. J., & Nezu, A. (1982). Social problem solving in adults. In P. C. Kendall (Ed.), *Advances in cognitive-behavioral research and therapy* (Vol. 1; pp. 202–274). New York: Academic Press.

D'Zurilla, T. J., & Nezu, A. M. (1990). Development and preliminary evaluation of the Social Problem-Solving Inventory (SPSI). Psychological Assessment. *A Journal of Consulting and Clinical Psychology, 2,* 156–163.

D'Zurilla, T. J., & Nezu, A. M. (2007). *Problem-solving therapy: A positive approach to clinical intervention* (3rd ed.). New York, NY: Springer Publishing.

D'Zurilla, T. J., Nezu, A. M., & Maydeu-Olivares, A. (2002). *Manual for the Social Problem-Solving Inventory-Revised.* North Tonawanda, NY: Multi-Health Systems.

D'Zurilla, T. J., Nezu, A. M., & Maydeu-Olivares, A. (2004). Social problem solving: Theory and assessment. In E. C. Chang, T. J. D'Zurilla, & L. J. Sanna (Eds.), *Social problem solving: Theory, research, and training* (pp. 11–27). Washington, DC: American Psychological Association.

Ell, K., Katon, W., Xie, B., Lee, P., Kapetanovic, S., Guterman, J., & Chou, C. (2010). Collaborative care management of major depression among low-income, predominantly Hispanic subjects with diabetes. *Diabetes Care, 33*, 706–713.

Ell, K., Xie, B., Quon, B., Quinn, D. I., Dwight-Johnson, M., & Lee, P. (2008). Randomized controlled trial of collaborative care management of depression among low-income patients with cancer. *Journal of Clinical Oncology, 26*, 4488–4496.

Elliott, T. R., Brossart, D., Berry, J. W., & Fine, P. R. (2008). Problem-solving training via videoconferencing for family caregivers of persons with spinal cord injuries: A randomized controlled trial. *Behaviour Research and Therapy, 46*, 1220–1229.

Ellis, A. (2003). Cognitive restructuring of the disputing of irrational beliefs. In W. O'Donohue, J. E. Fisher, & S. C. Hayes (Eds.), *Cognitive behavior therapy: Applying empirically supported techniques in your practice* (pp. 79–83). New York, NY: Wiley.

Esposito, C. L., & Clum, G. A. (2002). Psychiatric symptoms and their relationship to suicidal ideation in a high-risk adolescent community sample. *Child & Adolescent Psychiatry, 41*, 44–51.

Falloon, I. R. H. (2000). Problem solving as a core strategy in the prevention of schizophrenia and other mental disorders. *Australian and New Zealand Journal of Psychiatry, 34*(Suppl.), S185–S190.

Falloon, I., Boyd, J., McGill, C., Razani, J., Moss, H., & Gilderman, A. (1982). Family management in the prevention of exacerbations of schizophrenia. *The New England Journal of Medicine, 306*, 1437–1440.

Fawzy, F. I., Cousins, N., Fawzy, N. W., Kemeny, M. E., Elashoff, R., & Morton, D. (1990). A structured psychiatric intervention for cancer patients: I. Changes over time in methods of coping and affective disturbance. *Archives of General Psychiatry, 47*, 720–725.

Feinberg, E., Stein, R., Diaz-Linhart, Y., Egbert, L., Beradslee, W., Hegel, M. T., & Silverstein, M. (2012). Adaptation of problem-solving treatment for prevention of depression among low-income, culturally diverse mothers. *Family and Community Health, 35*, 57–67.

Ferguson, K. E. (2003). Relaxation. In W. O'Donohue, J. E. Fischer, & S. C. Hayes (Eds.), *Cognitive behavior therapy: Applying empirically supported techniques in your practice* (pp. 330–340). New York, NY: Wiley.

Fitzpatrick, K. K., Witte, T. K., & Schmidt, N. B. (2005). Randomized controlled trial of a brief problem-orientation intervention for suicidal ideation. *Behavior Therapy, 36*, 323–333.

Frankl, V. E. (1984). *Man's search for meaning.* New York, NY: Pocket Books.

Frye, A. A., & Goodman, S. H. (2000). Which social problem-solving components buffer depression in adolescent girls? *Cognitive Therapy and Research, 24*, 637–650.

Gallagher-Thompson, D., Lovett, S., Rose, J., McKibbin, C., Coon, D., Futterman, A., & Thompson, L. W. (2000). Impact of psychoeducational interventions on distressed caregivers. *Journal of Clinical Geropsychology, 6*, 91–110.

García-Vera, M. P., Labrador, F. J., & Sanz, J. (1997). Stress-management training for essential hypertension: A controlled study. *Applied Psychophysiology and Biofeedback, 22,* 261–283.

García-Vera, M. P., Sanz, J., & Labrador, F. J. (1998). Psychological changes accompanying and mediating stress-management training for essential hypertension. *Applied Psychophysiology and Biofeedback, 23,* 159–178.

Gatt, J. M., Nemeroff, C. B., Schofield, P. R., Paul, R. H., Clark, C. R., Gordon, E., & Williams, L. M. (2010). Early life stress combined with serotonin 3A receptor and brain-derived neurotrophic factor valine 66 to methionine genotypes impacts emotion brain and arousal correlates of risk for depression. *Biological Psychiatry, 68,* 818–824.

Gellis, Z. D., & Bruce, M. L. (2010). Problem solving therapy for subthreshold depression in home healthcare patients with cardiovascular disease. *American Journal of Geriatric Psychiatry, 18,* 464–474.

Gellis, Z. D., McGinty, J., Horowitz, A., Bruce, M., & Misener, E. (2007). Problem-solving therapy for late-life depression in home care: A randomized field trial. *American Journal of Geriatric Psychiatry, 15,* 968–978.

Gendron, C., Poitras, L., Dastoor, D. P., & Pérodeau, G. (1996). Cognitive-behavioral group intervention for spousal caregivers: Findings and clinical considerations. *Clinical Gerontologist, 17,* 3–19.

Gibbs, L. M., Dombrovski, A. Y., Morse, J., Siegle, G. J., Houck, P. R., & Szanto, K. (2009). When the solution is part of the problem: Problem solving in elderly suicide attempters. *International Journal of Geriatric Psychiatry, 24,* 1396–1404.

Given, C., Given, B., Rahbar, M., Jeon, S., McCorkle, R., Cimprich, B., . . . Bowie, E. (2004). Does a symptom management intervention affect depression among cancer patients: Results from a clinical trial. *Psychooncology, 13,* 818–830.

Glasgow, R. E., Toobert, D. S., & Hampson, S. E. (1996). Effects of a brief office-based intervention to facilitate diabetes dietary self-management. *Diabetes Care, 19,* 835–842.

Glynn, S. M., Marder, S. R., Liberman, R. P., Blair, K., Wirshing, W. C., Wirshing, D. A., . . . Mintz, J. (2002). Supplementing clinic-based skills training with manual-based community support sessions: Effects on social adjustment of patients with schizophrenia. *American Journal of Psychiatry, 159,* 829–837.

Goodman, S. H., Gravitt, G. W., & Kaslow, N. J. (1995). Social problem solving: A moderator of the relation between negative life stress and depression symptoms in children. *Journal of Abnormal Child Psychology, 23,* 473–485.

Gouin, J. P., Glaser, R., Malarkey, W. B., Beversdorf, D., & Kiecolt-Glaser, J. (2012). Chronic stress, daily stressors, and circulating inflammatory markers. *Health Psychology, 31,* 264–268.

Graf, A. (2003). A psychometric test of a German version of the SPSI-R. Zeitschrift für. *Differentielle und Diagnostische Psychologie, 24,* 277–291.

Graham, J. E., Christian, L. M., & Kiecolt-Glaser, J. K. (2006). Stress, age, and immune function: Toward a lifespan approach. *Journal of Behavioral Medicine, 29,* 389–400.

Grant, J. S., Elliott, T. R., Weaver, M., Bartolucci, A. A., & Giger, J. N. (2002). Telephone intervention with family caregivers of stroke survivors after rehabilitation. *Stroke, 33,* 2060–2065.

Gross, J. J., & Thompson, R. A. (2007). Emotion regulation: Conceptual foundations. In J. J. Gross (Ed.), *Handbook of emotional regulation* (pp. 3–24). New York, NY: Guilford.

Grossman, P., Niemann, L., Schmidt, S., & Walach, H. (2004). Mindfulness-based stress reduction and health benefits: A meta-analysis. *Journal of Psychosomatic Research, 57,* 35–43.

Grover, K. E., Green, K. L., Pettit, J. W., Monteith, L. L., Garza, M. J., & Venta, A. (2009). Problem solving moderates the effects of life event stress and chronic stress on suicidal behaviors in adolescence. *Journal of Clinical Psychology, 65,* 1281–1290.

Gunnar, M. R., Frenn, K., Wewerka, S. S., & Van Ryzin, M. J. (2009). Moderate versus severe early life stress: Associations with stress reactivity and regulation in 10–12-year-old children. *Psychoneuroendocrinology, 34,* 62–75.

Gutman, D. A., & Nemeroff, C. B. (2011). Stress and depression. In R. J. Contrada & A. Baum (Eds.), *The handbook of stress science: Biology, psychology, and health* (pp. 345–357). New York, NY: Springer Publishing.

Halford, W. K., Goodall, T. A., & Nicholson, J. M. (1997). Diet and diabetes (ii): A controlled trial of problem solving to improve dietary self-management in patients with insulin dependent diabetes. *Psychology and Health, 12,* 2310238.

Hammen, C., Kim, E. Y., Eberhart, N. K., & Brennan, P. A. (2009). Chronic and acute stress and the prediction of major depression in women. *Depression and Anxiety, 26,* 718–723.

Hansen, D. J., St. Lawrence, J. S., & Christoff, K. A. (1985). Effects of interpersonal problem-solving training with chronic aftercare patients on problem-solving component skills and effectiveness of solutions. *Journal of Consulting and Clinical Psychology, 53,* 167–174.

Hassink-Franke, L. J. A., van Weel-Baumgarten, E. M., Wierda, E., Engelen, M. W. M., Beek, M. M. L., Bor, H. H. J., . . . van Weel, C. (2011). Effectiveness of problem-solving treatment by general practice registrars for patients with emotional symptoms. *Journal of Primary Health Care, 3,* 181–189.

Havas, D. A., Glenberg, A. M., Gutowski, K. A., Lucarelli, M. J., & Davidson, R. J. (2010). Cosmetic use of botulinum toxin-A affects processing of emotional language. *Psychological Science, 21,* 895–900.

Hawkins, D., Sofronoff, K., & Sheffield, J. (2009). Psychometric properties if the Social Problem-Solving Inventory-Revised Short Form: Is the short form a valid and reliable measure for young adults? *Cognitive Therapy and Research, 33,* 462–470.

Heim, C., Mletzko, T., Purselle, D., Musselman, D. L., & Nemeroff, C. B. (2008). The dexamethasone/corticotropin-releasing factor test in men with major depression: Role of childhood trauma. *Biological Psychiatry, 63,* 398–405.

Heim, C., & Nemeroff, C. B. (2001). The role of childhood trauma in the neurobiology of mood and anxiety disorders: Preclinical and clinical studies. *Biological Psychiatry, 49,* 1023–1039.

Hill-Briggs, F., & Gemmell, L. (2007). Problem solving in diabetes self-management and control: A systematic review of the literature. *Diabetes Educator, 33*, 1032–1050.

Houts, P. S., Nezu, A. M., Nezu, C. M., & Bucher, J. A. (1996). A problem-solving model of family caregiving for cancer patients. *Patient Education and Counseling, 27*, 63–73.

Huband, N., McMurran, M., Evans, C., & Duggan, C. (2007). Social problem-solving plus psychoeducation for adults with personality disorder: Pragmatic randomized controlled trial. *The British Journal of Psychiatry, 190*, 307–313.

Jacobson, N. S., & Follette, W. C. (1985). Clinical significance of improvement resulting from two behavioral marital therapy components. *Behavior Therapy, 16*, 249–262.

Kaiser, A., Hahlweg, K., Fehm-Wolfsdorf, G., & Groth, T. (1998). The efficacy of a compact psychoeducational group training program for married couples. *Journal of Consulting and Clinical Psychology, 66*, 753–760.

Kant, G. L., D'Zurilla, T. J., & Maydeu-Olivares, A. (1997). Social problem solving as a mediator of stress-related depression and anxiety in middle-aged and elderly community residents. *Cognitive Therapy and Research, 21*, 73–96.

Kasckow, J., Brown, C., Morse, J. Q., Karpov, I., Bensasi, S., Thomas, S. B., . . . Reynolds, C. (2010). Racial preferences for participation in a depression prevention trial involving problem-solving therapy. *Psychiatric Services, 61*, 722–724.

Katon, W. J., Von Korff, M., Lin, E. H. B., Simon, G., Ludman, E., Russo, J., . . . Bush. T. (2004). The pathways study: A randomized trial of collaborative care in patients with diabetes and depression. *Archives of General Psychiatry, 61*, 1042–1049.

Katon, W., Von Korff, M., Lin, E., Unützer, J., Simon, G., Walker, E., . . . Bush, T. (1997). Population-based care of depression: Effective disease management strategies to decrease prevalence. *General Hospital Psychiatry, 19*, 169–178.

Katon, W. J., Von Korff, M., Lin, E. H. B., Simon, G., Ludman, E., Russo, J., Ciechanowski, P., Walker, E., & Bush. T. (2004). The Pathways Study: A randomized trial of collaborative care in patients with diabetes and depression. *Archives of General Psychiatry, 61*, 1042–1049.

Keinan, G. (1987). Decision making under stress: Scanning of alternatives under controllable and uncontrollable threats. *Journal of Personality and Social Psychology, 52*, 639–644.

Kendler, K. S., Karkowski, L. M., & Prescott, C. A. (1999). Causal relationship between stressful life events and the onset of major depression. *American Journal of Psychiatry, 156*, 837–841.

Kendrick, T., Simons, L., Mynors-Wallis, L., Gray, A., Lathlean, J., Pickering, R., . . . Thompson, C. (2005). A trial of problem-solving by community mental health nurses for anxiety, depression and life difficulties among general practice patients. The CNP-GP study. *Health Technology Assessment, 9*, 1–104.

Kiecolt-Glaser, J. K., & Glaser, R. (2001). Stress and immunity: Age enhances the risks. *Current Directions in Psychological Science, 10*, 18–21.

Kiecolt-Glaser, J. K., McGuire, L., Robles, T. F., & Glaser, R. (2002). Emotions, morbidity, and mortality: New perspectives from psychoneuroimmunology. *Annual Review of Psychology, 53*, 83–107.

Ladouceur, R., Dugas, M. J., Freeston, M. H., Léger, E., Gagnon, F., & Thibodeau, N. (2000). Efficacy of a cognitive-behavioral treatment for generalized anxiety disorder: Evaluation in a controlled clinical trial. *Journal of Consulting and Clinical Psychology, 68*, 957–964.

Lang, A. J., Norman, G. J., & Casmar, P. V. (2006). A randomized trial of a brief mental health intervention for primary care patients. *Journal of Consulting and Clinical Psychology, 74*, 1173–1179.

Largo-Wight, E., Peterson, P. M., & Chen, W. (2005). Perceived problem solving, stress, and health among college students. *American Journal of Health Behavior, 29*, 360–370.

Lazarus, R. S. (1999). *Stress and emotion: A new synthesis.* New York, NY: Springer Publishing.

LeDoux, J. (1996). *The emotional brain.* New York, NY: Simon & Schuster.

LeDoux, J. (2002). *Synaptic self: How our brains become who we are.* New York, NY: Penguin Books.

Lerner, M. S., & Clum, G. A. (1990). Treatment of suicide ideators: A problem-solving approach. *Behavior Therapy, 21*, 403–411.

Leykin, Y., Roberts, C. S., & DeRubeis, R. J. (2011). Decision-making and depressive symptomatology. *Cognitive Therapy and Research, 35*, 333–341.

Liberman, R. P., Eckman, T., & Marder, S. R. (2001). Training in social problem solving among persons with schizophrenia. *Psychiatric Services, 52*, 31–33.

Liberman, R. P., Falloon, I. R., & Aitchison, R. A. (1984). Multiple family therapy for schizophrenia: A behavioral, problem-solving approach. *Psychosocial Rehabilitation Journal, 7*, 60–77.

Liberman, R. P., Wallace, C. J., Falloon, I. R. H., & Vaughn, C. E. (1981). Interpersonal problem-solving therapy for schizophrenics and their families. *Comprehensive Psychiatry, 22*, 627–630.

Lin, E. H. B., Katon, W., Von Korff, M., Tang, L., Williams, J. W., Jr., Kroenke, K., . . . Unützer, J. for the IMPACT Investigators. (2003). Effect of improving depression care on pain and functional outcomes among older adults with arthritis: A randomized controlled trial. *JAMA, 290*, 2428–2429.

Loewe, B. K., Breining, S., Wilke, R., Wellman, S., Zipfel, S., & Eich, W. (2002). Quantitative and qualitative effects of Feldenkrais, progressive muscle relaxation, and standard medical treatment in patients after acute myocardial infarction. *Psychotherapy Research, 12*, 179–191.

Londahl, E. A., Tverskoy, A., & D'Zurilla, T. J. (2005). The relations of internalizing symptoms to conflict and interpersonal problem solving in close relationships. *Cognitive Therapy and Research, 29*, 445–462.

Loumidis, K. S., & Hill, A. (1997). Training social problem-solving skill to reduce maladaptive behaviours in intellectual disability groups: The influence of individual difference factors. *Journal of Applied Research in Intellectual Disabilities, 10*, 217–237.

Lynch, D. J., Tamburrino, M. B., & Nagel, R. (1997). Telephone counseling for patients with minor depression: Preliminary findings in a family practice setting. *Journal of Family Practice, 44*, 293–298.

Malouff, J. M., Thorsteinsson, E. B., & Schutte, N. S. (2007). The efficacy of problem solving therapy in reducing mental and physical health problems: A meta-analysis. *Clinical Psychology Review, 27,* 46–57.

Marder, S. R., Wirshing, W. C., Mintz, J., McKensie, J., Johnston, K., Eckman, T. A.,. . . . Liberman, R. P. (1996). Two-year outcome of social skills training and group psychotherapy for outpatients with schizophrenia. *American Journal of Psychiatry, 153,* 1585–1592.

Maydeu-Olivares, A., & D'Zurilla, T. J. (1995). A factor analysis of the Social Problem-Solving Inventory using polychoric correlations. *European Journal of Psychological Assessment, 11,* 98–107.

Maydeu-Olivares, A., & D'Zurilla, T. J. (1996). A factor-analytic study of the Social Problem-Solving Inventory: An integration of theory and data. *Cognitive Therapy and Research, 20,* 115–133.

Maydeu-Olivares, A., Rodríguez-Fornells, A., Gómez-Benito, J., & D'Zurilla, T. J. (2000). Psychometric properties of the Spanish adaptation of the Social Problem-Solving Inventory-Revise (SPSI-R). *Personality and Individual Differences, 29,* 699–708.

McCraty, R. M., Atkinson, W. A., Tiller, G., Rein, E., & Watkins, A. (2003). The impact of a workplace stress reduction program on blood pressure and emotional health in hypertensive employees. *Journal of Alternative and Complementary Medicine, 9,* 355–369.

McDonagh, A., Friedman, M., McHugo, G., Ford, J., Sengupta, A., Mueser, K., . . . Descamps, M. (2005). Randomized trial of cognitive-behavioral therapy for chronic posttraumatic stress disorder in adult female survivors of childhood sexual abuse. *Journal of Consulting and Clinical Psychology, 73,* 515–524.

McGuire, J. (2005). The Think First programme. In M. McMurran & J. McGuire (Eds.), *Social problem solving and offending: Evidence, evaluation and evolution* (pp. 183–206). Chichester, England: Wiley.

McLeavey, B. C., Daly, R. J., Ludgate, J. W., & Murray, C. M. (1994). Interpersonal problem-solving skills training in the treatment of self-poisoning patients. *Suicide & Life-Threatening Behavior, 24,* 382–394.

McMurran, M., Nezu, A. M., & Nezu, C. M. (2008). Problem-solving therapy for people with personality disorders. *Mental Health Review, 13,* 35–39.

Melchior, M., Caspi, A., Milne, B. J., Danese, A., Poulton, R., & Moffitt, T. E. (2007). Work stress precipitates depression and anxiety in young, working women and men. *Psychological Medicine, 37,* 1119–1129.

Miner, R. C., & Dowd, E. T. (1996). An empirical test of the problem solving model of depression and its application to the prediction of anxiety and anger. *Counseling Psychology Quarterly, 9,* 163–176.

Mischel, W., & Shoda, Y. (1995). A cognitive-affective system theory of personality: Reconceptualizing situations, dispositions, dynamics, and invariance in personality structure. *Psychological Review, 102,* 246–268.

Mishel, M. H., Belyea, M., Gemino, B. B., Stewart, J. L., Bailey, D. E., Robertson, C., & Mohler, J.(2002). Helping patients with localized prostate carcinoma manage uncertainty and treatment side effects: Nurse delivered psychoeducational intervention over the telephone. *Cancer, 94,* 1854–1866.

Monroe, S. M., Slavich, G. M., & Georgiades, K. (2009). The social environment and life stress in depression. In I. H. Gotlib & C. L. Hammen (Eds.), *Handbook of depression* (pp. 340–360). New York, NY: Guilford Press.

Monroe, S. M., Slavich, G. M., Torres, L. D., & Gotlib, I. H. (2007). Major life events and major chronic difficulties are differentially associated with history of major depression. *Journal of Abnormal Psychology, 116,* 116–124.

Monroe, S. M., Torres, L. D., Guillaumont, J., Harkness, K. L., Roberts, J. E., Frank, E., & Kupfer, D. (2006). Life stress and the long-term treatment course of recurrent depression: III. Nonsevere life events predict recurrence for medicated patients over 3 years. *Journal of Consulting and Clinical Psychology, 74,* 112–120.

Mooney, R. L., & Gordon, L. V. (1950). *The Mooney Manual: Problem Checklist.* New York, NY: Psychological Corporation.

Murawski, M. E., Milsom, V. A., Ross, K. M., Rickel, K. A., DeBraganza, N., Gibbons, L. M., & Perri, M. G. (2009). Problem solving, treatment adherence, and weight-loss outcome among women participating in lifestyle treatment for obesity. *Eating Behaviors, 10,* 146–151.

Muscara, F., Catroppa, C., & Anderson, V. (2008). Social problem-solving skills as a mediator between executive function and long-term social outcome following paediatric traumatic brain injury. *Journal of Neuropsychology, 2,* 445–461.

Mynors-Wallis, L., Davies, I., Gray, A., Barbour, F., & Gath, D. (1997). A randomized controlled trial and cost analysis of problem-solving treatment for emotional disorders given by community nurses in primary care. *British Journal of Psychiatry, 170,* 113–119.

Mynors-Wallis, L. M., Gath, D. H., Day, A., & Baker, F. (2000). Randomised controlled trial of problem solving treatment, antidepressant medication, and combined treatment for major depression in primary care. *British Medical Journal, 320,* 26–30.

Mynors-Wallis, L. M., Gath, D. H., Lloyd-Thomas, A. R., & Tomlinson, D. (1995). Randomised controlled trial comparing problem solving treatment with amitriptyline and placebo for major depression in primary care. *British Medical Journal, 310,* 441–445.

Newberg, A., & Waldman, M. R. (2009). *How God changes your brain.* New York, NY: Ballantine Books.

Newman, C. F. (2003). Cognitive restructuring: Identifying and modifying maladaptive schemas. In W. O'Donohue, J. E. Fisher, & S. C. Hayes (Eds.), *Cognitive behavior therapy: Applying empirically supported techniques in your practice* (pp. 89–95). New York, NY: Wiley.

Nezu, A. M. (1986a). Efficacy of a social problem solving therapy approach for unipolar depression. *Journal of Consulting and Clinical Psychology, 54,* 196–202.

Nezu, A. M. (1986b). Negative life stress and anxiety: Problem solving as a moderator variable. *Psychological Reports, 58,* 279–283.

Nezu, A. M. (1987). A problem-solving formulation of depression: A literature review and proposal of a pluralistic model. *Clinical Psychology Review, 7,* 121–144.

Nezu, A. M. (2004). Problem solving and behavior therapy revisited. *Behavior Therapy, 35,* 1–33.

Nezu, A. M. (2009, November). *Problem-solving skills training to enhance resilience.* Invited address presented at the 2nd Annual Warriors' Resilience Conference sponsored by the Department of Defense's Centers of Excellence for Psychological Health and Traumatic Brain Injury, Norfolk, VA.

Nezu, A., & D'Zurilla, T. J. (1979). An experimental evaluation of the decision-making process in social problem solving. *Cognitive Therapy and Research, 3,* 269–277.

Nezu, A., & D'Zurilla, T. J. (1981a). Effects of problem definition and formulation on decision making in the social problem-solving process. *Behavior Therapy, 12,* 100–106.

Nezu, A., & D'Zurilla, T. J. (1981b). Effects of problem definition and formulation on the generation of alternatives in the social problem-solving process. *Cognitive Therapy and Research, 6,* 265–271.

Nezu, A. M., & D'Zurilla, T. J. (1989). Social problem solving and negative affective conditions. In P. C. Kendall & D. Watson (Eds.), *Anxiety and depression: Distinctive and overlapping features* (pp. 285–315). New York, NY: Academic Press.

Nezu, A. M., & Nezu, C. M. (Eds.). (1989). *Clinical decision making in behavior therapy: A problem-solving perspective.* Champaign, IL: Research Press.

Nezu, A. M., & Nezu, C. M. (2009). *Problem-solving therapy.* APA DVD Series on Systems of Psychotherapy (J. Carlson, producer). Washington, DC: American Psychological Association.

Nezu, A. M., & Nezu, C. M. (2010a). Problem-solving therapy for relapse prevention in depression. In S. Richards & M. G. Perri (Eds.), *Relapse prevention for depression* (pp. 99–130). Washington, DC: American Psychological Association.

Nezu, A. M., & Nezu, C. M. (2010b, July). *Problem-solving training.* Paper presented at the Department of Veterans Affairs Mental Health Conference: Implementing a Public Health Model for Meeting the Mental Health Needs of Veterans, Baltimore, MD.

Nezu, A. M., & Nezu, C. M. (2012, April). *Moving forward: A problem-solving approach to achieving life's goals.* Workshop presented at the Department of Veterans Affairs Education/Training Conference, Philadelphia, PA.

Nezu, A. M., Nezu, C. M., & Cos, T. A. (2007). Case formulation for the behavioral and cognitive therapies: A problem-solving perspective. In T. D. Eells (Ed.), *Handbook of psychotherapy case formulation* (2nd ed., pp. 349–378). New York, NY: Guilford Press.

Nezu, A. M., Nezu, C. M., & D'Zurilla, T. J. (2007). *Solving life's problems: A 5-step guide to enhanced well-being.* New York, NY: Springer Publishing.

Nezu, A. M., Nezu, C. M., Faddis, S., DelliCarpini, L. A., & Houts, P. S. (1995, November). *Social problem solving as a moderator of cancer-related stress.* Paper presented at the Annual Convention of the Association for Advancement of Behavior Therapy, Washington, DC.

Nezu, A. M., Nezu, C. M., Felgoise, S. H., McClure, K. S., & Houts, P. S. (2003). Project Genesis: Assessing the efficacy of problem-solving therapy for distressed adult cancer patients. *Journal of Consulting and Clinical Psychology, 71*, 1036–1048.

Nezu, A. M., Nezu, C. M., Felgoise, S. H., & Zwick, M. L. (2003). Psychosocial oncology. In A. M. Nezu, C. M. Nezu, & P. A. Geller (Eds.), *Health psychology* (pp. 267–292), Volume 9 of the *Handbook of Psychology*, Editor-in-Chief: I. B. Weiner. New York, NY: Wiley.

Nezu, A. M., Nezu, C. M., Friedman, S. H., Faddis, S., & Houts, P. S. (1998). *Helping cancer patients cope: A problem-solving approach.* Washington, DC: American Psychological Association.

Nezu, A. M., Nezu, C. M., Friedman, S. H., Faddis, S., & Houts, P. S. (1997, November). *Problem-solving therapy for distressed cancer patients.* Paper presented at the Annual Convention of the Association for Advancement of Behavior Therapy, Miami, FL.

Nezu, A. M., Nezu, C. M., Houts, P. S., Friedman, S. H., & Faddis, S. (1999). Relevance of problem-solving therapy to psychosocial oncology. In J. A. Bucher (Ed.), *The application of problem-solving therapy to psychosocial oncology* (pp. 5–26). Binghamton, NY: Haworth Medical Press.

Nezu, A. M., Nezu, C. M., & Jain, D. (2005). *The emotional wellness way to cardiac health: How letting go of depression, anxiety, and anger can heal your heart.* Oakland, CA: New Harbinger.

Nezu, A. M., Nezu, C. M., & Jain, D. (2008). Social problem solving as a mediator of the stress-pain relationship among individuals with noncardiac chest pain. *Health Psychology, 27*, 829–832.

Nezu, A. M., Nezu, C. M., Lee, M., Haggerty, K., Salber, K. E., Greenberg, L. M., . . . Foster, E. (2011, November). *Social problem solving as a mediator of posttraumatic growth and quality of life among patients with heart failure.* Paper presented at the Annual Convention of the Association of Behavioral and Cognitive Therapies, Toronto, Canada.

Nezu, A. M., Nezu, C. M., & Lombardo, E. R. (2001). Cognitive-behavior therapy for medically unexplained symptoms: A critical review of the treatment literature. *Behavior Therapy, 32*, 537–583.

Nezu, A. M., Nezu, C. M., & Lombardo, E. R. (2004). *Cognitive-behavioral case formulation and treatment design: A problem-solving approach.* New York, NY: Springer Publishing.

Nezu, A. M., Nezu, C. M., & Perri, M. G. (1989). *Problem-solving therapy for depression: Therapy, research, and clinical guidelines.* New York, NY: Wiley.

Nezu, A. M., Nezu, C. M., Saraydarian, L., Kalmar, K., & Ronan, G. F. (1986). Social problem solving as a moderator variable between negative life stress and depressive symptoms. *Cognitive Therapy and Research, 10*, 489–498.

Nezu, A. M., Nezu, C. M., Tenhula, W., Karlin, B., & Beaudreau, S. (2012). *Problem-solving training to enhance readjustment among returning veterans: Initial evaluation results.* Paper presented at the Annual Convention of the Association of Behavioral and Cognitive Therapies, National Harbor, MD.

Nezu, A. M., & Perri, M. G. (1989). Social problem solving therapy for unipolar depression: An initial dismantling investigation. *Journal of Consulting and Clinical Psychology, 57,* 408–413.

Nezu, A. M., Perri, M. G., & Nezu, C. M. (1987, August). *Validation of a problem-solving/stress model of depression.* Paper presented at the Annual Convention of the American Psychological Association, New York.

Nezu, A. M., Perri, M. G., Nezu, C. M., & Mahoney, D. (1987, November). *Social problem solving as a moderator of stressful events among clinically depressed individuals.* Paper presented at the Annual Convention of the Association for Advancement of Behavior Therapy, Boston.

Nezu, A. M., & Ronan, G. F. (1985). Life stress, current problems, problem solving, and depressive symptomatology: An integrative model. *Journal of Consulting and Clinical Psychology, 53,* 693–697.

Nezu, A. M., & Ronan, G. F. (1988). Stressful life events, problem solving, and depressive symptoms among university students: A prospective analysis. *Journal of Counseling Psychology, 35,* 134–138.

Nezu, A. M., Wilkins, V. M., & Nezu, C. M. (2004). Social problem solving, stress, and negative affective conditions. In E. C. Chang, T. J. D'Zurilla, & L. J. Sanna (Eds.), *Social problem solving: Theory, research, and training* (pp. 49–65). Washington, DC: American Psychological Association.

Nezu, C. M., D'Zurilla, T. J., & Nezu, A. M. (2005). Problem-solving therapy: Theory, practice, and application to sex offenders. In M. McMurran & J. McGuire (Eds.), *Social problem solving and offenders: Evidence, evaluation and evolution* (pp. 103–123). Chichester, United Kingdom: Wiley.

Nezu, C. M., Fiore, A. A., & Nezu, A. M. (2006). Problem-solving treatment for intellectually disabled sex offenders. *International Journal of Behavioral Consultation and Therapy, 2,* 266–276.

Nezu, C. M., Nezu, A. M., & Areán, P. A. (1991). Assertiveness and problem-solving training for mildly mentally retarded persons with dual diagnosis. *Research in Developmental Disabilities, 12,* 371–386.

Nezu, C. M., Palmatier, A., & Nezu, A. M. (2004). Social problem-solving training for caregivers. In E. C. Chang, T. J. D'Zurilla, & L. J. Sanna (Eds.), *Social problem solving: Theory, research, and training* (pp. 223–238). Washington, DC: American Psychological Association.

Nock, M. K., & Mendes, W. B. (2008). Physiological arousal, distress tolerance, and social problem-solving deficits among adolescent self-injurers. *Journal of Consulting and Clinical Psychology, 76,* 28–38.

Nugent, N. R., Tyrka, A. R., Carpenter, L. L., & Price, L. H. (2011). Gene-environment interactions: Early life stress and risk for depressive and anxiety disorders. *Psychopharmacology, 214,* 175–196.

Olff, M. (1999). Stress, depression and immunity: The role of defense and coping styles. *Psychiatry Research, 85,* 7–15.

Pace, T. W. W., Mletzko, T. C., Alagbe, O., Musselman, D. L., Nemeroff, C. B., Miller, A. H., & Heim, C. M. (2006). Increased stress-induced inflammatory responses in male patients with major depression and increased early life stress. *American Journal of Psychiatry, 163*, 1630–1633.

Pandey, A., Quick, J. C., Rossi, A. M., Nelson, D. L., & Martin, W. (2011). Stress and the workplace. In R. J. Contrada & A. Baum (Eds.), *The handbook of stress science: Biology, psychology, and health* (pp. 137–149). New York, NY: Springer Publishing.

Parker, K. J., Buckmaster, C. L., Schatzberg, A. F., & Lyons, D. M. (2004). Prospective investigation of stress inoculation in young monkeys. *Archives of General Psychiatry, 61*, 933–941.

Pennebaker, J. W. (2004). Theories, therapies, and taxpayers: On the complexities of the expressive writing paradigm. *Clinical Psychology: Science and Practice, 11*, 138–142.

Perri, M. G., McAdoo, W. G., McAllister, D. A., Lauer, J. B., Jordan, R. C., Yancey, D. Z., & Nezu, A. M. (1987). Effects of peer support and therapist contact on long-term weight loss. *Journal of Consulting and Clinical Psychology, 55*, 615–617.

Perri, M. G., Nezu, A. M., McKelvey, W. F., Shermer, R. L., Renjilian, D. A., & Viegener, B. J. (2001). Relapse prevention training and problem-solving therapy in the long-term management of obesity. *Journal of Consulting and Clinical Psychology, 69*, 722–726.

Pessoa, L. (2010). Emotion and cognition and the amygdala: From "what is it?" to "what's to be done?" *Neuropsychologia, 48*, 3416–3429.

Post, R. M. (2007). Kindling and sensitization as models for affective episode recurrence, cyclicity, and tolerance phenomena. *Neuroscience and Biobehavioral Reviews, 31*, 858–873.

Priester, M., & Clum, G. A. (1993). Perceived problem-solving ability as a predictor of depression, hopelessness, and suicide ideation in a college population. *Journal of Counseling Psychology, 40*, 79–85.

Provencher, M. D., Dugas, M. J., & Ladouceur, R. (2004). Efficacy of problem-solving training and cognitive exposure in the treatment of generalized anxiety disorder: A case replication series. *Cognitive and Behavioral Practice, 11*, 404–414.

Radley, J. J., Rocher, A. B., Miller, M., Janssen, W. G., Liston, C., Hof, P. R., . . . Morrison, J. H. (2006). Repeated stress induces dendritic spine loss in the rat medial prefrontal cortex. *Cerebral Cortex, 16*, 313–320.

Rath, J. F., Simon, D., Langenbahn, D. M., Sherr, R. L., & Diller, L. (2003). Group treatment of problem-solving deficits in outpatients with traumatic brain injury: A randomised outcome study. *Neuropsychological Rehabilitation: An International Journal, 13*, 461–488.

Rivera, P. A., Elliott, T. R., Berry, J. W., & Grant, J. S. (2008). Problem-solving training for family caregivers of persons with traumatic brain injuries: A randomized controlled trial. *Archives of Physical Medicine and Rehabilitation, 89*, 931–941.

Robinson, R. G., Jorge, R. E., Moser, D. J., Acion, L., Solodkin, A., Small, S. L., . . . Arndt, S. (2008). Escitalopram and problem-solving therapy for prevention of post-stroke depression: A randomized controlled trial. *JAMA, 299*, 2391–2400.

Rogers, R., & Monsell, S. (1995). The costs of a predictable switch between simple cognitive tasks. *Journal of Experimental Psychology: General, 124*, 207–231.

Ross, R. R., Fabiano, E. A., & Ewles, C. D. (1988). Reasoning and rehabilitation. *International Journal of Offender Treatment and Comparative Criminology, 32*, 29–35.

Rovner, B. W., Casten, R. J., Hegel, M. T., Leiby, B. E., & Tasman, W. S. (2007). Preventing depression in age-related macular degeneration. *Archives of General Psychiatry, 64*, 886–892.

Rudd, M. D., Rajab, M. H., & Dahm, P. F. (1994). Problem-solving appraisal in suicide ideators and attempters. *American Journal of Orthopsychiatry, 64*, 136–149.

Sahler, O. J. Z., Varni, J. W., Fairclough, D. L., Butler, R. W., Noll, R. B., Dolgin, M. J., . . . Mulhern, R. K. (2002). Problem-solving skills training for mothers of children with newly diagnosed cancer: A randomized trial. *Developmental and Behavioral Pediatrics, 23*, 77–86.

Salkovskis, P. M., Atha, C., & Storer, D. (1990). Cognitive-behavioural problem solving in the treatment of patients who repeatedly attempt suicide. A controlled trial. *British Journal of Psychiatry, 157*, 871–876.

Sato, H., Takahashi, F., Matsuo, M., Sakai, M., Shimada, H., Chen, J., . . . Sakano, Y. (2006). Development of the Japanese version of the Social Problem-Solving Inventory-Revised and examination of its reliability and validity. *Japanese Journal of Behavior Therapy, 32*, 15–30.

Scheier, M. F., Matthews, K., Owens, J., Magovern, G., Lefebvre, R., & Abbot, R. (2003). Dispositional optimism; coronary artery bypass surgery; physical recovery; psychological well-being; physical well-being. *Social psychology of health, 342*–361.

Scholey, A., Haskell, C., Robertson, B., Kennedy, D., Milne, A., & Wetherell, M. (2009). Chewing gum alleviates negative mood and reduces cortisol during acute laboratory psychological stress. *Physiology & Behavior, 97*, 304–312.

Schreuders, B., van Marwijk, H., Smit, J., Rijmen, F., Stalman, W., & van Oppen, P. (2007). Primary care patients with mental health problems: Outcome of a randomised clinical trial. *British Journal of General Practice, 57*, 886–891.

Seery, M. D. (2011). Resilience: A silver lining to experiencing adverse life events. *Current Directions in Psychological Science, 20*, 390–394.

Shaw, W. S., Feuerstein, M., Haufler, A. J., Berkowitz, S. M., & Lopez, M. S. (2001). Working with low back pain: Problem-solving orientation and function. *Pain, 93*, 129–137.

Siu, A. M. H., & Shek, D. T. L. (2005). The Chinese version of the Social Problem Solving Inventory: Some initial results on reliability and validity. *Journal of Clinical Psychology, 61*, 347–360.

Slavich, G. M., Monroe, S. M., & Gotlib, I. H. (2011). Early parental loss and depression history: Associations with recent life stress in major depressive disorder. *Journal of Psychiatric Research, 45*, 1146–1152.

Snyder , C. R., Rand, K. L., & Sigman, D. R. (2002). Hope theory: A member of the positive psychology family. In C. R. Snyder & S. Lopez (Eds.), *Handbook of positive psychology* (pp. 257–276). New York: Oxford.

Spence, S. H., Sheffield, J. K., & Donovan, C. L. (2003). Preventing adolescent depression: An evaluation of the problem solving for life program. *Journal of Consulting and Clinical Psychology, 71*, 3–13.

Stanovich, K. E., & West, R. F. (2000). Individual differences in reasoning: Implications for the rationality debate? *Behavioral and Brain Sciences, 23,* 645–726.

Stetler, C., & Miller, G. E. (2011). Depression and hypothalamic-pituitary-adrenal activation: A quantitative summary of four decades of research. *Psychosomatic Medicine, 73,* 114–126.

Stillmaker, J., & Kasser, T. (2012). Instruction in problem-solving skills increases the hedonic balance of highly neurotic individuals. *Cognitive Therapy and Research.* Published on line June 16, 2012. doi:10.1007/s10608-012-9466-3

Tarrier, N., Yusupoff, L., Kinney, C., McCarthy, E., Gledhill, A., Haddock, G., & Morris, J. (1998). Randomised controlled trial of intensive cognitive behaviour therapy for patients with chronic schizophrenia. *British Medical Journal, 317,* 303–307.

Tenhula, W. N. (2010, Fall). Problem-solving training. *Health Power Prevention News,* 3–4.

Teri, L., Logsdon, R. G., Uomoto, J., & McCurry, S. M. (1997). Behavioral treatment of depression in dementia patients: A controlled clinical trial. *Journals of Gerontology, Series B: Psychological Sciences and Social Sciences, 52B,* 159–166.

Toobert, D. J., Strycker, L. A., Glasgow, R. E., Barrera, M., & Bagdade, J. D. (2002). Enhancing support for health behavior change among women at risk for heart disease: The Mediterranean Lifestyle Trial. *Health Education and Research, 17,* 574–585.

Tranel, D., & Hyman, B. T. (1990). Neuropsychological correlates of bilateral amygdala damage. *Archives of Neurology, 47,* 349–355.

Tymchuk, A. J., Andron, L., & Rahbar, B. (1988). Effective decision-making/problem-solving training with mothers who have mental retardation. *American Journal on Mental Retardation, 92,* 510–516.

Uchida, S., Hara, K., Kobayashi, A., Funato, H., Hobara, T., Otsuki, K., . . . Watanabe, Y. (2010). Early life stress enhances behavioral vulnerability to stress through the activation of REST-4-mediated gene transcription in the medial prefrontal cortex of rodents. *The Journal of Neuroscience, 30,* 15007–15018.

Unützer, J., Katon, W., Williams, J. W., Callahan, C., Harpole, L., Hunkeler, E. M., . . . Langston, C. A. (2001). Improving primary care for depression in late life: The design of a multicenter randomized trial. *Medical Care, 39,* 785–799.

van den Hout, J. H. C., Vlaeyen, J. W. S., Heuts, P. H. T., Stillen, W. J. T., & Willen, J. E. H. L. (2001). Functional disability in non-specific low back pain: The role of pain-related fear and problem-solving skills. *International Journal of Behavioural Medicine, 8,* 134–148.

van den Hout, J. H. C., Vlaeyen, J. W. S., Heuts, P. H. T., Zijlema, J. H. L., & Wijen, J. A. G. (2003). Secondary prevention of work-related disability in nonspecific low back pain: Does problem-solving therapy help? A randomized clinical trial. *The Clinical Journal of Pain, 19,* 87–96.

van Straten, A., Cuijpers, P., & Smits, N. (2008). Effectiveness of a web-based self-help intervention for symptoms of depression, anxiety, and stress: Randomized controlled trial. *Journal of Medical Internet Research, 10,* e7.

Wade, S. L., Walz, N. C., Carey, J., McMullen, K. M., Cass, J., Mark, E., & Yeates, K. O. (2011). Effect on behavior problems of teen online problem-solving for adolescent traumatic brain injury. *Pediatrics, 128,* e947–e953.

Wade, S. L., Wolfe, C., Brown, T. M., & Pestian, J. P. (2005). Putting the pieces together: Preliminary efficacy of a web-based family intervention for children with traumatic brain injury. *Journal of Pediatric Psychology, 30*, 437–442.

Wakeling, H. C. (2007). The psychometric validation of the Social Problem-Solving Inventory-Revised with UK incarcerated sexual offenders. *Sex Abuse, 19*, 217–236.

Wallace, C. J., & Liberman, R. P. (1985). Social skills training for patients with schizophrenia: A controlled clinical trial. *Psychiatry Research, 15*, 239–247.

Walusinski, O. (2006). Yawning: An unsuspected avenue for a better understanding of arousal and interoception. *Medical Hypotheses, 67*, 6–14.

Warmerdam, L., van Straten, A., Twisk, J., Riper, H., & Cuijpers, P. (2008).Internet-based treatment for adults with depressive symptoms: Randomized controlled trial. *Journal of Medical Internet Research, 10*, e44.

Weinberger, M., Hiner, S. L., & Tierney, W. M. (1987). In support of hassles as a measure of stress in predicting health outcomes. *Journal of Behavioral Medicine, 10*, 19–31.

Wetherell, M. A., Hyland, M. E., & Harris, J. E. (2004). Secretory immunoglobin A reactivity to acute and cumulative acute multi-tasking stress: Relationships between reactivity and perceived workload. *Biological Psychology, 66*, 257–270.

Wichers, M., Jacobs, N., Kenis, G., Peeters, F., Derom, C., Thiery, E., . . . van Os, J. (2009). Transition from stress sensitivity to a depressive state: longitudinal twin study. *The British Journal of Psychiatry, 195*, 498–503.

Wilhelm, K., Siegel, J. E., Finch, A. W., Hadzi-Pavlovic, D., Mitchell, P. B., Parker, G., & Schofield, P. R. (2007). The long and the short of it: Associations between 5-HTT genotypes and coping with stress. *Psychosomatic Medicine, 69*, 614–620.

Wilkinson, P., & Mynors-Wallis, L. (1994). Problem-solving therapy in the treatment of unexplained physical symptoms in primary care: A preliminary study. *Journal of Psychosomatic Research, 38*, 591–598.

Williams, J. M. G., Teasdale, J. D., Segal, Z. V., & Soulsby, J. (2000). Mindfulness-based cognitive therapy reduces overgeneral autobiographical memory in formerly depressed patients. *Journal of Abnormal Psychology, 109*, 150–155.

Williams, J. W., Barrett, J., Oxman, T., Frank, E., Katon, W., Sullivan, M., . . . Sengupta, A. (2000). Treatment of dysthymia and minor depression in primary care: A randomized controlled trial in older adults. *Journal of the American Medical Association, 284*, 1519–1526.

Williams, J. W., Katon, W., Lin, E. H., Noel, H., Worchel, J., Cornell, J., . . . Unützer, J. (2004). The effectiveness of depression care management on diabetes-related outcomes in older patients. *Annals of Internal Medicine, 140*, 1015–1024.

Xu, A., Liu, X., Xia, Y., Peng, M., & Zhou, R. (2010). Effect of chewing gum on emotion and cognitive tasks. *Chinese Journal of Clinical Psychology, 18*, 407–410.

Yang, B., & Clum, G. A. (1994). Life stress, social support, and problem-solving skills predictive of depressive symptoms, hopelessness, and suicide ideation in an Asian student population: A test of a model. *Suicide and Life-Threatening Behavior, 24*, 127–139.

Instructions for Scoring the Problem-Solving Test

Scales of Effective Problem Solving

1. Positive Problem Orientation (PPO)
   - Add scores for items 5, 8, 15, 23, & 25
2. Planful Problem Solving (PPS)
   - Add scores for items 2, 9, 12, 17, & 18

Explanation of Scores

- For both scales, scores below 12 suggest that this individual is in need of problem-solving education, training, and practice in order to improve his or her psychological resilience to deal with the stress of daily problems.
- Scores between 12 and 18 indicate that he or she has some strengths but can probably benefit from some training to improve.
- Scores greater than 18 indicate that this individual has strong positive attitudes and/or strong planful problem-solving skills.

Scales of Ineffective Problem Solving

1. Negative Problem Orientation (NPO)
   - Add scores for items 1, 3, 7, 11, & 16
2. Impulsive/Careless (IC)
   - Add scores for items 4, 13, 20, 22, & 24
3. Avoidance (AV)
   - Add scores for items 6, 10, 14, 19, & 21

Explanation of Scores

- For all these three scales, note that higher scores are indicative of a higher level in that scale (i.e., the higher the NPO score, the more negative one's orientation; the higher the IC score, the more he or she is impulsive/careless; the higher the AV score, the more avoidant the person).

- Scores above 12 indicate that one has some characteristic way(s) of dealing with problems that can frequently get in the way of his or her problem-solving efforts. Scores lower than 12 on any of these scales suggest the absence of any concerns regarding these areas.

- A *Negative Orientation* score of 12 or higher indicates that one has the tendency to think about problems in ways that are inaccurate, as well as experiencing difficulty managing the emotions that are often present when under stress. The higher the score above 12, the more negative the person's orientation.

- An *Impulsive/Careless* score of 12 or higher indicates that this individual may have the tendency to "look before he/she leaps" and may often make decisions that are not in his or her best interest. The higher the score above 12, the more impulsive the person.

- An *Avoidance* score of 12 or higher indicates that one has the tendency to avoid problems. This is the type of individual who often withdraws or leaves the room when engaged in an interpersonal argument, or pushes thoughts and feelings out of his or her head when worried or sad. Scores higher than 12 are suggestive of particular difficulties with avoidance.

APPENDIX TWO

Patient Handouts:
Figures, Forms, and Worksheets

Date:

Problem-Solving Self-Monitoring Form

What was the problem? (Describe the situation; be sure to indicate who was involved, why it was a problem for you, and your goal or objectives in the situation)

What was your emotional reaction to the problem? (Be sure to note your initial feelings, as well as your emotions throughout—did they change?)

What did you do to handle the problem? (Describe what you tried to do to solve or cope with the problem; try to be as specific as possible, describing your thoughts and actions)

What was the outcome? (Describe what happened after you tried to handle the problem; be sure to indicate your emotional reactions to this outcome, how satisfied you were with this outcome, and whether you believe the problem was solved)

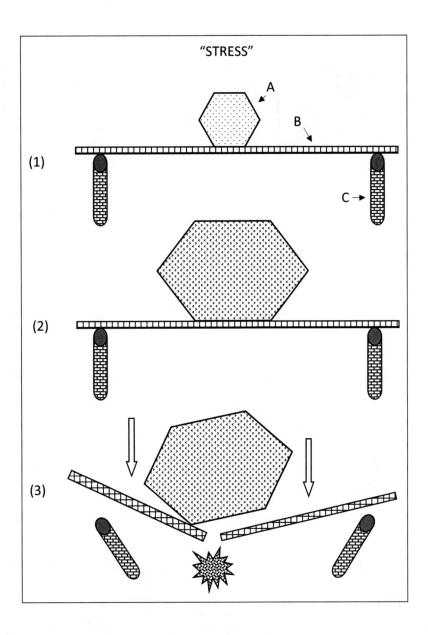

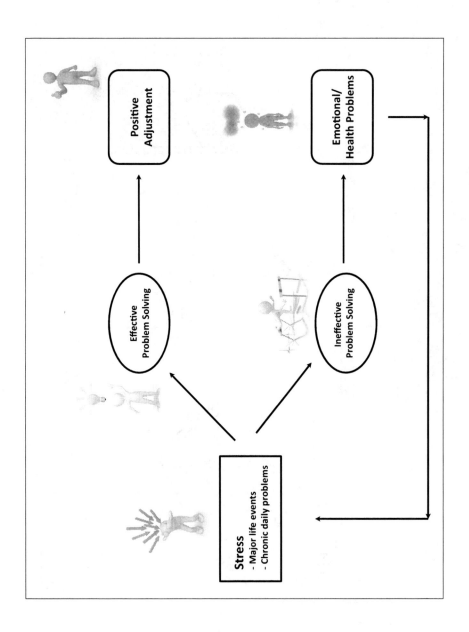

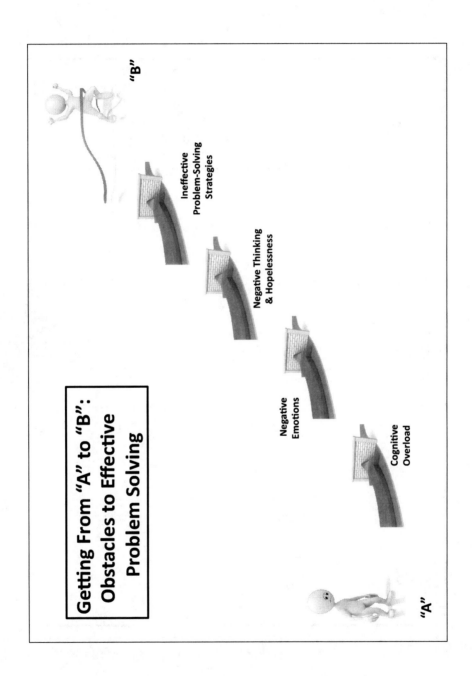

Reactions to Stress

Event	Thoughts	Affect	Physical Sensations	Behavior

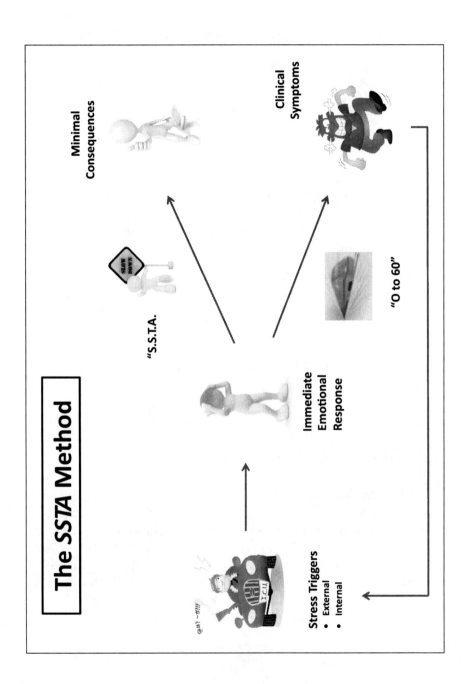

The *SSTA* Method

Minimal Consequences

Clinical Symptoms

"S.S.T.A."

"0 to 60"

Immediate Emotional Response

Stress Triggers
- External
- Internal

LISTENING TO FEELINGS: WHAT YOUR EMOTIONS MIGHT BE TELLING YOU

EMOTION: FEAR/ANXIETY

Ways People Describe This Emotion: *Nervous, jittery, "on edge," scared, anxious, restless, uncomfortable, worried, panicked.*

Information to Look For: *Any sense of impending hurt, pain, threat or danger. Anxious or nervous thoughts; sweating, dry mouth, upset stomach, dizziness, shallow breathing; urge to run away and hide, avoid situations.*

Examples of What the Information May Reveal:

- You fear physical or emotional injury for yourself or others.
- You fear that you are inferior to others and your sense of self-esteem is threatened (examples include fears about your intelligence, talents, physical skill, or outward appearance).

Why This Information Is Important:

- You can now work on better managing your fears, rather than trying to avoid them.
- You can examine the fears you have and see if they are realistic.
- You can face your fears and work on ways to reduce them. Similar to facing a schoolyard bully, facing your fears often leads to greater self-confidence, even if you sustain a bruise or two.

FEELING: ANGER

Ways People Describe This Emotion: *Frustrated, irritated, enraged, mad, "pissed off," angry, states a desire to break something or hurt someone.*

Information to Look For: *Being blocked from getting what you want—the block can be due to circumstances or specific people.*

Examples of What the Information May Reveal:

- You want success, achievement, or to be the best, but you see someone or something in the way.
- You want a relationship, but it seems like hard work, or you see the other person as creating problems.
- You want to be loved or admired, but others do not appreciate you.
- You want to be able to control circumstances or the reactions of others, but it is impossible to have that much control over situations or people.

Why the Information Is Important:

- You may discover that your anger is less about the other person and more about yourself, your pride, or what you want. Rather than focusing on your anger, you can direct your energies toward making your own life better.
- You may have unrealistic expectations regarding others or yourself. It may be time for you to "get real"—give yourself and others a break from such harsh standards.

FEELING: SADNESS

Ways People Describe This Emotion: *"Let down," disappointed, devastated, hurt, unhappy, depressed, drained, miserable, downcast, heartbroken.*

Information to Look For: *Losing something or holding the belief that you have lost something or someone important to you.*

Examples of What the Information May Reveal:

- You have lost a person (such as a friend, lover, or partner) in one of the following ways—a move, illness, death, disagreement, estrangement, or the person chooses to be with other people.
- You have lost something other than a person. This may refer to something tangible (e.g., money, job, physical health, leisure time) or something intangible (e.g., a position or role in the family or work, respect from others).

Why the Information Is Important:

- You can begin to work on increasing pleasant or joyful moments in your life to help you heal from a loss.
- You may have the opportunity to see that your worth is more than the objects of loss. For example, your wealth is not a measure of your self-esteem; your physical strength is not equal to your spirit.

FEELING: EMBARRASSMENT

Ways People Describe This Emotion: *Humiliated, vulnerable, "feel like crawling in a hole," "self-conscious."*

Information to Look For: *You feel very vulnerable.*

Examples of What the Information May Reveal:

- You are concerned that others can see your imperfections, mistakes, and problems.

Why the Information Is Important:

- You can begin to focus less on imperfection and more on accepting yourself for the person you are.

FEELING TYPE: GUILT

Ways People Describe This Emotion: *Ashamed, "feel bad," "screwed up," failed.*

Information to Look For: *You regret something you did.*

Examples of What the Information May Reveal:

- You have hurt others through your own actions.
- You have not done anything wrong, but you or someone else is telling you that you were wrong and you have self-doubts.

Why the Information Is Important:

- You can work on ways to communicate your regret and make a plan for personal change for the better.
- In the case of self-doubt, you can begin to change your inner voice, such that you do not require the approval of others 100 percent of the time.

WHAT ARE YOUR UNIQUE TRIGGERS?

Personal

Affect:

Conflict:

Thoughts/memories/images:

Physical sensations:

Urge to act differently:

Environmental/social

Interpersonal:

Physical:

Additional:

POSITIVE SELF-STATEMENTS

Use the following positive self-statements to help you "dispute" or argue against negative and irrational thinking.

- I can solve this problem!
- I'm okay—feeling sad is normal under these circumstances.
- I can't direct the wind, but I can adjust the sails.
- I don't have to please everyone.
- I can replace my fears with faith.
- It's okay to please myself.
- There will be an end to this difficulty.
- If I try, I can do it!
- I can get help from _____ if I need it.
- It's easier once I get started.
- I just need to relax.
- I can cope with this!
- I can reduce my fears.
- I just need to stay on track.
- I can't let the worries creep in.
- Prayer helps me.
- I'm proud of myself!
- I can hang in there!

Can you think of any others?

ABC THOUGHT RECORD

Situation or Event (A)	Thoughts (B)	Emotional Reactions (C)	Intensity Rating (1-10)

"MINDING YOUR MIND"
Identifying Negative Self-Talk &
Converting to Positive Self-Talk

SIGNS THAT YOU ARE USING NEGATIVE SELF-TALK

- Using "judgmental" words such as "must" and "should"
- Using *catastrophizing* words for circumstances NOT related to life and death matters
- Overgeneralizing

STRATEGIES FOR "DISPUTING" NEGATIVE SELF-TALK

- Argue against negative self-talk with logic
- Argue against "should" or "ought" with "why should I?"
- Question catastrophic words and assess real damage potential of situation
- Challenge overgeneralizations
- Use challenging POSITIVE self-statements

PROBLEM-SOLVING WORKSHEET

Briefly describe the problem (Can it be changed?):

State your problem-solving goal (BE REALISTIC):

Describe the major obstacles to achieving your goal at this time:

a.

b.

c.

Think of alternative ways to achieve your goal. Be creative. List at *least* 3 solution ideas:

1.

2.

3.

4.

5.

What are the major "pros" or positive consequences of these differing alternatives?

What are some of the "cons" or negative consequences?

Decide which alternatives are the best by choosing the ones with the best *positive* consequences and fewest *negative* consequences. Write down your action plan.

Carry out the plan & observe the consequences: Are you satisfied that your plan worked?

GETTING THE FACTS!

To better define and understand the nature of your problem, you may need to gather additional facts. Remember to determine which piece of information is a *fact* (what we know to be true) versus an assumption (what we may *think* is true but has not yet been verified).

In order to gather the most useful types of facts, try to answer the following questions and write them down in user-friendly and unambiguous language:

Who is involved?

What happened (or did not happen) that bothers you?

Where did it happen?

When did it happen?

Why did it happen? (i.e., known causes or reasons for the problem)

How did you respond to the situation? (i.e., actions, thoughts, and feelings)

Problem Map: What Makes This A Problem?

A

B

What's Preventing You From Getting from A to B?
What are the barriers?"

_____

_____

_____

_____

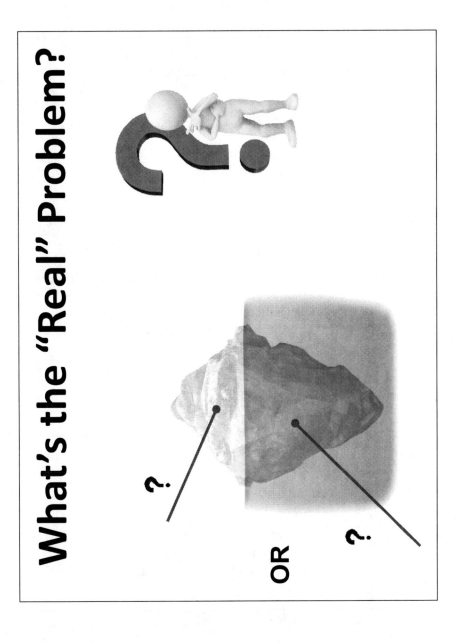

DEFINING THE PROBLEM

Use this worksheet to help you better define your problem. Try to answer the questions below using unambiguous and user-friendly language. Use additional paper if necessary.

What are the facts? Describe the problem here. Remember to separate facts from assumptions.

Why is this a problem for you? If you are unable to improve this situation or the way you are feeling, what are the consequences? Why is this an important problem for you to improve? How will improving this problem improve your life (even in a small way)?

What are your goals? Be sure to make them realistic and attainable! Start with small goals that are steps to your larger goals.

What are the major obstacles to your goal? What is actually getting in the way with your ability to work toward your goals?

GENERATING ALTERNATIVE SOLUTIONS

Use this worksheet to write down your list of alternative solution ideas to your problem. Remember to use the following "brainstorming" principles: "Quantity Leads to Quality"; "Defer Judgment"; and "Think of a Variety of Ideas." Try to come up with at least 3 to 5 ideas. Remember to use unambiguous and user-friendly language.

1.

2.

3.

4.

5.

6.

7.

8.

Use the back of this page for additional ideas.

DECISION-MAKING WORKSHEET

1. List your alternatives below.
2. For each idea, rate the likelihood that (a) it will help solve the problem; (b) you can carry this idea out optimally; (c) it will have positive immediate consequences; and (d) it will have positive long-term consequences. Use a scale of "minus" (−) to indicate a *low* likelihood, a "plus" (+) to indicate a *high* likelihood, and a "zero" (0) to indicate neither a low nor high likelihood. Use additional worksheets if necessary.

Alternative Solution Ideas	Will it Work?	Can I Carry it Out?	Personal Effects	Social Effects

"MOTIVATIONAL" WORKSHEET

If you are having difficulty deciding whether you should carry out your action plan, complete this worksheet.

Consequences If You Did Nothing at the Present Time	Predicted Consequences of Carrying Out Your Action Plan

ACTION PLAN OUTCOME EVALUATION WORKSHEET

1 = not at all
2 = a little
3 = somewhat
4 = much
5 = very much

Using the above rating scale, circle the number that represents your feelings.

1. How well does your solution plan meet your goals?

   1   2   3   4   5

2. How satisfied are you with the effects on you?

   1   2   3   4   5

3. How well do these results match your original prediction about personal consequences?

   1   2   3   4   5

4. How satisfied are you with the impact on others involved in the problem?

   1   2   3   4   5

5. How well do these results match your original prediction about the consequences concerning others?

   1   2   3   4   5

6. Overall, how satisfied are you with the results of your action plan?

   1   2   3   4   5

APPENDIX THREE

Patient Handouts:
Brief Instructional Booklets

STRESS, HEART FAILURE, AND DEPRESSION

Heart failure (HF) is the medical condition where the heart has significant difficulty in keeping blood flowing throughout the body to supply various organs. Common symptoms include fatigue, breathing problems, swelling, sleep difficulties, persistent coughing, lack of appetite, nausea, confusion, and increased heart rate.

Unfortunately, HF can be very stressful. HF-related problems can include physical and social limitations, limited capacity to perform activities of daily living, reduced ability to take care of other family members, reduced sexual activity, decreased mobility, and limited social relationships. As such, the quality of life for patients with HF is often greatly impaired. In fact, a recent review of the research literature suggests that patients with HF experience poorer overall quality of life than most other medical patient groups.

Research also suggests that **depression** is very common among individuals with HF. Estimates suggest that between 24% and 42% of all patients with HF experience significant depression that should be treated. But depression in patients with HF often goes unrecognized and undertreated. This is unfortunate, because depression can negatively impact the heart condition itself. For example, research has shown that depression can lead to a worsening of HF symptoms, an increased chance of being rehospitalized, and an increased risk of death. This can occur for physical reasons (e.g., depression can lead to elevated levels of stress hormones), as well as psychological reasons (e.g., being depressed can lead to poor adherence to the health care team's medical advice).

The **COPING WITH HEART FAILURE** program aims to help individuals with HF to better handle the common stresses and problems associated with this diagnosis and its treatment. The basic idea is to help them better cope with stressful problems as a means of decreasing their depression. Reducing depression is an important goal in and of itself, but alleviating depressive symptoms might also lead to an improvement in one's physical health. This is an important research question we hope to answer in the future by conducting these types of studies.

Interviews with patients with HF have revealed common stressful problems they experience, including

- Feeling tired all the time
- Being bothered by medication side effects
- Feeling that "no one understands me"
- Getting angry at small things
- Feeling helpless
- Not being able to do things that used to be enjoyable
- Feeling like a burden to their family
- Having difficulties sticking to a diet
- Problems with exercising even a little bit
- Worrying about death
- Relationship problems (with spouse, partner, family, friends)

What type of problems are *you* experiencing that are related to feelings of stress and depression? Which ones would you like to tackle first? List 2 or 3 problems below, for now—these might be ones to focus on with your counselor.

1. _____

2. _____

3. _____

So What Do I Do?

Learn to be an effective problem solver! The *COPING WITH HEART FAILURE* program provides *PROBLEM-SOLVING TRAINING* (PST). **PST** is a counseling program that teaches individuals how to adapt better to stressful circumstances. It is an interactive, skill-based approach to help people to cope better with stress by dealing with difficult problems. PST has been found to be highly effective as treatment for depression, as well as an approach to enhance the ability to cope with other types of medical problems, such as cancer, hypertension, diabetes, pain, and traumatic brain injury.

Our program is designed to help teach individuals with HF to better adapt to problems such as those listed above, as well as any stressful concerns unique to a given person. These skills should not only be applicable to HF-related issues but also to other problems in living (e.g., financial difficulties, sexual problems, work problems).

Dealing with depression is an important goal for your overall health. As one patient with HF, HK, once told us—"if you do not deal with the depression, it can become paralyzing; your mental state of health in dealing with heart failure is as important as your heart-related medical treatment."

WHAT IS EFFECTIVE PROBLEM SOLVING?

"We cannot direct the wind
but we can adjust the sails"

Life *is* full of problems, but as Helen Keller once said, "it is also full of overcoming them." These types of quotes underscore the idea that even though you might be experiencing many stressful difficulties, you *can* adjust to the multiple challenges they represent. As one client told us- "these are the cards I was dealt, now I have to play the hand, win, lose, or draw; I have to 'fight' the problems—I can't fight the reality that these problems exist!"

Research has demonstrated that individuals who are better at adapting to stressful circumstances by solving difficult problems they encounter experience less depression, a better quality of life, and enhanced physical well-being. Such individuals can be considered effective problem solvers, that is, people who tend to

- Look to see where opportunities for growth exist rather than react to problems as *major* threats
- Have self-confidence in their ability to tackle stressful situations
- React to difficult problems in a thoughtful and planful manner, rather than trying to go for the "quick fix," avoiding dealing with them, or responding with overwhelming negative emotions

The good news is that these are *skills*, not personality traits that we are born with! Just like driving, various sports, or hobbies, **these skills can be learned**.

What are **effective problem-solving skills**? People who are successful at coping with stressful difficulties are said to have a positive orientation toward problems in living, and engage in a planful problem-solving style when dealing with problems.

A **positive problem orientation** involves a set of attitudes to

- View a problem *and* negative emotional reactions more as a challenge than a threat
- Be *realistically* optimistic and believe problems *are* solvable
- Have the self-confidence in oneself to tackle such difficulties
- Believe that difficult problems take persistence and effort (Einstein once said—"It's not that I'm so smart, it's just that I stay with problems longer")
- Commit oneself to tackling problems

A **planful problem-solving style** involves a thoughtful and systematic way of dealing with problems. People using such an approach tend to

- Set realistic goals and try to determine what obstacles exist that prevent one from reaching that goal
- Creatively think of multiple ways of overcoming these obstacles and challenges
- Compare the pros and cons of these various options in order to identify effective solution ideas
- Carry out the solution as best as one can and monitor the outcome

On the other hand, **ineffective problem solvers** tend to have a negative orientation toward problems in living and engage in either an impulsive-careless or avoidant problem-solving style.

A **negative problem orientation** involves the general tendency to

- View problems as major threats to one's well-being
- Doubt one's ability to cope with problems
- Become overwhelmed with emotional distress when confronted with problems

An **impulsive-careless problem-solving style** involves the strong tendency to

- Go for the "quick fix"
- See the problem through narrow, "tunnel vision"
- Be incomplete and careless

An **avoidance style** is characterized by the strong tendency to

- Procrastinate
- Be passive
- Deny the existence of problems
- Rely on others to fix things rather than trying oneself

What kind of problem solver are *you*?

Do you *generally* see problems with a positive or a negative orientation? Do you *generally* react to problems with a planful style, an impulsive style, or an avoidant style?

People often react to problems with differing orientations or styles depending on the problem. For example, sometimes people use a more constructive way of dealing with problems at work but experience difficulty handling relationship or family problems (or vice versa). In addition, sometimes problems are so new, so complex, so overwhelming, or at times, even life-threatening that it becomes difficult to know what to do—our previously effective strategies don't seem to work. That's when we may need to learn new skills!

In thinking about the two types of orientations, which one describes you best?

- Positive orientation
- Negative orientation

Think about a problem you recently experienced—are you correct in describing your orientation?

Now think–which one of the 3 problem-solving styles best describes you?

- Planful problem solving
- Impulsive problem solving
- Avoidant problem solving

Go back to that same problem—are you correct in describing your style?

Francis Bacon once said—"knowledge is power!" We believe that self-knowledge is even more powerful; that is, if we are able to correctly understand our strengths and areas in need of improvement, we are better able to improve our strong points and overcome our limitations.

A first step toward becoming an effective problem solver is to better determine *your* particular problem-solving strengths and limitations. In that way, you can help your counselor to develop a learning program best suited for you!

PROBLEM-SOLVING MULTITASKING

*"The brain is a lot like a computer. You may have
several screens open at once on your desktop, but
you're able to think about only one at a time."*

—William Stixrud

Sherlock Holmes, the famous fictional detective who possessed great intelligence, would often characterize very difficult problems as a "three pipe problem," meaning that it would take smoking at least three pipes worth of tobacco before he would be able to solve it. This suggests that solving stressful real-life problems, in-and-of themselves, can often be difficult to handle. But what makes it even more of a challenge is our ability to multitask. This expression has become popular in the current computer age to describe the act of performing several tasks at the same time. Although a powerful computer can be a successful multitasker, due to the limited capacity of the human brain, this becomes difficult for us when attempting to solve real-life problems. In fact, science has shown that we actually cannot multitask efficiently!

Research has shown that our brains are limited in that they cannot perform all the activities required to solve problems efficiently at the same time, especially when the problem is particularly complex or stressful. Often, one activity interferes with another. For example, when we try to remember important information about a problem, this very act can actually interfere with our ability to think of ways to solve it.

Given this limited capacity (unfortunately we cannot go out to a computer store and buy a better brain), what can we do when faced with a stressful or complex problem in life?

Ways to Facilitate Problem-Solving Multitasking

Because our brains really can't do two things at the same time without affecting the accuracy of our attempts (even though we think we can), we need additional ways to help our minds perform better, especially when tackling complex or emotionally arousing problems.

We recommend three strategies:

- Externalization
- Visualization
- Simplification

These strategies are basic activities that can help us to become better problem solvers in general. Think of them as skills that are important building blocks required for other skills to develop. For example, proper breathing and stretching is important as basic skills required when we wish to exercise correctly or play a sport successfully.

Externalization

This strategy involves displaying information *externally* as often as possible. Simply put—write ideas down, draw diagrams or figures to show relationships, make lists. This procedure relieves our brains from having to actively display information being remembered, which allows one to concentrate more on other activities, such as attempting to better understand what obstacles stand in our way of solving the problem, creatively thinking of various solutions, or making effective decisions. That's why we need calendars, BlackBerry's "to do lists," iPods, grocery lists, maps, and even audiotape recorders.

The construction worker needs the blueprints to properly build the house—without them, it would be impossible to remember all the details required regarding measurements, materials, and decorations. Having written materials can help us solve problems more effectively!

To practice this strategy, we strongly recommend that you purchase a small notebook, journal, or notepad.

Visualization

Visualization involves using your "mind's eye" in the following ways that can help you solve a problem:

- **Clarifying the problem**—visualize a problem in order to look at it from differing perspectives, break it down into different components, and "map out" ways of getting from "A" to "B." It can also help us to remember details better.

- **Imaginal rehearsal**—rehearse carrying out a solution in your mind to improve upon it and get more practice. Sports figures do this all the time to improve performance; for example, skiers "imagine" going down the slopes; basketball players "imagine" how to jump in order to get the ball into the hoop from certain angles.
- **Stress management**—visualizing a "safe place" to go to, such as a relaxing vacation spot, in one's mind, can be a powerful stress management tool. It can also help you to "slow down," an important concept that is part of this program.

Simplification

This strategy involves breaking down or simplifying problems in order to make them more manageable. Rather than trying to solve the big problem, one should try to break it down into smaller parts representing smaller steps. For example, rather than trying to deal with the problem of "how am I going to pay for four years of college?" one can break the problem into smaller steps, beginning with "how can I pay for my first year of college?"

In addition, simplification involves focusing only on the most relevant information, and translating complex, vague, and abstract concepts into more simple, specific, and concrete terms. One way to practice this rule is to write down a brief description of a problem that you are experiencing (which means that you would also be practicing the "externalization" rule)—now read it over and ask yourself the question—"if a friend read this description, would he or she understand it, or did I use vague, ambiguous language and ideas?" If the answer is "no," go back and try to rewrite the information using the simplification strategy. If that proves difficult, try to visualize talking to your friend to better determine what kinds of words or ideas you should use in order to really get your points across. Write this down, look it over, and try to simplify once again!

**Use these multitasking strategies
when trying to solve stressful problems!**

GO ON A VACATION IN YOUR MIND:
VISUALIZE TO REDUCE STRESS

This visualization exercise, often called "guided imagery," is a stress management tool that you can use to decrease negative emotions or arousal. Basically, you will be asked to use your "mind's eye" to vividly imagine a scene, one that represents a "safe place," similar to a favorite vacation spot. Think of it as "taking a vacation in your mind" in order to relax and calm your body and mind. Your safe place is there for you to relax, feel safe and secure, "let go," and completely be yourself. Under times of stress, it can be extremely helpful in reducing distress. It's like "turning down the 'stress' volume." This tool can also put you in a relaxed state of mind in anticipation of undergoing an upcoming difficult situation. In addition, the more you practice, the more you will be able to reap the positive benefits of relaxation more quickly and profoundly. It can also be used to help you to "***SLOW DOWN.***"

Preparation

We suggest that either you or a friend make a tape recording of the script contained in this handout in order to practice the exercise at home by yourself. In doing so, be sure to read slowly, pausing at places where you are being asked to concentrate, and think of a certain image. Try to visualize the scene as best as possible using your *mind's eye* and all of your other senses, such as touch, sound, taste, and even smell. Try to *experience* the situation as best as you can. By recording it, you can listen to the instructions at your leisure and not have to be distracted by trying to remember all of the directions. You can even add some of your own favorite relaxing instrumental music playing softly in the background. This way, you will be able to have your own visualization tape that you can use over and over again.

Find a comfortable location to practice this visualization exercise, such as a recliner, couch, bed, or soft floor covering. Remember to loosen your clothing, remove glasses or contact lenses, and lower the lights to create a more calming effect in your environment. Practice once every day for at least one week. Practicing this tool is important—like learning any other skill (e.g., driving a car, using a computer, playing a piano), the more you practice, the better you get! Trying this strategy only once or twice will **not** produce the kind of results that leads to significant reductions in anxiety or negative arousal. Therefore, practicing is important. A single session will take about 10–15 minutes to complete. The more you practice, the less you will need the tape to help guide you. In that way, you can be able to use this exercise in places outside your home where you have some privacy when you especially need to relax. This exercise can also be helpful when you are having difficulty falling asleep. Try it the next time you can't fall asleep.

Visualization Script

Let your eyes shut gently. Shut out the world and begin a voyage inward. Relax. It is important to get the most out of visualization.

Now you are going to go to your safe place. Take a nice slow, deep breath. Now put your palms gently over your closed eyes and gently brush your hands over your eyes and face. Place your hands at your sides and allow your body to become relaxed all over. You are about to allow yourself to privately enter your own special place that is peaceful, comfortable, and safe. You will fill your imagination of this place with rich detail. You will experience this place close up, looking off into the distance and through all of your senses. You can also allow room for another person, such as your spouse, friend, or family member, to be with you in this place—but only if you choose to do so.

Your safe place may be at the end of a boardwalk leading to a beach. Sand is under your feet, the water is about 20 yards away, and seagulls, boats, and clouds are in the distance. You feel the coolness of the air as a cloud passes in front of the sun and seagulls are calling to each other. The sun is shimmering on the waves continually rolling to the shore, and there are smells of food coming from the boardwalk. If this is a safe place for you, try to imagine it as best you can. What do you feel? What do you see? What do you smell? What do you hear? Try to visualize this scene in great detail. Enjoy this safe place—enjoy this vacation.

A different safe place might be a warm, wood-paneled den, with the smell of cinnamon buns baking in the oven in the kitchen. Through a window you can see fields of tall dried corn stalks or a forest of beautiful, lush trees. There is a crackling fire in the fireplace. A set of candles emit the aroma of lavender and there is cup of warm tea on the table for you.

You may have a different safe place than these two scenes. Take a few seconds to identify your safe place. It can be the beach or a warm house, on a boat, or in your own backyard. It can be anywhere. Maybe a safe place is a vacation spot you have already been to that was relaxing. Where was it? Go to this place now using your mind's eye.

Continue to close your eyes, allowing your breathing to be slow and deep. Walk slowly to your safe and quiet place. Let your mind take you there. Your place can be inside or outside. But wherever it is, it is peaceful and safe. Picture letting your anxieties and worries pass. Look to the distance . . . what do you see? Create a visual image of what you see in the distance. What do you smell? What do you hear? Notice what is right in front of you—reach out and touch it. How does it feel? Smell it . . . listen for any pleasant sounds. Make the temperature comfortable. Be safe here—look around for a special, private spot. Feel the ground or earth under your feet—what does it feel like? Look above you. What do you see? What do you hear? What do you smell?

Now walk a bit further and stop. Reach out and touch something lightly with your fingertips. What is the texture of what you are touching? This is your special place and nothing can harm or upset you here. Notice how relaxed you are. Notice how good this feels. Be mindful of how you feel—relaxed and calm. Say that to yourself—"I feel relaxed and calm." Say it slowly. Think of these words—"I feel relaxed and calm." You can come here and relax whenever you want. Stay in this safe and peaceful place for as long as you wish, allowing yourself to breath slowly and deeply and become relaxed all over.

Is there anyone else you wish to be with you? If so, imagine that he or she is now with you, also enjoying the peace and calm of your safe place. If not, that's fine—remember, this is your vacation.

Remain in your safe place for as long as you wish. Continue to be mindful of what you see, feel, hear, smell, and touch. Take slow, deep breaths. Relax and enjoy.

When you wish to, slowly rise and leave your safe place by the same path or steps that you used to enter. Do this slowly. Notice your surroundings . . . say to yourself the following words—"I can relax in my safe place. This is my special place and I can come here whenever I wish." Now slowly open your eyes and get used to your surroundings, but bring back "home" the nice feelings of relaxation.

Remember to practice!
Enjoy your vacation!

STOP, SLOW DOWN, THINK, & ACT THE *S.S.T.A.* METHOD

If you are having difficulty coming up with new ideas.
Then slow down.

—Natalie Goldberg

Here's a Question

When's the best time to make an important decision? When you are upset, right? Of course not! The worst time to try to solve a difficult problem is when you are under stress, feel upset, feel unmotivated, or not thinking your best!

Even if you have great problem-solving skills, putting them to work when trying to cope with lots of stress can be very challenging to even the best of problem solvers. In particular, three common barriers exist when trying to deal with stressful problems. These include

- **Negative feelings**
- **Negative thinking**
- **Feelings of hopelessness**

Negative feelings, such as sadness, guilt, tearfulness, or anxiety, when intense and overwhelming, often interfere with our ability to identify effective ways of coping with problems. They can take over our ability to think logically and serve to mask what such feelings are truly trying to tell us ("there's a problem to be solved"). **Negative thinking** that focuses on the bad things that have happened or may happen in the future can run over and over in our heads, leaving little room for *constructive* thinking. When negative emotions and negative thinking occur, it isn't long before a sense of **hopelessness** takes over and significantly reduces our motivation to believe that anything can improve our situation—when that happens, we often stop trying! When we're thinking logically, it makes sense that quitting *guarantees* failure. BUT, when we're feeling down and hopeless, it just feels like nothing can be done!

The good news is that there are ways to learn how to be an effective problem solver in *spite* of these obstacles!

When confronted with negative feelings, negative thinking, and feelings of hopelessness, there are things you can do to keep solving problems effectively. The following acronym best captures our overall approach:

"S. S. T. A."

This acronym stands for

STOP:	notice your feelings when facing a problem,
SLOW DOWN:	give your brain and body a chance to lower the intensity of your negative arousal,
THINK:	use your planful problem-solving skills to try to cope with the problem, and
ACT:	put your problem-solving ideas into action.

Stopping the negative feelings from taking over is an important first step! Negative feelings, such as sadness, in response to stress, is fairly common—it's when the sadness turns into depression that significant difficulties can occur! Or when feeling tense turns into anxiety or panic, or the sensation of being "ticked off" turns into anger and hostility! The best way to prevent such initial feelings from turning into strong and overwhelming emotions is to **"STOP, SLOW DOWN, THINK, & ACT."**

It's very difficult to stop a train if it has already left the station and increasingly gaining speed. However, putting the brakes on *early* can allow you to stop it before it goes too far. **Note that this is a skill that you can learn!**

How Can I STOP and SLOW DOWN if I'm Upset and Stressed Out?

Your PST counselor will teach you a set of skills that will help you to *STOP and Slow Down*. These include

1. **Becoming more aware of your reactions to stress.** These include feelings (sadness), thoughts ("I can't handle this situation"), physical responses (headaches, sweaty hands, fatigue), and changes in behavior ("wanting to run away"). Becoming more aware can help you to better know when to *STOP* and try to determine what is actually bothering you and to deal with that situation rather than becoming more upset. When you experience these reactions, that's when to say to yourself—***STOP!***
2. **Becoming aware of your "unique triggers."** These would be your "hot" buttons or switches—those people, events, situations, thoughts, sights, sounds, etc., that most often "get to you. Examples might include someone cutting in front of you on a long line, crowds, hearing a song that has special meaning for you in a sad way, or getting yelled at by someone. Knowing your triggers can also help you to ***STOP & Slow Down.***
3. **Slowing Down.** Once you are able to STOP, the next step is to try to "slow down" the arousal, that is, to try to "slow the train down enough that is doesn't leave the station."

Strategies to Slow Down

Below is a list of tools your counselor can help you with. Some may seem strange or unusual ("fake yawning"). But before you dismiss them, talk to your counselor. Others you may have learned to do already, for example, deep breathing. All have been found to reduce stress and help people to "slow down." Because we believe in the idea—"different strokes for different folks"—we wanted to provide you with a group of tools, rather than just one or two.

- Counting
- Deep breathing
- Visualization
- "Fake" smiling
- "Fake" yawning
- Meditation
- Muscle relaxation
- Exercise/mindful walking

- Talking to someone
- Gum chewing
- Prayer
- Can you think of any others

Think & Act

The last two steps involve planful problem solving—that is, thinking creatively of a plan that will help you to solve the stressful problem, as well as carrying it out.

However, before you can do this, your mind *and* body needs to be calm and cool!

Talk to your counselor about practicing the **S-S** process. Learn which "slow down" tools seem to work for you!

DEEP BREATHING

Deep or *diaphragmatic* (meaning breathing from your diaphragm instead of from your chest) breathing is one of the simplest, cheapest, and safest ways to help our bodies calm down. According to doctors who specialize in mind and body interactions, breathing is an incredibly powerful health tool that we have available to us at all times.

Follow the steps below to learn how to make more effective use of your breathing in order to better manage stress.

Step 1. Lie down or sit in a comfortable position and close your eyes.

Step 2. Place your hands gently on your body. Put your right hand on your stomach, just under your rib cage and about even with your waistline. Put your left hand on the center of your chest, just under your neck.

Step 3. Become aware of your breathing. Notice how you are breathing. Which hand rises the most? If the hand on your stomach or belly is moving up and down, then you are breathing more from your diaphragm or abdomen. This is the best way to breathe. Practice doing this now, keeping your hands on your belly. As you take in your breath, imagine that your entire abdomen, just below your rib cage, is a balloon that is filling up with air. When you exhale, let all the air out of the belly slowly, and feel it collapse, just like a balloon that is letting out air.

Step 4. Follow the breathing directions for about 5 minutes.

- Inhale *slowly* and *deeply* through your nose into your abdomen, filling all the spaces in your belly with air (if you have difficulty breathing through your nose, go ahead and breathe through your mouth).
- Now exhale through your mouth, making a quiet, exhaling "whooshing sound" like the wind, as you gently and slowly blow out. Purse your lips, forming an "O" and release your breath, as if you were trying to make a paper sailboat glide *slowly* across the water. Take long, slow, deep, breaths.
- Feel your belly rise and fall.
- Repeat a phrase (silently or out loud) with each breath, such as "I take in life" with each breath in and "I am giving life" with each breath out (another phrase can include "I am taking in a good breath and now I am releasing the tension").
- Continue to breathe this way for approximately 5 minutes.

Try to practice this breathing exercise at least once a day—it only takes 3–5 minutes! As you get better at this skill, you can try to use it to calm your body down during times of stress without having to close your eyes and place your hands on your stomach. It may come in handy, for example, while waiting in a long line at the supermarket, getting caught in traffic, right before a major presentation at work, or in the middle of a difficult exam. Apply this skill especially when you are feeling increased stress when attempting to solve a problem.

MINDFUL MEDITATION

An important goal of mindful meditation is to be able to adopt a point of view where one attempts to distance oneself from one's experiences. This independent observer pays close attention to his or her thoughts and feelings as they occur but attempts to separate such thoughts and feelings in a way that helps the person come to believe that *"I am not my thoughts; I am not my feelings."* In this way, you can observe your thoughts and feelings as you experience them but begin to realize that you don't have to allow these thoughts and feelings influence you to behave in a certain way. For example, the following thought, "I feel so stupid today for forgetting my planning book at home," should be considered *just a thought* and not reality! You can note that you had this thought but realize that you don't have to *react* to such a thought as if it is the "universal truth" and then feel bad about yourself. You can simply acknowledge, with *detached acceptance,* that you had the thought. You had the thought but the thought neither "owns" you nor "defines" you— it's *just a thought.*

We have found that the metaphor of looking at movies of yourself or hearing tape recordings of your voice can be a useful way to help you to become a detached observer. Seeing a movie of yourself allows you to see yourself "outside of your own body." You are actually seeing yourself say and do things— *but it really isn't you.* If you can refrain from evaluating these actions, but rather simply note that you are engaged in them, then you can begin to see your thoughts and feelings from a distance. If you have ever taken any home movies, try to look at them and observe yourself. Try to observe yourself without any judgments, being more accepting and forgiving of any actions you previously would have felt embarrassed (or even proud) by. Simply observe—don't judge.

Being able to detach yourself from negative thoughts and feelings can help you to "slow down" negative arousal by accepting that these experiences are just experiences and do not represent the "truth."

Instructions for Mindful Meditation

The following are instructions that can help you to engage in mindful meditation.

You can practice this meditation with your eyes open or closed. Initially, plan on about 10 minutes to engage in this mindful meditation exercise. You can extend the time after you have practiced a bit. Similar to other stress management strategies in this book, you may wish to tape record the following instructions in order to free you from having to remember them.

Begin by feeling your breadth—do not *think* about it—just feel it come in.

1. Focus your attention on your breathing; notice how it stops, it reverses, then it flows out.
2. There is no special way to breathe. Anyway you breathe is natural—it is your life force.
3. Think of your breath like a rising wave—it happens on its own—just stay with that—be mindful of the breath in your own body.
4. Your mind is not going to want to stay on the breath for very long. When that happens and you drop your focus on your breathing, just let the mind go off—but let it also come back.
5. Leave your body still.
6. Feel the breath.
7. Breathe in . . . breathe out.
8. As you breathe in, focus on the "in" breath.
9. As you exhale, focus on the "out" breath.
10. "Ride" the breath.
11. Flow with the breath.
12. Feel it in your nostrils.
13. Feel your abdomen rise and fall (place your hands on your stomach area if you prefer to feel the flow of your breath).
14. Rest your mind on the simple, regular, calming wave of breathing that your body is experiencing.
15. Notice the sensation in you nostrils, abdomen, and shoulders.
16. Notice any thoughts that bubble up to the surface of your mind. Notice them and simply let them go. Visualize these thoughts floating away, like leaves floating down a gentle stream of water. Remember that these thoughts are "not you"—you are not defined by your thoughts.

17. Settle in the present moment. Stay aware of actual moment-to-moment happenings—a slight pain in your shoulder or various sounds, such as a train passing by, the wind rustling through the trees, or people's voices.
18. Let your concentration deepen.
19. Don't try to suppress your perceptions, feelings, awareness—simply notice what is happening and then let it dissolve as the new moment begins.
20. Stay awake (even if your eyes are closed), remain alert . . . pay attention.
21. Breathe in . . . breathe out. Stay focused.
22. Let go of each breath. Let go of each thought—don't hang on. Let them float away down the stream.
23. Note your thoughts—notice them and let them go. With each breath, let go of any thoughts a little bit more. Let them simply pass by in the stream.
24. Notice where your mind is when it's not on your breathing.
25. Make no judgment, just notice where it is and come back to the breath
26. Allow each moment to be fresh and new.

After engaging in several practice sessions, it is likely that you will have experienced several moments in which you were able to let the "noise of your mind" fade in the background and experience "the present moment." Try to practice this tool several times during the next week. We suggest that you consider practicing this tool once a week for the rest of your life.

DEEP MUSCLE RELAXATION

Deep muscle relaxation, also known as *progressive muscle relaxation*, is a stress management technique that reduces physiological tension in the muscles. When we experience anxious thoughts or feelings, our bodies often respond with muscle tension. This muscle tension then gets interpreted by our brains as a sign of more anxiety. Thus, begins a vicious cycle between the mind and body. This strategy can release muscle tension and give a feeling of warmth and well-being to the body. This is interpreted by our brain as "everything is okay." Deep muscle relaxation can be a very strong antistress medicine and break the above cycle.

Preparation

Essentially, progressive muscle relaxation teaches you to first tense a particular muscle group (e.g., your left hand) and then to "release that tension" in order to feel relaxed and calm. You then progress in a similar manner throughout several muscle groups in your entire body. You will then be taught to foster a sense of overall relaxation without tensing any muscles.

Note that when you are asked to tense a given muscle, you should not do so as to cause a cramp or create pain. Rather, tense the muscle only in order to feel the tension. Try to concentrate on the particular muscle group that is being addressed and not any others. For example, when asked to "make a fist," do so simply by clenching your hand into a fist but not raising your entire arm.

Ask someone with a *calming* voice to make a tape recording of the script provided in the following pages or you may want to make the tape yourself. You can even add some of your own favorite relaxing instrumental music playing softly in the background. This way, you will be able to have your own progressive muscle relaxation tape that you can use over and over again.

Now, practice this relaxation tool in a comfortable place. Loosen your clothing, remove glasses or contact lenses, and lower the lights to create a more calming effect in the room environment. Make sure that your legs are not crossed and your head is supported, as your body may experience a sense of heaviness that would be uncomfortable if your legs or arms were in a crossed position. Practice once every day for at least one week. Practicing this tool is important—like learning any other skill (e.g., driving a car, using a computer, playing a piano), the more you practice, the better you get! A single session will take about 25–30 minutes to complete.

Script Instructions (*read softly and slowly*)

Let yourself go now, getting deeply relaxed all over. Start by taking a deep breath, feeling the air flow in, way down to your lower stomach, and filling your whole abdomen region. Now exhale slowly, and as you do, feel the air slowly releasing from your lower abdomen region and allow yourself to float down into your chair. Close your eyes and focus on the sensations of breathing. Imagine your breath rolling in and out—like waves coming onto the shore.

Think quietly to yourself—I am going to let go of tension . . . I will relax and smooth out my muscles . . . I will feel all of the tightness and the tension dissolve away.

Now we will begin the progressive muscle relaxation procedure. Your first muscle group will be your hands, forearms, and biceps. First, clench your right fist . . . tighter . . . study the tension and discomfort as you do so. Keep it clenched and notice the tension in your fist, hand, and forearm. Hold this tension in your right fist for a few seconds (reader—pause for 3 seconds). Now relax . . . feel the looseness in your right hand.

Notice the contrast with the tension. Repeat the procedure with your right fist again, always noticing as you relax that this is the opposite of tension . . . relax and feel the difference.

Now, clench your left fist, tighter and tighter, studying the tension and discomfort as you do so. Keep it clenched and notice the tension in your fist, hand, and forearm. Hold this tension in your left fist for a few seconds (reader—pause for 3 seconds). Now relax . . . feel the looseness in your left hand . . . notice the contrast with the tension (reader—pause for 5 seconds).

Now repeat the entire procedure with your left fist, then both fists at once. Clench both fists, tighter and tighter, studying the tension and discomfort as you do so. Keep them clenched and notice the tension. Hold this tension in both fists now for a few seconds (reader—pause for 3 seconds). Now relax . . . feel the looseness in your hands . . . allow warmth and relaxation to spread all over. Now bend your elbows in order to tense your biceps. Tense them now and observe the feeling of tension and tightness (reader—pause for 3 seconds). Now relax . . . let your arms straighten out. Let relaxation flow in and feel the difference between the tension and strain in your arms when it was tensed and how it felt when it was relaxed, loose and limp. Now repeat this procedure. Bend your elbows and tense your biceps. Tense them now and observe the feeling of discomfort (reader—pause for 3 seconds). Now relax . . . let your arms straighten out. Let relaxation flow in and feel the difference between the tension and strain in your arms when it was tensed and how it felt when it was relaxed.

Your next muscle group will be your head, face, and scalp. Turning attention to your head, wrinkle your forehead (reader—pause for 3 seconds). Now relax and smooth it out. Imagine that your entire scalp is becoming smooth and relaxed . . . at peace . . . at rest. Now frown and notice the tightness and strain spreading throughout your forehead (reader—pause for 3 seconds). Now let go . . . allow your brow to become smooth and soft again. Close your eyes now and squint them tighter. Notice the tension, the discomfort (reader—pause for 3 seconds). Now relax your eyes and allow them to remain gently closed (reader—pause for 3 seconds). Now clench your jaw, bite down like your trying to hold something in your teeth (reader—pause for 3 seconds). Now relax your jaw. When your jaw is relaxed, your lips may be slightly parted and you might feel your tongue loosely in your mouth. Now press your tongue against the roof of your mouth. Feel the slight ache it creates in the back of your mouth (reader—pause for 3 seconds). Now relax . . . feel your tongue soft and loose in your mouth. Press your lips now, purse them into an "O" as if you were blowing bubbles (reader—pause for 3 seconds). Now relax your lips. Notice that your forehead, scalp, eyes, jaw, tongue, and lips are all relaxed (reader—pause for 5 seconds).

Your next muscle group will be your head, neck, and shoulders. Press your head back as far as you can and observe the tension in your neck. Roll it from right to left and notice the changing location of the stress. Straighten your head forward, pressing your chin to your chest. Feel the tension in your throat and the back of your neck (reader—pause for 3 seconds). Now relax . . . allow your head to return to a comfortable position. Let the relaxation spread over your shoulders (reader—pause for 3 seconds). Now shrug your shoulders. Keep the tightness and tension as you hunch your head down between your shoulders. Feel how uncomfortable this position is (reader—pause for 3 seconds). Now relax your shoulders. Drop them back and feel relaxation spreading throughout your neck, throat, and shoulders; pure relaxation, deeper and deeper (reader—pause for 5 seconds). Your next muscle group will be your chest and abdomen. First, give your entire body a chance to relax. Feel the comfort and the heaviness. Now breathe in and fill your lungs completely. Hold your breath and notice the tension (reader—pause for 3 seconds). Now exhale . . . let your chest and abdomen become loose while the air is coming out. Continue relaxing and let your breathing become calm and natural (reader—pause for 3 seconds). Repeat the deep breath once more and notice the tension leave your body as you exhale (reader—pause for 5 seconds).

Now tighten your stomach as if you are trying to "suck it in" and make it hard and flat. Hold it (reader—pause for 3 seconds). Notice the tension. Now relax. Arch your back (without straining). Notice the tension in your lower back and hold this position for a few seconds (reader—pause for 3 seconds). Focus on the tension in your lower back. Now relax, gently lowering your back down and relaxing all over (reader—pause for 5 seconds).

Your next muscle group will be your legs and buttocks. Tighten your buttocks and thighs. Flex your thighs by pressing down on your heels (reader—pause for 3 seconds). Now relax and feel the difference (reader—pause for 3 seconds). Now point your toes like a ballet dancer and make your calves tense. Study the tension and hold it (reader—pause for 3 seconds). Now relax . . . notice the difference between the relaxed feeling in your legs and the discomfort that you experienced a moment ago. Bend your toes toward your face, creating tension in your shins. Pause and hold it (reader—pause for 3 seconds). Now relax again (reader—pause for 5 seconds). Feel the heaviness and warmth throughout your lower body as the relaxation spreads all over you. Relax your feet, ankle, calves, shins, knees, thighs, and buttocks. Now let the relaxation spread to your stomach, lower back and chest (reader—pause for 3 seconds). Let go of the tension more and more (reader—pause for 3 seconds). Experience the relaxation deepening in your shoulders, arms, and hands. Deeper . . . and deeper. Notice the feeling of looseness and relaxation in your neck, jaw, and all your facial muscles (reader—pause for 3 seconds). Say to yourself—my muscles are relaxed, warm, and smooth . . . I am letting go of all my tension . . . I am deeply relaxed . . . my muscles are relaxed, warm, and smooth . . . I am letting go of all my tension . . . I am deeply relaxed. Enjoy these feelings of relaxation for the next few moments (reader—pause for 2 minutes, during which you can occasionally say—"more and more relaxed, deeper and deeper into a state of relaxation").

Now bring your focus back to the present time and place while I count from 1 to 5. With each increasing number, try to become more alert to your surroundings, open your eyes, but keep the feelings of relaxation in your body (Reader—slowly count from 1 to 5).

REMEMBER TO PRACTICE!

MINDFUL WALKING:
TAKING A "WABI-SABI" WALK

Wabi-sabi is a Japanese concept that is somewhat difficult to translate into English but essentially represents a particular type of "world view" or way of thinking about the world. A wabi-sabi perspective acknowledges the beauty in objects, things, or people things that are *imperfect, impermanent,* or *incomplete.*

As an example, when we look at a tree, the lines in the bark, the tree's color, as well as the foliage, all tell us unique characteristics about that tree. Thus, each tree is uniquely beautiful. Similarly, it is the lines in a person's face that lets us know how much they have laughed, thought deeply, experienced pain, or was kind to others. Wabi-sabi offers a philosophy that fosters an appreciation of our surroundings each moment. It can also help us to slow down by becoming more aware of the beauty all around us.

Instructions for Taking a Wabi-Sabi Walk

Allow yourself at least 20 minutes to take this type of walk. This is not a walk for physical exercise—and you can feel free to sit down at any time during this activity. The importance of this exercise is that you will have an opportunity to practice a walking meditation. Try taking such a walk at least once a week—perhaps for the rest of your life. As you go on this walk, engage in the following:

1. Begin by engaging in mindful breathing.
2. As you breathe in, be aware that you are "receiving life."
3. As you exhale, be aware that you are "giving something back to the world."

4. Stay in the present.
5. Clear all thoughts of the past or future.
6. Stay in touch with your breathing.
7. As thoughts come into your mind, simply observe them and let them pass.
8. Let any of these thoughts go and refocus on the present.
9. The purpose is to be present and aware of your breathing and walking.
10. Be aware of your feet as you walk, one foot in front of the other.
11. Walk gently on the earth—be aware that with every step you are placing your footprint on the earth.
12. You can coordinate your breathing with your steps by talking an "in" breath every 3 or 4 steps, followed by an "out" breath every few steps. You may quietly whisper "in" and "out" to yourself as you go along your path.
13. Be aware of all other sights, smells, and life in your surroundings—the car horns, the birds, the traffic noises, the leaves on a tree, the blades of grass, the concrete walkway, the park bench, or the mall parking lot.
14. Notice that everything you see is *imperfect, impermanent,* and *incomplete.* The tree's bark has cracks in it indicating its age or the conditions under which it grew.
15. As you walk along the concrete path you may notice that it is cracked, covered with leaves, debris, or animal droppings.
16. Be aware of people. Notice how *imperfect, incomplete,* or *impermanent* they are.
17. Visualize how you are connected to each person in some way or they to each other.
18. Now what is present in your surrounding that you cannot see? Perhaps a squirrel that is climbing on the other side of the tree, the pain experienced by the elderly gentleman who crosses the street with his cane, or the bulbs of spring flowers that are still under a frozen ground. Be aware that even though you may be aware of all that you observe, it is possible that there are objects present that you cannot see with your eyes.
19. As you return from your walk, be aware of all those things that you may have missed on previous walks—make a commitment to become more mindful as you go through your day.
20. Enjoy the walk!

POSITIVE VISUALIZATION FOR GOAL ATTAINMENT

This handout contains a series of "visualization lessons" that can help you to lay out various goals for the future and feel more motivated to try to reach them. Follow the described below in a step-by-step manner beginning with Lesson 1.

Move on to the next visualization lesson when you are ready. You can take anywhere from 1 day to several weeks to get through the 8 lessons. If you decide to take some time with any one of the lessons, just make sure to practice the visualization exercise that is described in that lesson at least once each day.

Lesson 1: Develop a Specific Visual Picture of the Future

Many times our personal goals are too vague and cloudy. For example, if your goal is to improve your health, what is your *visual* picture of this goal? Do you see yourself eating 3 well-balanced meals a day? Do you picture yourself completing 10 push-ups and running 2 miles? Do you picture yourself with a blood pressure of 120 over 75, smoke free, or meditating in the park? Do you picture playing catch with your grandchildren in the park? Likewise, a goal for more financial security may include increasing your savings to a certain amount, starting a retirement plan, or picturing yourself in your own home or apartment.

It is very important that you develop your visualization of the future in very *specific and concrete mental pictures*. Try it out right now. Describe the mental picture of what you wish to accomplish and write down a description of that picture. For example, individuals who want to learn how to scuba dive might picture themselves in warm, clear water, wearing a wet suit and scuba gear, slowly following the path of a beautiful fish. They approach the surface with a sense of enjoyment and satisfaction. Later, they picture themselves sitting in the warm sun on the deck of the boat, sharing the experience with friends.

Lesson 2: Break Down Your Visual Picture of the Future Into Small Steps

It is important to have both *short-* and *long-*term goals to visualize (Remember to "simplify!"). For example, if your long-range visualization is seeing yourself smoke-free and walking 1 mile each day, make a series of visual images that are steps to this goal. For example, in this situation, a person may have a short-range goal of initially cutting-out smoking while on the telephone and walking at least two blocks each day. The next step might include no smoking after meals and walking 5 blocks a day. And so on . . . practice visualizing your goals by creating both short- and long-term goals in your visual images.

Lesson 3: Develop Different Types of Goals

Remember to visualize your goals in terms of things that you can accomplish. You can only make changes in yourself. For example, if your overall goal is to improve your marriage, goals such as "my husband will not complain so much," "my wife will not drink too much," or "my husband will find me attractive" may not be reachable because they are not in your control. However, "I will be more patient," "I will communicate my concerns and disagreement with her behavior more effectively," or "I will feel more confident about the way I look" are goals that can be achieved because they involve things that you have control over. In the same way, goals involving physical or athletic accomplishments should be focused on improving your performance, not simply winning a game or an event. Winning involves other players' performances—something over which you have no control. In this way, your goals are actually reachable.

Lesson 4: Remove the Barriers to Your Goals Through Visualization

In this lesson, you will travel, in your imagination, to the future, and visit yourself 5 years from now. In this image, remember that anything goes—so picture it just the way that you want it to be. You will look around at your possessions, notice your accomplishments, see who you are with, be aware of how you spend your leisure time, and so on. Remember, it is a good idea to have a friend or family member with a calming voice tape record the script below.

Before you begin, find a comfortable location to practice visualization, such as a recliner, couch, bed, or soft floor covering. Remember to loosen your clothing, remove glasses or contact lenses, and lower the lights to create a more calming effect in the room environment. Practice once every day for at least one week. Practicing this tool is important—trying this strategy only once or twice will not produce the kind of results that leads to significant reductions in anxiety, depression, or feelings of hopelessness. Therefore, practicing is important. A single session will take about 10–15 minutes to complete. Use positive statements or affirmations when you begin the visualization. These should be short, positive statements that state your intention to yourself. Examples include the following:

- "I will experience success in my mind"
- "I can peace within myself"
- "A goal is a possible future"
- "If I can dream it, I can do it"
- "I can put distractions aside for now"
- Think of some new ones yourself

Visualization Instructions

(Reader: read softly and slowly—pause between sentences throughout).

"Close your eyes and relax—let go of any tension in your body. Now go to a safe and tranquil place in your mind—a special, outdoor place. Look around, take note of what you see nearby, as well as in the distance. Describe the scene silently to yourself. Now look for a path—this is your path toward the future. Notice a tree stump or log branch across the path. Imagine that this piece of wood in front of the path is getting in the way of your ability to walk down the path. This piece of wood is your own hesitation or fear of changing and walking toward your goals. Step over it, step over this log and visualize overcoming your hesitation, overcoming your fears.

Now, as you walk along the path, you come across a steep hill. This hill is your own doubts about yourself. Slowly, keep walking up the hill, even though you are not absolutely sure of what you will find at the top of the hill. With each step, begin to let yourself become more self-confident that you will reach your goals. When you reach the top, you walk through a dark forest of trees that block out the sunlight. This forest has all the obstacles that block you from seeing your final goals—interference from others, day-to-day problems that keep you from working on your goals, or your own fears that you don't deserve what you want. However, you push past the trees to a clearing and you are now in a sunny field. You can see your home in the distance. This is your home 5 or 10 years in the future. Go into your home and look around. What do you see? How many rooms are there? How are they decorated? What things do you own? What pictures or photographs do you see? Look at yourself in the mirror. What do you look like? What are you wearing? Look at your family come in. How do they act toward each other? Listen to yourself as you picture yourself to be five years older. Listen to yourself as you talk to people or make phone calls—what do you say?

Follow yourself to work or school. What are your achievements? What are your activities? Watch yourself at leisure. What are you doing? For example, maybe you're watching TV, race car driving, sailing, fishing, listening to classical music?

Now ask yourself how you feel. In other words, look back over your life of the last 5 years—what are you especially glad that you had the chance to experience? What are you most proud of? Maybe you gave a successful speech, ran a marathon, had several good friends, raised self-confident children, or people knew that they could count on you. Anything is possible.

Remember—visualize what you hope and wish to be in the future—not what is going on now!

When you have finished exploring, let your images fade away and come back to the present—here and now. Open your eyes and make a brief list with your images still fresh in your mind. Pick one or two major goals for your future and write down the details and the specific visual images that come to mind."

Lesson 5: Write Down Your 5-Year Goal

Choose just one image that you had from the previous visualization exercise and write down your 5-year goal. It could be a personal, physical, career, family, or social goal. Remember to be very specific and concrete, as explained in the first lesson.

Lesson 6: Break Your Goal Into 1-Year Goals

Look at the goal again, and break it down into smaller 1-year goals—one goal for each year. These would be smaller steps leading to your larger goal. Write these down—externalize!

Lesson 7: Break Your First Year Goal Into Smaller Steps

Now look at your first 1-year goal and break it down one more time into several steps to reach over the course of a year. Write these down. Once again, remember to be very concrete and specific.

Lesson 8: Create a Daily Visualization

Create a visualization for each day to accomplish the steps toward these goals. In your imagination, picture yourself clearly carrying out the steps for your immediate goals. For example, you might be picturing yourself exercising 2 days per week for the next four months. If so, visualize yourself in workout clothes, imagine that you will experience a sense of pride in arranging for enough time to spend at the gym. Imagine your favorite music playing on a personal tape player; visualize your body feeling strong and the perspiration dripping off your skin as you are working hard.

As you reach each goal that you have visualized, begin daily visualizations of the next step in your series of goals, leading finally up to your 1-year goal. After that, develop a series of visualization steps toward the next year's goal. In general, use the basic strategy of visualizing future goals in order to develop a road map of steps that you need to take in order to achieve such goals, whether it involves solving a particular stressful problem at present, reaching toward a goal that involves only a week, or going for something that involves a much longer time. In developing such road maps, write down both overall goals, as well as smaller steps or objectives leading to these goals.

Visualize reaching each step and then "go for it!"

Remember though—sometimes we set unrealistic initial goals or set goals that depend on other people. If either of these situations occur, maybe you need to redesign your smaller goals to those that are reachable in a smaller period of time and involve situations that you have control over and do not necessary require others to change.

PLANFUL PROBLEM SOLVING

Planful problem solving involves several steps or activities that serve as guides to help people approach problems in a reasoned, deliberate, and systematic way. It is a powerful means of helping individuals to reach their goals. When attempting to deal with problems that are particularly stressful, remember that this toolkit should be used in combination with the directive to **STOP and SLOW DOWN**. You simply can't think logically when you are feeling stressed out!

The tasks involved in **Planful Problem Solving** includes the following 4 steps:

Step 1. Define the problem and set realistic goals.
Step 2. Generate alternative solutions to solve the problem.
Step 3. Decide which ideas are the best.
Step 4. Carry out the solution and determine whether it worked or not.

Step 1: Define the Problem

There is an old saying—"measure twice, cut once." John Dewey, the American philosopher and psychologist, suggested that "a problem well-defined, is half solved!" Both quotes suggest that if we take the time to fully understand the nature of the problem we are experiencing, solving it will take less time and effort. Defining a problem is similar to laying out a course or route to travel. We need to know our destination, what resources we have to get there, and what barriers exist that might make the trip difficult. Accurately defining the problem, then, involves the following activities:

■ **Seek important facts** about the problem (that is, answer questions such as "who," "what," "when," "where," & "how").

- **Describe the facts in clear language**.
- **Separate "facts" from "assumptions."**
- **Set realistic goals**—break down a complex problem into smaller ones if necessary.
- **Identify barriers** or obstacles to your goal.

Problems That Are Changeable Versus Problems That Cannot Be Changed

One thought about goals—it's important to remember that we cannot always solve a problem by "fixing it." Sometimes, the best solution for dealing with a problem is to accept that the problem exists. On a small scale, this means that we cannot change the weather to better suit our plans; we may just have to accept that it's going to rain during a ballgame we waited a long time to see. On a larger scale, as one former client told us—"accepting reality often helps me to get past feeling sorry for myself or to keep from trying over and over to change something that can't be changed; especially people who don't want to change!"

Step 2: Generate Alternative Solutions

The next step is to creatively think of a *variety* of solution alternatives or ways to solve the problem. Doing so can increase your chances of coming up with a great idea, make you feel more hopeful (imagine if there was only one alternative to choose among for each decision we had to make), decrease "black and white" thinking, and minimize the tendency to act impulsively. This step directs you to creatively think of multiple ideas—at least 3 to 5, more if possible.

To carry out this step effectively, we suggest that you use various brainstorming principles. *Brainstorming* increases your flexibility and creativity, which actually improves the quality *and* quantity of the solutions that you generate. Brainstorming also helps you to better deal with strong negative emotional reactions. Strong emotions can frequently dominate or influence your thinking by giving you "tunnel vision," leaving you with only one or two ideas, and ones that are likely not even to be ultimately effective. When emotions do seem to become overwhelming, brainstorming can help you to get "back on track." There are 3 brainstorming rules we recommend:

- **"Quantity leads to quality"** (the more ideas you think of, the better your chances of thinking of really good ones).

- **"Do Not Judge"** (trying to evaluate each idea, one at a time, only limits your ability to be real creative).
- **Think of "variety"**—try to think of different kinds of ideas.

Step 3: Decision Making

In thinking of differing solution alternatives, we suggested that you "defer judgment." In this step, judgment is the key activity used to make sound decisions. Making decisions about how to handle difficult problems can be hard. However, we offer several guidelines that can help you. There are 4 important tasks involved in making good decisions:

- **Screen out** obviously ineffective solutions.
- **Predict** the positive and negative consequences of each solution idea.
- **Evaluate** the impact of these consequences (weigh the pros and cons of these solutions).
- **Develop an action plan to carry out as your solution** (the plan includes those ideas that are the most effective ones based on the above cost-benefit analysis).

When thinking about consequences—be sure to consider *personal* (the effects on oneself), as well as *social* consequences (the impact on others), and *short-term*, as well as *long-term* consequences.

Step 4: Carry Out the Action Plan & Evaluate its Success

Now that you developed an action plan, the next step is to carry it out. However, that's not necessarily where you stop. It becomes important to determine whether your plan was successful; if not, to determine where you need to revise your plan. The specific tasks in this last Planful Problem-Solving step include the following:

- **Motivate** yourself to carry out your solution (think about the pros and cons of "doing nothing" vs. the possible success of solving the problem; **visualize** how you would feel if you persist and solved the problem).
- **Carry out** your action plan.
- **Observe and monitor** the actual outcome.
- **Reward yourself** for making an effort (you *do* deserve it), especially if the problem is solved.
- **Circle back** to the previous activities if the problem is *not* solved to your satisfaction.

To help develop an action plan geared to solve your problem, ask your problem-solving counselor for a "Problem-Solving Worksheet," a form that can help guide you to carry out these important problem-solving tasks.

Our program also has numerous additional helpful hints, suggestions, and guidelines to help improve one's problem-solving skills. If you find that you are having difficulty engaging in 1 or more of the tasks described above, be sure to ask your counselor for more help.

Index

Note: Page references followed by "*f*" and "*t*" denote figures and tables, respectively.